The Century after CORTÉS

The Century after
CORTÉS

BY FERNANDO BENÍTEZ

TRANSLATED BY JOAN MACLEAN

THE UNIVERSITY OF CHICAGO PRESS | CHICAGO & LONDON

Translated from:
Los primeros Mexicanos: La vida criolla en el siglo XVI
© Ediciones ERA, S. A., Mexico, D. F.
Published by Ediciones ERA 1962

Reproductions of the murals of Diego Rivera
were made available through the courtesy of Ediciones ERA

Library of Congress Catalog Card Number: 65–25121
The University of Chicago Press, Chicago & London
The University of Toronto Press, Toronto 5, Canada
English translation © 1965 by The University of Chicago
All rights reserved. Published 1965
Printed in the United States of America
Decorations by Theo. Jung

Contents

010103

1

An Old City and a New World

New Spain happened once and only once in all history, for before another Mexico and its land may be discovered, we shall see the past and the present come together in body and soul before the Lord of Heaven and Earth on that universal day of the Last Judgment.

Juan Suárez de Peralta

On August 13, 1521, San Hipólito's Day, the Spaniards took the young Emperor Cuauhtémoc prisoner, and the city of Tenochtitlán fell into their hands. Suddenly the shouts that had sounded throughout the many days of siege were cut short, the heroic last stand of the Aztecs was ended and a silence like death pressed down over the ruins. The Conquistadors, unable to stand the stench of their dead enemies, decided to leave the charnel city and set up their camp in the neighboring village of Coyoacán.

The city remained faithful to Tláloc, the four-eyed god of rain. The colors of the forested mountains still dominated it, untouched. The swamp cypresses of Xochimilco competed for dominion over the valley with the *ahuehuetes*—the old men of the water, hung with Spanish moss—the cedars, and the bright-branched ash trees. Masses of verdure grew to the shore of the lake in which the cypresses had taken root beneath the water to form a vegetable city of small floating gardens called *chinampas*. As a consequence of this profuse vegetation, the rains came with clocklike regularity. From midday on, the spirits that attend on Tláloc were busy with their sticks, cracking open the great casks of the clouds, which shattered with the roar of thunder, and a violent downpour began. In the afternoons and evenings, the sky would let fall a soft and monotonous rain, and its gentle murmur on the lake provided an accompaniment to the oboes, the horns, and the muted flutes of the frogs. The next morning a world of tender greens and deep blues would glow in the valley, lighted by the sun above the high plateau. Water slid down the faces of the gods in the ruins of the abandoned city, flooded the broken paving stones of the Plaza Mayor, and glided along the painted stucco of the temples. The city looked like a submerged Atlantis in ruins. Gods, columns, palaces, and pagan temples lay wrecked, awash in a sea of mud, with the great, mutilated pyramids towering above them.

Tenochtitlán might have lain there like a gigantic archeological display, if Hernán Cortés had not decided to found the capital of New Spain upon the ruins. The labor of building it began in the early days of 1522, and shortly afterward Alonso García Bravo drew up the plan for the new city. The pattern was tentative, a mere sketch on paper, which started with various fixed sites in Tenochtitlán as points of reference. On the spot near where the temple of Huitzilopochtli had stood, a cross was drawn to indicate the site of the cathedral; the square followed the old sacred perimeter; and the causeway of Tacuba along which the Spaniards had fled on the Noche Triste became, like the other old-time arteries, a main street, a wall, and a bridge.

Before long, García Bravo's sketch had shaped up into a simple machine for living. Quantities of cut stone were everywhere, heavy timber was within hand's reach, and, most important, there were thousands of slaves highly trained as sculptors, painters, carpenters, masons, and gardeners. Building European-style houses turned out to be child's play for the indigenous artisans, once they had chisels and iron hammers. "The seventh plague that was visited upon the Indians," Motilinia writes, "was the building of the great city of Mexico, in which more people were engaged during the early years than in the erection of the Temple of Jerusalem." A walk through the streets became an undertaking. Hundreds of Indians, chanting in their own tongue, dragged enormous blocks of stone or tree trunks. Everything smelled of fresh mortar and newly hewn wood. A temple would be torn down in one spot while the walls of a house were rising in another or a church was being roofed.

Building, always left to the Indians, moved ahead rapidly. "They do the work and supply the materials at their own cost, and they pay for the stonemasons and carpenters, and if they do not bring their own food, they go hungry." The columns of the arches on the great square, which was intended for jousts and tournaments, had begun to fall into line. In the background was the temporary cathedral; facing it, the city hall; in the center, the pillory and the gibbet—convincing symbols of the municipal jurisdiction. Here and there were monasteries and convents, their chapels crowned with cupolas and the trees of the orchards arching over their extensive walls. On the main streets rose the houses of the Conquistadors, the lawyers, and the merchants.

It was a city designed exclusively for white men. Communities for the Indians were established outside its boundaries, with their own temples, laws, and authorities. These were two worlds, planned to maintain themselves as separate entities. The world of the Spaniards lacked gateways and outer walls but was actually as well protected as Ávila or Burgos ever had been during the time of the Moors. The monasteries, the churches, and the houses had battlements and buttresses, heavily grilled windows, and nail-studded doors. The old Indian canals served as natural moats, and at the least sign of rebellion, drawbridges were raised, and the warrior's helmet, the iron gauntlet, the arquebus, and the crossbow would peer from behind each battlement.

That small white seignorial city lacked none of the requisites of Christian civilization. It had a viceroy and an archbishop, a cathedral and a monastery, and in time, a university, a press, and a theater. The lawyer, the soldier without a war, "that special type of mercenary," the newly arrived adventurer, the officer of the crown, the lady in her litter, and the halberdier with his lance over his shoulder—all came and went through its streets.

Humanism in Action

We owe the first description of our city to the Latinist Don Francisco Cervantes de Salazar, the friend and companion of Luis Vives, who came to New Spain in 1533, when he was already an old man. Neither Archbishop Montúfar nor his successor, Moya de Contreras, held him in high esteem. Indeed, the latter characterized him as "in no way a churchman, nor a man to be entrusted with business, ambitious for honor and fond of flattery"; but for all these adverse judgments, he managed to get himself appointed dean of the cathedral, within the Church. Shortly after his arrival he was given the chair of rhetoric in the Royal and Pontifical University, to which he was an adviser, and later rector, from 1567 to 1568.

In 1554, Juan Pablos published three Latin dialogues by Cervantes, all dealing with the city of Mexico. This was not his first book, nor would it be his last. He had already published some works in Alcalá de Henares, and later he wrote in Mexico some laudatory epistles and a chronicle of New Spain, which remained unpublished for many years. Although his epistles with their rhetorical flourishes have not been rescued from oblivion, his memoirs of our city have. His idle pen delighted in sketching guidebooks to the environs for learned strangers and in recording their strolls in his company through the streets, squares, and fields. If Macrobius could say that Vergil destroyed and razed a great city with the verse

The fields where Troy once stood

Cervantes reconstructed ours through his Latin conversations as it lay before his eyes one peaceful day in 1554.

Three centuries after the *Dialogues* were written, Don Joaquín García Icazbalceta decided to reissue them, not because he was carried away by the charms of the prose, but for the sake of the information they contained concerning the physical appearance of the primitive city. We are forced to recognize that it was a scurvy trick on the part of the gods. The Latin that Cervantes de Salazar was so proud of had become a mere topographical map, a simple document in urban history. The Humanist never succeeded in capturing the life that was bubbling in

Mexico; for all his virtuosity, whatever he touched with his pen was turned to stone. We can see his figure in the distance, pointing with a rigid forefinger, describing in his high-flown style the small town markets, the palace hangers-on, and the fatuous students of the university—all the outward manifestations of an entity whose real essence escaped him.

In the "First Dialogue" he brings two actors onto the stage: Meza, an old-time resident of the city, and Gutiérrez, a recently arrived Spaniard. The first thing they come to is a building situated on the corner of the Plaza Mayor and the street we still know by the name of La Moneda. The two floors of the structure had plenty of window space, and many young men could be seen going in the door dressed in long gowns, with square caps jammed down over their ears.

"What building is that?" Gutiérrez asked.

Meza answered, "It is the university where the youth is being educated; the ones going in there are the students, the lovers of Minerva and the Muses."

Gutiérrez was all amazement. "There is still a place for learning in a land where greed reigns?"

Undoubtedly there was—"what is most valuable and powerful had conquered"—for that place was in fact the recently built University of Mexico.

The spacious courtyard was surrounded by the columns of the cloisters. The professors' daises had been assigned to them on the ground floor, with inscriptions designating the course of instruction; the chapel was "very nicely decorated"; and "the clock was something worth seeing, for not only does it strike the hours, but the quarters, too, by means of two sheep, which come to butt the bell in unison."

The beadle gravely walked the corridors in his long robe, his silver mace at his shoulder. In reality he was more of an ornament than a warden, for those students, unlike ours, employed their recesses and their free periods in endless discussions.

"My word," Gutiérrez says, "look how that fat student argues with the thin one! Such shouting, such waving of arms! See how he harries and presses him."

The masters were no less fond of argumentation than their students. The philosopher Negrete and Frías, the professor of Roman law, were a couple of fanatical polemicists. They loved to launch sophistries like trial balloons among the students, and when everyone finally agreed that what they were discussing was an irrefutable truth, the professors would prick them amid laughter at some pointed scholastic sally. They spent all their time thinking up problems for one another; they dressed up and stripped down allegations; they thrust and parried with the grace of fencers, their hands waving and their capes flying as they shouted and exchanged blows.

Every Tuesday in the theology classroom they would argue over conclusions to be drawn, "some problematical, some affirmative, others negative, and the dispute between defender and attacker was so hot that it would seem as if each was staking his life on it." A schoolmaster in academic dress presided over the debate "in his doctoral gown and hood," and it was he who directed the controversy and cleared up the moot points. In those fiery verbal fencing bouts, there were never any winners or losers. They delivered "mortal blows"; some of them tried to retract their clumsy thrusts; and when the defender flagged, the judge and the spectators took a hand in the combat "with much greater heat than there had been between the ones who had initiated the disputation." The roar of their voices was wafted over the city from the open balconies. Justo Sierra wrote with quiet humor: "It was the word, always the Latin word, the invisible shuttle that ran back and forth unceasingly through the endless warp of dialectical concepts. The exclamation of the Danish prince, 'Words, words, words,' should have been inscribed above the doors of the university of that day."

There was nothing new to discover, no room for doubt, for all the problems that confronted students and masters had already been "resolved by the authority of the Church beyond any possible revision of judgment." All that had been alive in Spain, all that had been debated in theology and law, would here be transformed into a verbal exercise. The word was beginning to lose its value; rhetoric for rhetoric's sake was filling that battlefield which was a vacuum, that empty solemnity which was to characterize the next two centuries.

We might seek the symbol of the university in the clock that hung above the turbulent cloister. The lovers of Minerva and the Muses railed furiously against the bell, but every attack on it was answered with a gentle chime. The hours of the colony glided away in this diversion.

From High on a Horse

In the "Second Dialogue," two citizens, Zuazo and Zamora, mounted on horseback, and the visitor Alfaro, on a black mule, begin their tour of the city through the streets of Tacuba. This was probably the only paved section of the city. The aqueduct that had its source in the forest of Chapultepec ran uncovered through the center, and the houses of the hidalgos, built of porous red stone, rose along its edges, looking like fortresses with their drawbridges, their escutcheons carved in stone, their grilled windows, and their battlements. All the houses were low, plain, and strong, to guard against earthquakes and Indian attacks.

In the spot once occupied by the palace of Axayácatl, Moctezuma's father, where the soldiers of Cortés were billeted, stood the house of the viceroy, crowned by a tower with clock weights hanging inside it. The two sidewalks leading to the Plaza Mayor were crowded with carpenters, blacksmiths, locksmiths, barbers, bakers, painters, stonecutters, tailors, buskin-makers, clog-makers, armorers, chandlers, crossbowmakers, sword-makers, pastry cooks, grocers, cabinet-makers, chairmakers, and wineskin-makers. The tanners' and leather-cutters' guild had its own side street. The cordwainers collected in a narrow lane on the western side of the cathedral, where they wove ropes "of whatever thickness was wanted," hempen thongs, shoemaker's thread, halters, and rope-soled sandals. The harness-makers fashioned chest coverings for horses, horse collars, stirrups, rowels with a cordovan heel strap, velvet sword belts, and sole-leather cases for arquebuses. The hatters—later grouped in an alley that debouched on San Fernando Plaza—offered hats of taffeta and French satin and Roman, Salamancan, and Castilian bonnets. The weavers turned out taffetas, damasks, and velvets, and the dyers used Mexican cochineal to turn the white silks red, as prescribed by ordinance.

The Plaza Mayor drew from Cervantes seven exclamations of admiration: "God, how fruitful and broad! How gay! How well adorned with tall, proud buildings at every compass point! What order! What beauty! What arrangement! What placing!" Zuazo explains:

It was built so wide that no one would find it necessary to carry anything for sale elsewhere; for what the markets for hogs, vegetables, and oxen, and the

Livia, the Julia, the Aurelia and Capedini Piazzas were to Rome, this one alone is to Mexico City. Fairs and market days are held here, and every kind of merchandise is available; merchants from all over the country gather here with their goods, and everything that is best in Spain comes to this square.

The place of prominence in the Plaza was occupied by the palace. Craftsmen had taken over the main floor—"What a racket and what a boiling crowd of people on foot and horseback!"—while the upper floor was reserved for the viceroy and the Audiencia. The palace, which since that time has been considered the center of colonial life, was a massive feudal castle flanked by two battlemented towers. Three single windows, a balustrade, and the columns at the door failed to soften the prevailing effect of crudeness and monotony, which still marked the *casas viejas* of Cortés in 1563.

"Who are those people," Alfaro asks, "who gather in the corridors of the palace in such numbers, and who walk now slowly, now rapidly, or stop dead, then run, who are as quick to shout as to stop talking, so that they seem like madmen?" Well, they were litigants, business agents, procurement officers, scriveners "waiting to appeal decisions of the lower courts to the Royal Audiencia," or mercenary soldiers awaiting a contract, or immigrants following a contingent of Indians and Creoles looking for work, making the corridors and the viceregal antechambers ring with their shouts and their tales of woe. We shall meet them later.

The visitors passed through the main post office, which was "filled with tables, benches, and scribes," along a passageway leading to the viceroy's apartments; then, after removing their hats, they glided noiselessly into the hall where hearings were held. There, on a thick carpet, in a chair canopied with lace-trimmed damask, sat the chief of state for the colony, surrounded by the oidores. Below him, on both sides, were grouped the attorney-general, the chief constable, the counsel for the poor—who was also the protector and defender of the Indians—the litigants, the secretary of the palace, and the clerk of the court, who read off the cases. Behind the wooden grille that divided the hall, "so the common, vulgar people may not go in and seat themselves with the others," stood "those who had the right to take a seat but did not wish to do so, as well as those who would like to but had not the right, because they did not enjoy that much pre-eminence." Nothing could be heard in the hall but the voice of the presiding officer of the week, for "silence enhances authority."

Alfaro notes, "With what respect that elderly lawyer rises in his place, his head uncovered, and defends his client!"

"And see," Zuazo whispers, "how that other man, with hair as white as the first, stands on the opposite side, and after asking with great respect to be heard, dissents and contradicts."

At that moment, the clerk of the court, having considered that the litigants had talked long enough, calls for silence, and our friends go through a large doorway to resume their tour.

"This," Zamora explains, "is the *medius Janus,* a place that has been provided for the merchants and businessmen, like the stairs in Seville and the Bourse in Antwerp, where Mercury holds sway."

"The visitor has come to the famous Merchants' Gateway, "where Claudius' gate spreads its elongated shadow," the only group of buildings on the Plaza Mayor that has not lost its name or its look of antiquity. The clerks in the dark shops are showing their customers Spanish brocades and Flemish damasks; by the end of the century they would be showing cold, heavy silks from China. All the laces and velvets, the plumes for hats, the jewels, the ornaments, the weapons, and the furniture which the sixteenth century loved so well were for sale in that gateway, considered the shopping center of Mexico. From the beginning, it constituted a kind of mercantile aristocracy. Not only were great fortunes amassed there, but a number of prosperous families destined to play important roles in the development of the city were established there too.

At one end of the plaza rose the city hall, symbol of the democratic system that has never quite succeeded in counterpoising Mexico's bias for political centralism. The building was noteworthy for its beautiful colonnaded gallery, which overlooked the main assembly hall. At the back of the structure were the city meat market and the city jail—and in the lower gateways was the foundry where "the officials who stamp out the silver work under lock and key like prisoners," and where public auctions were held and ingots weighed in order to collect His Majesty's 20 per cent duty. The dwelling of Martín López and the archbishop's palace completed the perimeter of the square; the only exception to its magnificence was the cathedral, which was lodged in a "small, humble, and poorly adorned" church.

Our friends did not end their tour here. The obliging guide had made up his mind that his guests were going to enjoy the morning to the hilt. Leaving the plaza behind them, they entered a street lined with magnificent residences. The richest families of New Spain, with the longest lineages, lived in this street, later given the name of Calle del Reloj—Clock Street. Don Luis de Castilla, the mining prodigy and adviser to viceroys, to whom we shall refer again; the Ávilas and the Benavides, dynasties of encomenderos who will play leading roles in our book; the eminent Mendozas, Zúñigas, Altamiranos, Estradas, Ávalos, Sosas, Alvarados, Saavedras, and Villafáñezes—these occupied the aristocratic section of the city.

Slaves dressed in livery stood guard at the doors, and the silence was broken from time to time when some lord went forth, clad in his burnished armor and followed by his pages, to take part in a tournament, or when his lady made her way to church in her sedan chair, surrounded by her ladies in waiting.

After passing the length of the street, Alfaro's tireless guides showed their guest the rude convent of Santo Domingo—an autonomous city within the Spanish city—then took the east side of the street that is now Belisario Domínguez, admired a new convent, the Concepción, and rested their tired mounts in front of the Franciscan monastery. The most noteworthy evangelical center in the New World was then a rustic spot that reflected the humility and simplicity of the early monks. A cross "so tall it seemed to touch the sky" rose in the inner courtyard, shaded by "well-tended leafy trees," and the open-air chapel, supported by lofty wooden pilasters, completed a picture of religious transition that ran from the ancient platforms where the ritual of the Indians was performed to the open courtyards where the faithful attended the divine services of the Catholic Church beneath the shade of the trees.

The secondary school for mestizo boys—"orphans," Zuazo explains, "born of Spanish fathers and Indian mothers"—stood in front of the Franciscan monastery.

"What do they do while they are shut up in there?" Alfaro asks.

"They read," Zamora explains. "They read and, what is more important, they are instructed in whatever has to do with divine worship.

They walk two by two in long robes, and many of them four by four because they are quite small."

"Now look at that proud and beautiful building," Zuazo adds, "There cannot be many like it in all the world. It is called *las tiendas de Tejada* (the textile shops), a name derived from the use for which it is intended and the people who built it."

"I have never seen anything more beautiful," Alfaro muses.

The building in question, two stories high, opens its doors to the street on one side and on the other faces the reservoir where "two small wharves" have been built, with stone steps leading down to them. From that spot they could again see the canals, and the apposite comparison was not slow to come to Alfaro's lips. "The number of boats, of freight canoes excellent for carrying merchandise, is so great that no one need feel homesick for Venice."

The Decline of the Markets

At the far end of the streets of San Juan de Letrán, then outside the boundaries of the plat, they came upon the Indians' hovels, which they had not been able to see as they were riding between buildings, "because they are so humble, scarcely rising above the ground." The market of San Juan stood nearby, which, together with the Tlatelolco and the San Hipólito, constituted one of the most important trading centers in the city.

The visitor's attention was caught by the exotic character of the market. A restless world spread out before them, overflowing with strange sound and stranger fruits, alongside the battlements, churches, and shops of the medieval city. Latin verses by the erudite Cervantes, hung above the lintel,

> India sent us her marble,
> the Sabine wharf its incense,

were like those classic ornaments that figure in travel books and other volumes wherein the Western mind has attempted to frame the picture of a new culture,

> With a face as varied
> as mankind's taste.

The indigenous markets had become greatly impoverished in thirty years. Market day at the San Juan bore little resemblance to the Tlatelolco *tianguez* described by Hernán Cortés in his Second Letter to Charles V. The jewel merchants had vanished. The silversmiths had been replaced by ostensibly converted Jews and Spaniards who operated shops in the street that still bears the name of their trade; the craftsmen who made mosaics and diadems of feathers, the illuminators of manuscripts, the dyers, and the salesmen who were as likely to offer the buyer a pheasant as the arms of a fallen warrior, the barbershops, and the ancient eating houses belonged to archeology. In their stead were some Indians sitting on the ground, selling red peppers, beans, avocados, mameys, sapodillas, and zocotes. Almost nothing was for sale except cereals, fruits, atole (a gruel of boiled ground corn)—the poor man's milk—and chía water in large clay pots beautifully decorated with flowers and grasses.

"My, what strange names!" Alfaro remarks.

"No more so than our names to the Indians," Zuazo answers.

Alfaro, an inquisitive man, had never stopped his flow of questions: "That black liquid they use to anoint their legs, which turns them blacker than an Ethiop's—what is it? And what is that black stuff that looks like mud with which they daub their heads? Tell me, why do they do that?"

"The Indians call the liquid *oglit,*" Zuazo tells him, "and they use it to protect themselves from the cold and the mange. They call the clay *zoquitl* or *quahtepuztli* in their own language. It is very fine for dyeing the hair black and for killing lice."

"I see they also have a large supply of worms for sale," Alfaro goes on. "I would like to know what they are used for. It seems laughable."

Zamora answers, "They are water worms, which they bring from the lagoon. The Indians call them *oquilin;* they eat them and feed them to their fowls."

"How very strange!" Alfaro murmurs, smiling in his beard. "Who would have believed worms would be used as human food, for the worms use men as food from the moment they die."

The visitor made the rounds of the market with his mouth open, not knowing which astonished him more, the figures and garments of the natives—among which he mentions petticoats and huipiles—or the things that "the universal mother" provides everywhere, as useful to the natives as they are harmful to the foreigners. The herb doctors, part medical men, part witch doctors, were there, as they had been in ancient times, selling their extraordinary remedies: *iztacpatli,* which drains off phlegm, *tlalcacahuatl* and *izticpatli,* which reduce fever, *culuzizicaxtli,* which clears the head, and *ololiuhqui,* "which heals ulcers and internal lesions."

"But those leaves," Alfaro asks, "so huge and thick, that end in a sharp point and are bordered with terrible spines along both sides—what tree do they come from?"

Zamora conscientiously enlightens him. "From what we call the maguey and the Indians call *metl,* which serves so many and important purposes that the ancient sword of Delphi could not equal its usefulness."

The sacred plant of the Indians, the green vegetable star of the mesa, has come onstage. Together with the prickly pear and the other cacti, it is the plant most common to our high and arid plateaus. After attempting to describe it, Zamora details with manifest satisfaction the many and varied uses the Indians make of the maguey:

They crush the green leaves and separate the fibers in water upon some stones. From them a kind of hemp is made, and from that thread a cloth is woven that takes the place of linen, and ropes both heavy and fine are twisted, too. The spine which outlines every leaf is hard as iron and does duty as a needle. The leaves serve as tiles to roof the houses; the shoots nearest the earth are white and tender, and the Indians prepare them in such a way that they prove most pleasing to the palate. When dry, they provide a fuel that gives forth a gentle, smokeless fire; they say the ashes are excellent for various uses. When the root is drawn from the center, it is placed on the roof instead of rafters; in the hollow that is left, surrounded by leaves, a sap is deposited, which is first used to make honey, then later wine, and finally vinegar. Sugar is made from the boiled honey; and, in sum, maguey is good in other ways that are so numerous they cannot be kept in mind, ways that neither Pliny nor Aristotle ever thought of, much less wrote about, however diligent students of nature they may have been.

Not much remains to be seen now in a visit to the impoverished market of San Juan de Letrán, but Zamora was still bent upon showing

Alfaro the sumptuous edifice of the Convent of San Agustín, then under construction—"a work that fame will rank above all others"—the unfinished hospital of Hernán Cortés, and the splendid house of Alonso de Villaseca, the Croesus or Midas of the city.

High noon struck, and the horses broke into a light trot.

"Why are you forcing the horses to such a pace?" Alfaro asks, curious and puzzled.

Zamora explains, "So as to be in time for dinner. It is past twelve already."

The tour was over. The church bells were ringing for noon, and the streets, hitherto lively, looked deserted. Zuazo invited his friends to dinner, and they accepted without needing much persuasion.

Zamora had the last word: "Seat yourselves at the table then, and I am sure your company will make the meal gracious as well as pleasing, the sort of meal that Varro would enjoy."

The Outskirts of Mexico City

In the afternoon the three friends Zuazo, Alfaro, and Zamora ordered their mounts again and made their way along the spacious causeway through the center of which the Chapultepec aqueduct ran.

Alfaro opens the conversation. "We have dined in the house of Lucullus, or even Apollo's hall, rather than in Zuazo's."

Zuazo remarks nostalgically, "You would have much greater reason to say that if you had arrived soon after this country was conquered."

"Now I declare, how can anything be better than the best?"

Zuazo sighs and is carried away by his memories. "The Sybarites' supper or the banquets in Syracuse could not have been more sumptuous."

Before the conversation could wander off into a discussion of the sensuous delights to which Cervantes de Salazar was surely no stranger, Alfaro's Humanistic observation about the causeway turned them back on their high-flown pedagogical course: "The Appian Way, which Cicero praises at several points in his defense of Milo, was never so thronged with people."

The public commons of the city opened before them, "very pleasing in their constant greenness," magnificent country houses, all of them surpassed by the one belonging to Hernán Cortés, and the plain where horses were trained in mock battle "so they will be ready when the real ones come."

Chapultepec, the favorite woodland of the Aztec emperors, was surrounded by high walls "to prevent the Indians from fouling the water and the hunters from killing or driving away the abundant game there: deer, boar, rabbits, and hares." The trio admired the reservoir—"the sun's rays and the shadows of the trees tint it with a thousand tones, and as it is not equally deep everywhere, many beautiful forms, more colorful than the rainbow, are reflected when the sun shines." Leaving their horses tethered to tree trunks, the three friends set out to climb the hill by the stone steps built during the reign of Moctezuma Xocoyotzin, the better to enjoy the panorama.

"My word!" Alfaro cries in one of his long and enthusiastic exclamations, as he comes to the crest of the hill above the crowns of the ahuehuete trees, "What a sight I see before me from here! How gladdening to the eye and spirit, and so beautifully varied that I venture to say with every reason that both worlds are contained and comprehended here. What the Greeks say about man, whom they call Microcosmus or the world in miniature, could be said about Mexico." The lake, with the city rising behind it, seemed covered with the Indians' boats and their fishing nets, and beyond, looking like the hulls of other scattered boats, the hills of the Peñón emerged, with their hot springs; Estrella Hill, one of the centers of Indian religion, resembled a game preserve. The landed estates and country houses, the plantings of trees, and, above all, the mountains formed a backdrop that lent our valley its remarkable beauty. Ajusco to the south; the Guadalupe range spreading to the north in a gentle circle; the cordillera to the east, with the sun glowing above it in the morning, and in between the deep blue harmonies of the cordillera and Ajusco; the ocher minerals of the sacred Santa Catalina range, the round flanks of the twin volcanoes, Popocatépetl and Iztaccíhuatl, crowned with snow—these completed the composition.

"The soil is so rich in iron that it yields bountiful harvests in many places." The game is so abundant "that even people who are not looking for it and are not hunters come upon eagles, royal herons, and wild geese; or it may be hares, rabbits, deer, boar, bears, and panthers."

In New Spain, Cervantes concludes, wool, cotton, grain, sugar, honey, and herds of ruminants both large and small are raised. The country is extremely rich in gold, silver, and other metals, and thanks to its good climate a man "can wear the same clothing on his person and his bed in winter and summer alike." The only things the Humanist found lacking in this opulent picture were olive oil, wine, and the conquest of Florida, land of the Fountain of Youth—one of the myths that still influenced Mexican life in 1554.

The City in 1580

A quarter century after Cervantes de Salazar made a tour of the city in the company of his hosts, the friar Alonso Ponce was commissioned to write a travel diary for the *comisario general* of the Franciscan order. He portrays a city constantly on the rise. "It is the most populous," he declares, "the noblest and most imposing in New Spain, even including Peru."

Even though the channels of many of the canals had become clogged, in 1580 the city had not lost its watery beauty. Two great reservoirs, like the ancient serpents that encircled the sacred recesses of the plazas, embraced the Spanish city. Ringed with green, spanned by bridges, the water glided up to the houses, penetrated the gardens of the convents, and formed huge pools that almost reached the Plaza Mayor, a most authentic and vigorous manifestation of Indian life.

Vegetables grown on the chinampas, the floating islands, hay for horses, charcoal and firewood, cereals, blankets, and pottery arrived daily in canoes propelled by long poles. The customs offices must have made a lively sight during the early hours of the morning. The shouts of the officials and the scurrying of the merchants, the unloading of so many and such varied products, the presence of hundreds of boats manned by Indians, composed a picture typical of the city that was to survive, without any essential change, until the nineteenth century.

The situation of Mexico City, built on land that was constantly being rescued from the marshes, gave rise to municipal problems very much like those of the present day. "The foundations are not sunk very deep," to borrow the words of the *Diario,* "because they soon strike water; instead they are commonly laid directly upon the earth and though the structures are tall and massive, they keep sinking little by little." In order to correct this drawback, the builders resorted to the use of piers beneath their great buildings, a device that our boundless love for skyscrapers has made familiar to us. The constant threat of floods and the "pestilential" odor emanating from the lagoon, "especially when it dries up somewhat in summer," did, however, exacerbate its marshy character.

What remarkable things did Mexico City have to offer in 1580, sufficient to compensate for such serious disadvantages? The *Diario* undertakes to list them: very fine houses and beautiful streets so regular they seem cast "from a single mold," beautiful children, and spirited horses. The Spanish poet Juan de la Cueva, who was in New Spain from 1574 to 1577, agrees completely with the historian-friar in his famous epistle addressed to the licentiate Sánchez de Obregón:

> *Seis cosas excelentes en belleza*
> *hallo escritas con C, que son notables*
> *y dignas de alabar en su grandeza:*
> *casas, calles, caballos admirables,*
> *carnes, cabellos y criaturas bellas*
> *que en todo extremo todas son loables;*
> *bien claro veis que no es encarecellas*
> *esto, y que pueden bien por milagrosas*
> *venir de España a México por vellas.*

> *Six things I find supreme in beauty,*
> *All of them beginning with C,*
> *All worthy of a poet's praise:*
> *Castles and causeways and cavalcades*
> *Children, carnal beauty, coiffured hair,*
> *If you leave Spain for Mexico you'll see*
> *Them here in elegance and plenty*
> *And grant such miracles can be.*

The houses, the streets, the horses, the children—here are the brush strokes that finally created a solid urban tradition. All of them were pictured repeatedly through the sixteenth century in bold freehand sketches and by scattered voices already singing an opening chorus to the full-voiced song of Mexican grandeur. What Juan de la Cueva expressed in a verse epistle were merely alluded to incidentally by Ponce and the English pirates, and furnished the material for a poem by Bernardo de Balbuena in which the buildings, the mettlesome stamping of the horses, the nobility of the streets, the courtesy and the virtue, the trades of the craftsmen, the government, and the religion were full of the breath of life, as on a baroque altar laden with burnished gold and sculptured images in high relief against a gold ground.

Hidalgos and dignitaries, "as many from Spain as born here," abounded in this small city which had fewer than four thousand white residents, supported by numberless Indians. They were all very courtly people, well spoken and better mannered. "Weighty" merchants—weighty in the broadest meaning of the term—lived there, an abundance of bureaucrats, then called officials, and "many rich men," though "the poor were always with them, too," as the *Diario* explains, "to round out the profile of that chivalric society." Indeed "they increase by the day and everyone keeps guard over his money."

The essential parts of the colonial machinery, which was to function without noticeable change through the passage of three hundred years, are the objects of close scrutiny in the *Diario*. At the highest level is the viceroy, the Audiencia, the chief officer of the court council, the prison, and the treasury where the public funds were stored. The mint coined hard money in pesos bound for the East Indies and the Orient; the printing press published catechisms, dictionaries, and grammars; and the recently established Inquisition tried those suspected of heresy.

Next door to the palace of the viceroy stood that of the archbishop. It contained the archepiscopal court and the prison, never empty of clergymen. While the walls and flying buttresses of the new cathedral were rising, the old one, restored and "almost like new," was used for the meeting of the recently formed Provincial Council.

Six hospitals—four of them for Spaniards, one for Indians, and the other for Negroes and mestizos—were in service, and seven convents of nuns and seven monasteries of monks were also operating. Besides the convents for the Reginists, the Santa Claras, the Conceptionists, the Marian, and the Jeroniman nuns, there were those for penitents and for recluses, the last-named being a sort of retreat from the world for divorced or widowed ladies. The dismal name by which the people habitually designated these ladies conveys all that need be said about them.

The nuns established a way of life in the religious regime of the colony that remained essentially vigorous over the space of fifty years. The presence of those enormous houses filled with pious virgins must have been a little disturbing. The odor of sanctity, a sense of chastity, emanated from them and conflicted with the open sensuality of the period. The double façades of their churches, the grilles in the choirs, bristling with barbs, their somewhat ethereal quality—all made up a world apart. If the regimens of the nuns failed to create a Saint Teresa, they did at least produce a great number of very skilled and original cooks during the lifetime of the colony. The best dishes of New Spain came from the hands of our religious women, whose influence can be traced not alone through the culinary art but through the language and many of the colonial customs as well. In fact the convent was a peaceful hearth, shorn of the vexations of marriage. The mystical brides of Christ lived a life absorbed, dedicated to the service of adoring the Lord. They made dresses for the ever-present images of their beloved Spouse, the Infant Jesus, and the saints; they wove, embroidered, and cooked; they chanted epithalamiums and cradle songs, almost always with no result, and from time to time they were authorized to sink into actual swoons of amorous ecstasy.

The monks also lived a communal life, in seven monasteries. One was that of the powerful Dominican order, empowered to exercise the functions of the Inquisition. The Augustinians operated two monasteries, although one of them was designed as a secondary school and was situated on the outskirts of the city. Two others belonged to the Franciscan branches of the barefoot monks of Saint Cosmus and Saint Damian and the Observants of Saint Francis; this last became the outstanding missionary center in New Spain. The sixth housed the Company of Jesus; the seventh the Carmelites, who had no more than arrived before they began to build the Indian quarter of San Sebastián under the patronage of the viceroy.

The presence in a small city of such a large number of monks—not to mention the priests—was marked by corruption and a sordid rivalry that became public knowledge. The days of the great Apostles were but a memory. The archbishop was in open conflict with the viceroy, the monks were hostile to the priests, and within the orders themselves violent disputes arose over who was to occupy the best positions. Fray Alonso Ponce himself fell a victim to these monastic intrigues, and his high investiture as the emissary of the head of the Franciscans availed him nothing whatsoever. After a while the provincial archbishop of Mexico refused to recognize him on the pretext that the powers granted him by the superior of the order had lapsed. Despite the fact that Fray Alonso Ponce succeeded in proving that his powers were still in force, the provincial archbishop declared war on him; Ponce then tried to protect himself by excommunicating the archbishop, and the viceroy, a partisan of the archbishop, had Ponce thrown in prison and exiled from Mexico.

Ponce's sufferings are not germane to our study. In the monastery of Tecamachalco he fell seriously ill—his champions were convinced that poison had been administered to him—and was taken to Puebla in a litter carried by Indians. The *Diario* states: "So great is the passion of some monks in the archdiocese of Mexico and so evil their intentions that although what had been stated concerning Father Ponce's illness actually did occur, and more besides, they dared to claim and to publish that he had feigned it." To be sure, the resistance of the Franciscan was remarkable. Among the remedies administered to him, mention is made of a sedative "of mouse dung . . . disguised in a little wine." The wonder is that Ponce, an old man, had managed to escape with his life from the hatred of his companions, the persecution of the viceroy, prison, and the barbarous pharmacopeia of his time.

Nature and the Indians

The European fruit trees already established in the convent orchards— orange, lemon, apple, clingstone peach, and pomegranate—flourished side by side with the cherry-like capulines, avocados, mamey, sapodilla, and custard apples, and it was easy to spot the silky leaves of banana trees shining like a lamp amid the variegated greens of the blossom. The shoots of the Mediterranean grapevine, the mulberry tree, which is home and nourishment to the silkworm, and the gray-green olive were beginning to sketch a classical landscape in outline when monopoly put a stop to their culture and deprived Mexico of olive oil and wine.

In general terms, the Valley of Mexico was felt to be a second Castile, although much more gentle and fertile. The trees of Spain—the willows and white poplars edging the water, liveoaks and pines on the uplands—grew in profusion. Owing to the absence of wolves and other carnivores, the fields were rich in cattle. Each village had its small butcher shop, and the ruminants multiplied to such a degree that "there are men who do their branding every year, even though many head are lost or become mavericks. . . ." The *Diario* concludes sarcastically, "It is a very vicious land for every kind of animal, though rational beings may be found among them."

Around the city washed a sea of rumor concerning the mysterious Indian life. The presence of the natives adds an impression of a disturbing force, something alien and barbaric, with little relation to the eloquent discourses of Cervantes, streets laid out in a straight line, or the escutcheons above the doors, and even less to the brocades and silks of the cavaliers who jousted for rings in the square.

The Indian men "went barefoot and barelegged," wearing shirts, trousers, and a cotton mantle "knotted over the shoulder." The women wore toques, huipiles, and skirts. They were seen on the scaffolds of buildings; in the black depths of the mines; stooping in the furrowed fields over the corn, issue of their ancestral tree of heaven; or with brush and pen, copying classical texts from the Romans or from the fathers of the Church. And those phantoms did all the work. They also gave a new shading to the language, peopled the architecture with flamboyant images, sang in the choirs; they were the craftsmen and the peasants, the backbone of the country, and the material from which to construct the Utopias of More and Don Vasco.

"They were approaching a sudden end. . . . we finish them off with a mere breath," Dorantes de Carranza confesses, and Ponce adds: "When Cortés arrived at Texcoco there were sixty thousand Indians; a few years later they numbered eighteen thousand. Thus they keep dwindling away throughout New Spain, as much through the epidemics and massacres that have occurred as through the ill treatment they have been accorded."

The Last Years of the Century

Mateo Rosas de Oquendo was a Spanish adventurer of the end of the sixteenth century, which is to say he was an adventurer quite unlike the men who came to the Indies at the beginning of the century. He had served as a soldier in Genoa and in Tucumán; he had been in Marseilles "where the easy women filled him with enthusiasm"; he had spent ten years in Peru as a servant to viceroy Don García Hurtado de Mendoza, and had left Lima in the year 1598 to live for some time in the city of Mexico. "According to his own confession," Alfonso Reyes writes, "his hair and beard were reddish, his eyes black, skin ruddy, and none of his ten wounds had proved mortal."

Rosas de Oquendo wore a sword at his belt, but he preferred to use the pen as a foil; he never stayed long in one place, for he was a wanderer of the world, like the wind that bloweth where it listeth, making sport of everyone; he was inclined to be sensual—in Lima "he left bastard children and had love affairs with married women"—and, unlike his contemporaries, he was never seduced by money.

A satirist by profession, Oquendo practiced his artful distortions on the most respectable figures in the Indies. Whereas his malicious portraits perhaps cannot be entirely believed, at least they are a mordant commentary on a milieu of dissemblers and hypocrites.

Oquendo sounds slightly foolish in his description of his own war exploits. Without wishing to make invidious comparisons, we can see he is the antithesis of Bernal Díaz de Castillo. Three days spent with some soldiers in Tucumán were enough time for him to found a city, "if four cattleyards are a city." And later the heroes "met together in Cabildo and wrote a parcel of nonsense to the viceroy, telling how they spent three successive days fighting against twenty thousand Capayan Indians, and as recompense for it they ask for privileges and exemptions. The truth was," he adds, "that the hapless natives gave us their land quite willingly, and their huts and their poor chattels, and not an ounce of blood was shed."

No doubt Rosas de Oquendo was a man who delighted in swimming against the current. Although Bernal Díaz, by his own account, took part in one hundred nineteen battles, it can safely be said that he spent even more time petitioning for his rewards; and Bernal was no exception, for all the Conquistadors did the same. They carried with them a detailed account of their hungry periods, their wounds, even their scratches; they talked incessantly about their perils and their incredible exploits; they composed moving stories of their immense efforts and sent them to the king. In exchange for so many sufferings, they solicited him for a small piece of land and a handful of Indians out of the millions they had won for him and for Christianity by the might of their swords.

To be sure, the Conquest had to be respected. Its chroniclers, both official and self-appointed, had spoken the last word on that epic, and the heroes' sons, in Peru, Santo Domingo, and Mexico, had racked their brains in unison trying to compress such extraordinary feats of arms into the eight lines of the puny *octava real*. And after all this literary consecration had built a poetic Everest, a scribbler took it into his head to make fun of the Conquest, the Conquistadors, and their reasonable requests!

Naturally a man like Oquendo, a soldier who fought the Indians and then made fun of his warfare, never had a cent. He went about shod in cowhide boots; he wore a little cape with two shoulder flaps and an English doublet; his breeches were patched, his hat was unlined, his hands coal-black—"I never wash my face," he confesses with obvious cynicism—and his fingernails

> . . . *are so long*
> *they serve me as the knife I lack.*

Oquendo's fondness for satirical poetry is unbridled. His crossings of the ocean, the worries of his daily life, his observations as a traveler, even his own person are topics for stinging jokes. The picture he composed of society in the Indies was also far from flattering:

> *It's a land of confusion,*
> *a chaos, a wasteland*
> *a scabby empire,*
> *an Antichrist in speech.*

Black faces peer out from all his couplets. Negroes in livery, Negro fruit and cake vendors, mulatto women with kerchiefs wound around their heads who dance the *chacona* and the *charumba* stipple the map of America with a new color. The women gossip in the confectioners' shops or, as in our own day, meet in their houses to play passionately at cards. Naturally adventurers were everywhere—Oquendo was one of them—and so were impostors. A great señor parades through the streets on festival days in a black doublet, a lace shirt, "an emerald on his chest," "a sword and gilded dagger" at his waist; the next morning he may be seen crossing the empty street with his breeches covered with filth and

> hands bound behind him
> as though trussed up to be roasted.

The general habit of truckling to the nobility is a dominant theme in Oquendo's couplets. All the Spaniards who went to the Indies were given to pompous display of their illustrious ancestors. "How kind the sea was!" the satirist exclaims. "It did for family trees what it does for wines,"

> making vinegar of the poor ones
> and perfecting the good!

According to their stories they came in search of adventure, certainly not to seek an easy fortune, leaving wealth and property behind them in Spain. The truth is that, like the early colonists and many of the Conquistadors, they emigrated to escape justice or poverty and, once arrived, they began to talk about trunks seized by pirates and shipwrecks in which their belongings were lost. These charlatans would conclude their bogus accounts—"Viceroy Marquis de Cañete thus bids ye set forth!"—with a modest petition for Arequipa or the Andes.

Well, that is the Indies for you. Overflowing with bastards carrying noble names:

> What do you give Pero Sanchez?
> Such a gift, Don Pero Sanchez!
> From lots of Hurtados and Pachecos
> Such a lot of Enriquezes and Guzmanes!
> From Mendozas and Leivas
> Such a lot of Velascos and Ardales,
> From Laras and from Cerdas,
> Buitrones and Salazares!

Before he quit the city of the kings, Oquendo wrote a sonnet in which he tried to express all he felt about Peru. He would have needed a million lines, but for lack of space, the coupleteer left only the following unimpeachable token of his gratitude toward the Limans, by way of farewell:

SONNET TO LIMA, PERU
A viceroy with thirty halberdiers,
scholars in decorous floods,
priests unordained and ordained,
vagabond, beardless cavaliers.
Gamesters and gamblers too many to number,
shopkeepers who've built on air;
constables ever light-fingered,
corners pre-empted by grocers.
A thousand weak-witted poets,
ladies whose honor is specious,
rascals and cuckolds by the score.
Yokels who dine on turnips and cabbage,
a sullen sun, a clouded birth—
that's Lima's everyday face.

Chronicle of a Satirist

Before the arrival of Oquendo, Mexico had no satirical poet. Gutierre de Cetina, Eugenio de Salazar, and Juan de la Cueva, all of whom were living in New Spain, not only had never laughed at our expense but had given the enthusiastic welcome, with laudatory verses or with good advice, that a city swarming with poets would usually offer foreign colleagues.

New Spain had its influence on Oquendo. Alfonso Reyes comments:

The man who was solely a satirist in Peru seems rapt in contemplation of the valleys and mountains of Mexico, somewhat melancholic, and very fond indeed of recalling his exploits of yesterday. Age may contribute to that in great measure. But it might be said that the atmosphere of Peru and Mexico makes itself felt from the first moment—the former satirical, the latter melancholic. As time goes by, each may indeed become the characteristic tone of these two literary provinces.

Like most satirists, Oquendo was at heart a sentimentalist. His eyes had been created to exaggerate the defects of society, and his cynicism was merely the most natural way for him to express his indignation toward the presumption and greed of the men who had come to America. In his verses, many of which are actually fables, in line with the tastes of his day, he vigorously condemns the self-interest "that prevails over everything," the vanity of the commoners, the glut of bad poets and thieving officials, and the old inconsistency of women who choose wealth and scorn virtue, two assets—the scoffing, contemptuous satirist suspects—that are seldom found in one man.

On the other hand, he had always been less devoted to letters than to live affairs, and advancing age inclined him to exaggerate his past exploits and to sigh rather more than was seemly for a professional satirist. No wonder, then, that nature in Mexico could turn him melancholic and that his verbal landscapes should show his state of mind transparently.

A famous Indian volcano
whose lofty temples
are crowned with spun snow
on sheets of alabaster;
thus the towering peaks
their straight spires piercing sky
compete for the reign of the heavens
with the green crests of the pines.
Thin hoarfrost lies so lightly
in pearly patterns of ice, and
melts in the warmth of my sighs
of longing that fly to their master.

We must not be misled by the tone of this and another ballad. Though he repents of his unfairness to Peru—his sonnet to Lima had opened a quarrel—and his increasing melancholy may appear to have vitiated the virulence of his sarcasm, he observes similarities between

Mexico City and Lima that lead him to lapse back into his old, uncorrected habits.

In the short chronicle which Oquendo dedicates to our city, he begins by closely approximating his earlier work. Silver, the metal that made Mexico famous in Europe and China, was foremost for him; he then mentions the herds that grazed over the woods and meadows and the stalks of wheat that tinge the fields with gold; lastly he mentions the famous squares and bridges, the temples and the fountains, the horses and the houses.

After thus setting the urban stage, Oquendo, inspired in its silence, describes to us the figures that enliven it. Gallant cavaliers emerge and

> *a throng of high-spirited ladies,*
> *. . . a concourse of merchants who,*
> *like everyone else, keep moving*
> *up and down like clock weights,*
> *some going up and others down;*
> *doctors in hood and tassel,*
> *many scholars of renown;*
> *canons who surpass Bártulos*
> *in the number of degrees,*
> *churchmen with a conscience*
> *kept apart and guarded:*
> *Even Salamanca has no more*
> *M.A.'s or Ph.D.'s.*

That portrait could scarcely be more flattering. But a little farther along, Oquendo, who had no such pedagogical proclivities as Cervantes de Salazar, creeps into a house where four women are playing cards in the shadows of the jalousies. A deluge of questions quickly overwhelms him.

> *Whom does he serve? What does he live on?*
> *Who is he, and what is his name?*
> *Is he married? A man of property?*
> *Is he cavalier to another young dame?*
> *How is our country treating him?*
> *Has he too much of something?*
> *Is he lacking in anything?*

The satirist mutters: "Devil take the girl!" and then raises his voice after the aside and begins his speech:

> . . . . *Joy of my soul,*
> *no man hires me, nor have I a wife.*
> *Jeronimo they call me,*
> *and the wealth I hold in fee*
> *would fit beneath my cloak entire.*
> *So now, milady, I'll comply*
> *with your request and try*
> *to tell you all I feel*
> *as to this country and my weal,*
> *my expectations, and my life.*

In Mexico City, he could see everywhere exotic fabrics, costly dress, rich jewels, "divine understanding," "white snow and fine mother-of-pearl." They say that Venus reigns there, but that opinion is false,

> *For to judge by what I've found*
> *and by what happens all around,*
> *love cannot possibly aspire*
> *to what self-interest does acquire.*

He almost always writes in the character of a gallant youth. It is not for him to speak of it, but he goes about dressed in brocade and fur; he is valiant, wise, and discreet; he knows how to court a lady, to dance and strum the guitar, and he hangs on the ladies' skirts:

> *The young girls call him "my life."*
> *The women call him "my soul."*
> *Wives say, "my glory and my goal."*

At the conclusion of his moral discourse, Oquendo tries to begin his conquest of the ladies with a salute to live, but one of them interrupts him with a gesture of annoyance.

> *Enough of your vain prating.*
> *Start a conversation*
> *and draw a hand for our game.*

The poetic interloper feels a chill:

> *And as in my pockets I was carrying not a copper,*
> *I changed my style and spoke improper*
> *so that if anyone had known me,*
> *he'd see my game had blown away*
> *ere I had seen my hand.*
> *Straightway I rose and told them,*
> *"If you ladies care to wait,*
> *I'll fetch my money, for my fate*
> *is being pleased to please.*

While the ladies are waiting for him to return, Oquendo, burning with rage, resumes his satirical activities. Each time he has the chance, he involves himself in drawing odious comparisons between Spain and the Indies. In Spain,

> *the good is held in esteem,*
> *but here, the bad is extolled.*

In his *Sátira que hizo un galán a una dama criolla que le alababa mucho a México* (*Satire Composed by a Gallant to a Creole Lady Who Praised Him Highly in Mexico*), Oquendo says:

> *What could Cortés or his Spaniards*
> *find in all this kingdom*
> *but barbarians*
> *dressed in feathers and shells?*
> *There were never horses,*
> *sheep, cattle, suckling pigs—*
> *nor oil, nor bread, nor wine,*
> *Nothing but* mameys *and* alotes.

The arrogance of Mexico, its boastful provincialism, led him to exclaim, "while invoking Spain":

> *Scourge this mad kingdom that,*
> *having naught but three little* zapotes,
> *yet ventures to compete with thee*

> *and tries to usurp thy armorial blazons,*
> *trying to convince us*
> *that no houses on earth*
> *can equal the Mexicans',*
> *thinking to make us adore them*
> *though in them I've never found*
> *the walls, the pyramids, or towers*
> *of Babylon and Egypt.*
> *And that is why they cry us down.*

The Indians, whom he accuses of speaking beastly Spanish, do not escape his satire:

> *Cada noche que amanece*
> *como la rana gritando*
> *cuanto saco mis biscueso*
> *lo presco piento poscando. . . ."* *

Even when they prate of love, the mestizos pretend to a smug superiority:

> *Ah, Señora Juana!*
> *forgive me, your ladyship,*
> *and listen to the plaints*
> *of a miserable mestizo.*
> *Although I go in shreds and patches*
> *still I'm a noble an hidalgo.*
> *My father and mother were*
> *born of the Conquistadors.*

One of his many failures on the field of love finally forces him to leave Mexico:

> *I'll forfeit your gardens in June*
> *and your Morisco feast in August;*

---

* This verse cannot be put into English. Oquendo wrote it to indicate the peculiarities of Spanish pronunciation in Mexico. (Translator.)

I'll forfeit the famous assemblies
of your lovely Mexican ladies;
I'll forfeit my deal at cards
and, dropping one from the pack,
I'll forfeit the chance that gives me
to drop it beneath your skirts.

"And so he says good-bye," writes Reyes, annotating the ballad that begins "Adrenio pastor humilde"—"to the sunlit sections of the city, to the martyr Catarina 'pierced by a thousand knives,' to the devout monasteries."

Illustrious city, farewell.
It breaks my heart
to think that my horse
will tread the paving-stones
of San Antón as I leave you . . .
Farewell, you beautiful markets
where bibulous ladies
will drink atole *until*
they've hoisted three sheets in the wind.
Farewell, Empedradillo;
farewell to your gallant captain.
Farewell, all you mule-thieves.
Farewell, unmiraculous men
who frolic along those beaches. . . .

It would be a mistake to think that Oquendo actually said good-bye to Mexico City in this romance. The incorrigible satirist was merely composing a sonnet expressing his opinions of the capital of New Spain, as he had when he left the city of Lima. The hendecasyllable—a metric line he uses only for special occasions—once more serves him to tie several outstanding persons hand and foot and offer them to us pickled in vinegar. Merchants swollen with covetousness, gentlemen longing to be cavaliers, upstart proprietors of low taverns, rebel Negroes, gentlemen who rule everywhere but in their own homes, women who gamble night and day, and a thousand claimants hanging to the viceroy like leeches all figure in the *Soneto del gachupín que maldice de Mexico*

(*Sonnet of the Lad Who Curses Mexico*). Real friends are few, but those who claim to be are many. Together with the markets, the auctions, and the confusion, there are also—can anyone doubt that Oquendo would leave them out?—

> *Women who sell themselves for gold*
> *and thus leave the better ones full of woe.*

The similarity between life in Peru and life in Mexico at the close of the century is evident. The rash of illustrious genealogies, the vanity and arrogance of the Spaniards in America, the indolence of the Creoles and their pretensions to a noble lineage, the passion for gambling, the prevalence of poets, literary men, and rich tavernkeepers are all characteristic of the colonial society of the two viceregencies.

Perhaps Oquendo's satiric influence was stronger in Mexico than any mark left by other Spanish poets. As we shall see in a later chapter touching on the poetry written by poets born in Mexico, the Creoles seized their chance to answer his insults, and the strength of their language rivaled Oquendo's own. In the rivalry that arose in the very beginning, between Spaniards born in the peninsula and those born in America, the Creoles came to regard Oquendo as an ally rather than an enemy. His sharp portrayal of the newcomer, a poor immigrant brimming with aristocratic notions and rodomontade, a rascal, hence an anti-hero, corresponded neatly with the resentment felt by the Creoles, who saw themselves being superseded. Oquendo offered them a weapon for revenge—most vendettas took a literary form at that time—and the yeoman service he thereby did moved them to pardon his other sins. Furthermore, the Creole writer's view of the Indies was no better than Oquendo's. He described America as hell and managed if possible to escape from it, though not without getting somewhat singed. The Creole poets, who could not possibly get away, were burning inwardly, with a slow fire.

The Mexico of the Rainbow Chasers

During the last third of the century, the north offered attractions enough to draw the adventurers who came streaming off the ships to spread over New Spain. To the gold seekers, the north was made up of one pinch of El Dorado and another of California. Prisons and missions lined the trail of mining. A fortress, a miserable little church spire, and a battlemented wall guarding the domestic buildings stretched lazily beneath the vast sky of the desert.

The mirage of the Seven Cities of Cíbola and the seductions of Baja California had added to the map of Mexico the absurd novelty of a desert that brought together on the same red soil—rich in cactus, death, and fortune—the nomad Indian in his savage state and the gamble of mining. Whereas the civilized Indians of the great empires had been enslaved without any great effort, the wild tribes of the north, who had never served kings in golden sandals, succeeded for centuries in keeping their age-old freedom. The savage hunter who decorated his war shield with the scalps and bushy beards of his enemies the white men had a phantasmal quality. He would burst impetuously from the bank of a river or the fringes of a forest and rout a troop of soldiers or a train of mules and covered wagons loaded with silver. And it might happen that a magistrate's wife was left in the middle of the desert, swooning in her satin litter, surrounded by dead men and howling Indians, while unheard-of tortures were going on.

Thanks to the influence of Ramón López, Zacatecas is regarded today as the model of a peaceful province. Forty years after its founding, it was the second most important city in the colony and the first in its ability to handle a wild and unstable way of life. Zacatecas had something for everyone. Hawkins' English pirates found sanctuary there; the Germans were able to devote themselves to alchemy and the transformation of metals; the Jews to usury and astrology, two sciences that usually go together; the Portuguese to commerce; and the Flemish to craftsmanship.

The orderliness of agricultural cities was unknown in that silver town. Life was lived on the fringe of the law, between the church and the tavern, gambling and quarreling, ruinous loss and riches. No one much honored the conventions, for in the lottery of the mines, yesterday's millionaire might gamble himself into beggary and today's ragamuffin might be tomorrow's magnate. Gaming had few rules, and the calculation of probabilities was unknown. Luck was in the hands of the gods. The miracle was a miracle made to order for the particular miner, a sign of divine grace, and it was compounded equally of danger and slightly sinister splendor of the adventure of prospecting for wealth. The famous Poor Man's Mine (Los Pobres) near Compostela in New Galicia, owed its origin to an episode typical of that environment. Doña Leonor de Arias, the widow of Captain Pedro Ruíz de Haro, had once given alms to a native beggar, and this man, in reality an angel dressed in rags, was so grateful to her that he revealed to her the whereabouts of the precious metal.

The lucky strike was often touchingly simple. Once when miners shifted the embers of a bonfire in the mountains, they found a very rich deposit of silver ore; in another case, a poverty-stricken soldier one night announced a mad premonition: "If it's God's will, we shall find here what we need to cure us all," and a vein of precious metal was found later on the spot where he had scraped the soil with his boot. And at times the gods were not above using ostentatious and macabre methods of communication; hidden treasure might claim its right to be exploited by causing skulls to whistle or some bandit hanged from a tree to speak with the strangled voice of James Joyce's famous hanged man.

In this heightened, atypical environment religion, omnipresent in New Spain, submitted to the peculiarities and the imperatives of life. From time to time, a poor Indian who had slipped and lost his footing would be rescued by his patron saint, who suspended him in the air; the Virgin did not hesitate to present herself in the taverns, interposing her divine body between the knives of two furious rivals. All the impulses, all the lusts, all the conflicts that are apparently regulated and under control in the great cities were manifest in the mining towns in all their naked crudity.

The Indians, brought en masse from their pueblos, were thrown mercilessly to the bottom of the mine shafts or lowered to the mine levels where mercury ate into their legs, leaving ulcers that would never heal. New jobs and new procedures were created for them. Indeed, diversification of the work resulted in the emergence of job classifications suggested by such words as watchmen, night guards, overseers, ditchers, boxers, ore carriers, muckers, washers, crushers, drillers, swampers, and loaders. All of them, however, could be grouped under the common heading of slaves.

Drawings by contemporary travelers, showing the drifts of the mines in cross section, have preserved for us a faithful picture of those dark and tortuous ant runs. They are the X-ray pictures of a mountain. The outside of it, its smooth turf covered with trees, looms over gentle valleys bathed in sunlight; but in its dark and steamy entrails, naked homunculi bore into the earth with picks and shovels, while others drain water from the mine and still others, with packs on their backs, ascend and descend like a living chain pump by the double ladders that lead into the tunnels. When their work was done, they would come out "faint with hunger, gasping with thirst, bathed in sweat, dazzled after the darkness they had been in, and worn out by their labors, to go and die of starvation along the roads or in their own poverty-stricken pigsties of some sickness they had contracted in those pits."

Gonzalo Gómez de Cervantes, an economist of the end of the sixteenth century, had seen the Indians carrying ore in their blankets from the mouth of the mine to the mill, from the mill to the crushers, from there to the graders, and finally to the smelters. Once a week they were paid four reales (about twenty cents), and as the blanket that had been ruined by the ore cost five or six reales, the Indian was "working for nothing and boarding himself." "Furthermore," Cervantes observes, "when the ore is taken from the mine it comes out coated with mud; yet when the wretched Indian lies down to sleep he has to use that same blanket, thick with mud and wet, to cover himself."

In a country with an abundance of untouched precious metals, the slave system permitted the accumulation of fabulous riches. Henry Hawkins remarks in his report:

The luxury and munificence of the mine-owners is something wondrous to see. As a rule the wife of a mining man goes to church escorted by a hundred servants and twenty ladies and maids in waiting. She keeps open house, and all who wish to do so may come to dine: a bell is rung for dinner and supper. Their houses are kept in princely style and they are liberal in all things.

Don Cristóbal de Oñate, one of the founders of Zacatecas, used to provide a public table to which everyone was called by a bell "so that as many as wished to might gather to dine, and the service was magnificent." Don Bartolomé Bravo de Acuña made fifteen million pesos, Don Agustín Zavala made four million, and the weekly income from a mining venture might easily add up to twenty thousand pesos. The smallest utensils in Don Luis de Castilla's kitchen were of silver, and Don Alonso de Villaseca, a mining man in Pachuca who made his name a synonym for wealth, turned over forty thousand pesos to the holy places in Palestine and ten thousand for the ransoming of captives. After his death a letter from Pope Pius V was found among his papers in which the pontiff thanked him for a donation of one hundred fifty thousand pesos to the basilica of Saint Peter's in Rome and for the poor of that same city.

The chain of bonanzas and strikes, popular legends, familiarity with death, and the mad appetite for pleasure created an atmosphere that was bound to have an influence on the evolving colonial society. Such popular sentiments as those shown on the baroque stage of Guanajuato in the light of the Revolution for Independence had originated in the primitive mining camps.

Zacatecas, Pachuca, Guanajuato, Taxco, and to some degree San Luis Potosí were all highly characteristic cities crossing the map of Mexico, all of them mingling to the highest degree the traits of colonial society. The apparent impermanence of material wealth in the Indies, the myths of miraculous sudden riches, and the contrasts between the splendor of the mine-owners and the slavery of the miners, all helped to construct those tiny worlds of cut stone and resplendent altars, of crowns and cloistered convents, of cold metal and warm, suffering flesh ruled by petty, cruel, pious monarchs.

A Parenthesis: Concerning the Countryside

Mexico has eluded the combined efforts of soldiers, geographers, and naturalists. A melange of arbitrary landscapes, featuring woods and rivers, strange animals and whimsical flowers, could not convey a clear idea of that varied region of the New World which suddenly shone like a mysterious jewel in the Spanish crown. Fifty years after its discovery, the uniqueness of Mexico was still setting its unmistakable stamp on forms and tastes, proving itself different from everything that was familiar in Europe and Africa. In this country one cannot hail the thrust of early primroses through the snow; the trill of the nightingale heralding spring cannot enrapture us as it did Rousseau during his first night at the Hermitage. But in exchange for such joys and many others merely imagined, nature has heaped many and exquisite gifts upon us.

To us, references by Europeans to the play of the seasons has an exotic ring, for we enjoy a perpetual autumn with very slight changes or, better still, an eternal mild spring. The rainy season with its clouds and cool weather and the dry season with its gifts of golden foliage and yellow meadows constitute our calendar, and we are in no sense bound to the seasons for our climatic changes. A slight descent can transform the severe and aristocratic landscape of the mesa and soften its austerity. With a short trip, one may live beneath another sky and enjoy another sun; the rhythm of the blood is quieted and the senses are relaxed, like the limbs of a shivering cat that discovers the grateful warmth of a fireplace, for to us the tropics are as the hearth to the European, the great glow of a flame that makes the trees grow and keeps the flowers forever blooming.

In a sense, Mexico may be compared to a tall house in which the climate corresponds to its several floors. Naturally, the warm and humid coast forms the ground floor. Its broad windows open on the warm, dazzling, empty blue sea, with seagulls screaming above it and blind, cruel pelicans diving after the silvery shadow of a fish. This ground floor is somewhat rude and untidy, full of palm trees, silk-cotton trees, and gigantic mangoes, of lush vegetation, of the wings of parakeets and herons, of poor villages, ruined pyramids, and great, dark, lonely rivers—rivers that are noisy and turbulent even during the night when the fireflies light their lamps, the drums of the huge frogs quicken their beat, and night birds flit from their hiding places.

The intermediate climate of the mountains is on the first floor. At an altitude of 3,500 feet, amid the silky needles of the oyamel and the dark sheen of the oaks, the cacao tree, the vanilla vine, the tobacco plant, orchids, orange and lemon trees, everything thrives beneath its misty ceiling; butterflies dart and bright birds flame.

The top floor is situated some 7,000 feet above sea level. This is the spot chosen as the dwelling place of the immigrant from the Indies and of the Spanish colonial. It is a panorama of blue valleys and yellow plains, burning sun and icy shade, where the creatures of the high plateau are stimulated by the thin air: The slender Indian with his thin voice, the *pirú* and the oak tree, the agave, the prickly pear, and the cacti.

This is Mexico, but it is not all of Mexico. In the north there is desert; in the southeast a chalky land without rivers or mountains; along the Guatemalan border, an impenetrable forest of sapodilla trees and valuable woods; along the Gulf of Campeche, a land of rivers and primeval swamps, called Tabasco; and on the Pacific a peninsula, Baja California, where pearl-rich, cold seas lap hot beaches that, themselves, stretch toward the bare spines of chalky mountain ranges.

The tone of this violent geography is set not by the valleys or the rivers or the forests but by the mountains unfolding in endless chains that press across the length and breadth of three-quarters of the Mexican earth.

The mountains represent chaos, the absence of order, the opponent of the sea, the defeat of the straight line. There are ranges of green mountains—the work of copper sulfate—and red mountains—the work of iron oxide; mountains of slate and sediment—the remains of other buried mountains—and mountains of graphite, of granite, of porphyry, of andesite, and of marble veined with the delicate skeletons of imprisoned plant life.

Mountains mean waterfalls, spring torrents, caves, fissures, gorges, summits, lava, snow, and volcanic smoke and gases. The mountain is the Mexican's neighbor, his witness for the defense, his enemy and his ally, his ladder, his cellar and his pantry, his aesthetic and his geometry. Everything comes from it: the gold spike, the silver rod, the green pine tree, the spores of fern, Noah's Ark; it is the realm of silence, the emblem of the country, the wailing wall, a solemn madness—wait; you too will find rest—the only place that vomits up its dead.

Life for us consists of climbing and descending, which means that we walk the same road twice. Actually, the Mexican is master of his terrain. A snow-topped volcano often overlooks a sugar cane plantation in the warm earth, and a stand of pine in the cool land may give a view of the gentle, rounded formations of a nature ruled by the benign, red, smiling sun.

In the mountainous regions, distance blends the near with the far, mingles the greens and the blues, brightens the minerals, and swells and diminishes forms by optical illusions. All this may have implanted in our consciousness a confusion between reality and hope, a spiritual milieu capable of any aberration.

The land of the Indians, whether it is of ancient cities buried in the jungle or new cities of skyscrapers and hearths, is an unpeopled landscape, regardless of the caprices of geography and climate. Man has wrought some destruction upon it, thus rendering it more tragic, but he has never succeeded in altering it or in transforming its demonic face. Where, can you tell me, does the mirage end and the reality begin?

The City in an Old Engraving

A new American city has been born, and is growing up before our eyes. It burgeoned from a sheet of paper, a stroke of the pen; it was not shaped by chance, as all cities are to some extent. In the course of the century, it has been described by a Humanist, a *comisario general* of the Franciscan order, and a satirical poet—all three of whom admired without reservation the houses and streets, the churches and convents, the children and horses. Feudal characteristics are so peculiar to it that, considering its relation to the surrounding landscape and the strange world whose center and capital it was, one gathers the impression that a sorcerer skilled in Oriental magic has transported a Castilian or Extremaduran town to our high plateau overnight.

It could hardly be otherwise. When the plat which García Bravo drew was converted into a city, the strict separation between the Spaniard and the aborigine followed the architect's rule. Materially it was "a huge enclave reserved for Europeans," the exclusive residence of the Conquistadors, the stone wall that must keep them and the Indians apart; spiritually also it was a white world set down in a world of color, a small island in a dark sea, a Spanish city that could not number even five thousand inhabitants in 1592, surrounded by millions of Indians.

The consequences of this new concept of a city are closely related to the history and constitution of our country. The children of the Conquistadors or of the first immigrants no longer resembled their parents even though they called themselves Spaniards. Loosely speaking, they were a new kind of men, designated by the name of Creoles. The mestizos, children of Spanish men and Indian women and almost all born out of wedlock, belonged to the other outstanding human type created by the city, albeit they were relegated during the sixteenth century to a lower social level than the Indians.

The presence of rebel Negro slaves, numerous in that century, and their unions with Indians and mestizos, which bore fruit—that clandestine fruit that combined a sense of the monstrous and the forbidden—resulted in a swarm of human beings on a descending scale of color who, without exception, played the role of the untouchables in New Spain.

Negroes, the mestizos, the children of quadroons and mulattos, known as *tente-en-el-aire, salta-pa-tras,* or *no-te-intiendo,* were of little significance compared with the enormous mass of the Indians themselves. The country teemed with them. Their brilliant eyes and slender figures flocked across the fields, the villages, the mines, and the plantations. Their gentle, resigned dignity, their silence and their docility, their genuine lack of resistance to evil in any form, made them ideal slaves. But these slaves, like the waves of the sea, washed daily against the walls of the city they encircled, infiltrated its houses in a thousand ways, taking the language apart, altering the color of the skin pigments, creating a diabolical cuisine, and introducing their sacred styles of life and art.

Let us leave these people in peace, for we shall meet them again many times in the course of this book, and let us take a final look at Mexico City. Viewed from the ideal distance of an engraving by an artist of the Renaissance, it spreads before our eyes its belfries and towers, its houses and battlemented monasteries springing up along the sparkling border of the lake. Carts and mule trains are coming down from the mountains and along the pavements, amid the whistles and shouts of the muleteers. They are bringing silver and gold from the mines; grains from the plantations; cloth, wine, oil, mercury, and books newly come across the Atlantic from Spain; or marbles and porcelains unloaded in Acapulco from a China ship after a voyage across the Pacific. Trade moves upon the tough hoofs of the mules. Within a short time, transportation by muleback has created a tradition of great houses smelling like stables, of round-bellied earthenware jars, of tooled leather, spurs and bridles, halters and hackamores, clothing with silver buttons and wide lace-

trimmed hats, of rawhide and latigos, of harness and smithies, of blasphemies, invocations, and the courtesies of the road.

The muleteer must answer the chant of the call boys at dawn, sleep on straw or in an open field, run the gantlet of other teams and pack trains, expose himself to the sun, the rain, and the attacks of bandits. His life, full of movement and adventure, may be summed up in the song of the medieval troubadour:

S'on me chasse, je fuirai,
et s'on me tue, je mourrai.

If I'm pursued, then I'll fly,
If someone kills me, then I'll die.

When the muleteers caught sight of the city, they set spur to their mounts so as to arrive before nightfall; the tinkle of the silver bell on the headstrap of the lead jenny quickens, and the train moves along in a cloud of dust turned to gold by the afternoon sun.

With luck, we might be able to witness the arrival of the new viceroy, with his retinue of brilliant local aristocrats and high colonial officials. Halberds gleam and the standard of the city, embroidered in silk and gold, flutters above the heads of the suits.

But we would witness another kind of scene with much greater frequency, a less sumptuous one but more familiar to the life of New Spain. A Spanish traveler, followed by an Indian carrying his bed on his back—the usual thing when covering short distances—stops his horse in front of our imaginary onlooker to give alms to two mendicant monks; several officers of the Inquisition are leading a heretic to the stake, tied hand and foot on a mule; the velvet palanquin of a magistrate, with its curtains drawn, joggles on the shoulders of its tired bearers; behind it a group of slaves captured in Pánuco are forced to walk with their heads and hands in stocks, like oxen beneath the yoke; a group of laughing Creole youths on horseback, dressed in dark traveling suits, fill the road.

A throng of Indians, whose quick, supple feet are taking them in the direction of the wharves, are almost hidden beneath loads of pottery, rolled-up *petates* (sleeping mats), and portable coops from which screeching turkeys thrust their red wattles. Behind them, their women look like a flock of doves in their cloaks and skirts rippled by the breeze. Along the edge of the road Indian vendors, beggars, and mestizos in rags watch the travelers go by, and their black eyes are full of bitterness and menace. Now the lake is all silver and liquid blues, and the mountains glow with the cool iridescence of pearls. A yellow sun, an age-old sun, turns the ocher of the fallow fields to fire, and the golden, sensuous light of the full moon is shed across the transparency of the sky.

2

Colonial Life

*Each time I am reminded that I am a man, I wish not to
have been, or that I did not have a man's sentiments.*
Fernán Pérez de Oliva

The capital of New Spain was patterned after the European feudal
model, then in its final agonies, and with few exceptions it too took its
keynote from that time when "all events assumed outward forms much
more pronounced than today."
 Sensitivity may often go hand in hand with extreme callousness.
Spectators who might be moved to tears by the funeral service of some
notable official were equally ready to hurl insults at a Jew or to straddle
the limb of a tree for hours as they watched the Jew burn slowly at the
San Hipólito stake.
 Some of the striking contrasts attributed by Huizinga to the life of the
fifteenth-century French were here in faithful replica. "The piercing
cold and the terrible winter nights" were unknown, of course, although
the hidalgos enjoyed wearing costly furs as trimming on their garments.
In a period dominated by the conventions of the Church, the display
and magnificence that we modestly confine to the ballet were seen daily
on the streets of Mexico City. Plumed hats, hose that revealed the
masculine figure from the waist down, hair in ringlets, lacy shirt fronts,
brocaded doublets, fluted ruffs, neck chains, and rings—all the elegance
that taught men to wear capes and women to bare their bosoms and

hoop their skirts were part of a style of living dominated by refined sensuality.

In women's dress, soft colors predominated—violet, olive green, or the silvery gray named for the feathers of the dove—and dresses were embroidered with silver and pearls. For more than fifty years the hoop petticoat, also known as the farthingale or *guardainfante,* enjoyed a great vogue in New Spain. This skirt was full and round, in the last medieval style of maternity dress; it filled out the abdomen and the hips, making them look like majestic balloons. From the moment of their appearance in Spain these skirts, so popular with women, had been the objects of mounting attack. Fray Hernando de Talavera, in his *Opúsculo contra la demasía de vestir y calzar* (*Short Treatise on Excess in Hose and Dress*), believes they should qualify wearers for excommunication; and he analyzes their drawbacks. He ascribes many miscarriages to their weight and he cites: their ugliness, because they make women look very fat; their failure to protect a woman's virtue, because they were hollow; their indecency even, owing to the ease with which they expose the legs. And with consistent ecclesiastical malice, our friar manages to slip in the theory "that it is commonly believed they were invented to conceal pregnant fornicators and adulterers, for the lines of the aforementioned garment lay it open to strong suspicion."

It seems that the farthingale began its sinful career in Valladolid, the birthplace of Fray Hernando de Talavera, thereby aggravating the patriotic clergyman's indignation. The scandal stirred up around that skirt was of such magnitude that the prelate of the Church did forbid women, large or small, married or maiden, to wear it under pain of excommunication, and he extended the penalty to cover the dressmakers who made it. Such serious censure did nothing, however, to prevent the wearing of the farthingale in Spain or its transplantation to the Indies, where for long decades it held its wide and rustling sway.

A passion for luxury was shared by aristocrats and plebeians alike. On festival days the craftsmen came forth in handsome dress, and at great public ceremonies the common people, without exception, decked themselves in clothing as gay as the celebration. The trade in costly fabrics was bound to be important. The gay colors of the dresses lent a joyous atmosphere to the city, like a fair or the celebrations of the medieval fortified towns.

Mourning, Tombs, and Responsories

The funerals as well as the festive celebrations of the mighty were remarkable for their solemnity. Descriptions and drawings have come down to us of the rich tomb erected by the city in 1559 to the memory of Charles V, in the atrium of the convent of San Francisco. The catafalque, in the Doric style, was built on two levels. The funeral urn rested on the first, "covered with a black cloth, and a cushion on which the crown rested" surrounded by flags; on the second level the Austrian eagle spread its enormous gilded wings beneath the sky of the plateau.

The influence of the Renaissance on the adornment of the catafalque is evident in several symbolic skeletons—"the great power of death that had vanquished such an invincible monarch"—and in the scenes of the overthrow of the natives. Pictures of "a goddess removing a garland from Ulysses and placing it on the Emperor"; of "the labyrinth of Dedalus, with a spike in the door and an iron ring hanging from the spike, to remind us that Charles V had emerged safely from so many difficult undertakings"; and "of an Apollo above the walls of the city of Mexico, symbolizing the university"—all were doubtless the inspiration of Dr. Cervantes de Salazar, who also wrote the description of the catafalque and composed the Latin poems published in the *Túmulo imperial.*

The architect, Claudio Arciniega, took three months to build the superb tomb, and the public was notified by the viceroy twenty days before the obsequies were to be held "that all men and all women, whatsoever their state and condition, must don mourning in token of the death of so grand a monarch." "You would not have believed," Cervantes writes, "that there were so many tailors and dressmakers in the city." One gentleman spent more than a thousand pesos on his clothes, and when November 30 arrived, the feast day of Saint Andrew Apostle, the city of Mexico appeared in deep mourning amid the pealing of bells and the rumble of oratory.

The funeral procession was led by the Indian rulers of Mexico City, Tacuba, Texcoco, and Tlaxcala. They were covered with black cloaks, their hems dragging in the mud; they carried standards that displayed embroidered coats of arms, their own and the emperor's. Next came the headmen of the villages, followed by two thousand Indian noblemen and four hundred monks and priests. Finally the archbishop came, beneath his sumptuous canopy, dressed in his pontifical robes, surrounded by clouds of incense and accompanied by the bishop of Michoacán, Don Vasco de Quiroga, and the bishop of New Galicia, Don Diego de Ayala.

The secular authorities, in their turn, displayed a pomp that would seem impossible today, accustomed as we are to the sight of grotesque parties of North Americans parading through our streets at the slightest pretext. Bernardino de Albornoz, who was entrusted with the city's banner, headed the civil section of the procession, followed by two mace bearers dressed in black damascene coats of mail, upon which the royal arms gleamed in gold and silver; the treasurer, Don Hernando de Portugal, carried the crown upon a damask cushion; the bursar, Ortuño de Ibarra, carried in his hand the unsheathed sword; the steward and inspector, Don García de Albornoz, the crossbow; and Don Luis Castillo, the imperial coat of mail. The viceroy, Don Luis de Velasco, with a chamberlain holding up the train of his cape, the oidores of the Audiencia, the chief exchequer, the head bailiff of the court, and the rector of the university closed the procession. The hoods, the swords, and the professors' wands, the magistrates and the mayors introduced a note of austerity that clashed with the final group of merchants in their ornate "long gowns and pointed hoods."

The day the viceroy himself, Don Luis de Velasco, died in 1564 the streets were packed with men, women, and children all dressed in black, who had come to watch his funeral cortege go by from the house of the official Ortuño de Ibarra, where he died, to the convent of San Francisco. Four bishops wearing copes and miters stiff with jewels carried the bier on their shoulders, and the Visitador Jerónimo de Valderrama led the mourning in company with the oidores of the Audiencia. The members of the city council, the chapter of the cathedral, Dominican and Franciscan friars, priests in long chasubles, and encomenderos with uncovered heads made up the cortege. Behind them the knight Gómez de Legazpi marched at the head of six hundred soldiers, the expeditionary force that was to conquer the Philippines. Muffled drums beat the funeral march in counterpoint to the tolling of the bells. Horses, unshod and lame, wore mourning panoply.

That was the period of the responsories. The inner conflict between religious feeling and a life devoted to avarice and sensuality created a thirst for salvation, for the remission of sin, and, like the pagans who surrounded their dead with the objects considered essential in another life, the people of the sixteenth century generally bade their departed godspeed with responsories. Bernal Díaz, a master of this genre, dedicates the following to the memory of Hernán Cortés, his old captain:

He had no good fortune in California, nor when he went to the Hibueras, nor in any other thing, ever since he completed his conquest of the earth, and perhaps that was so that he might find it in heaven, as I truly believe, for he was a fine gentleman and very devoted to the Virgin and the Apostle Saint Peter, and other saints. May God forgive him his sins and me mine.

End of the Period of Chivalry

Festivals, like funerals, went to extravagant lengths. Martín Cortés sponsored a series of brilliant fiestas to celebrate the baptism of his twin children. They started early in the day with native music and dancing, tournaments, religious ceremonies, and a masquerade ball, mock jousting, and elaborate fireworks were held at night. The cooks and pages of the marquis passed around a bullock and a huge number of birds that had been roasted at gigantic outdoor fireplaces, and they set two sixty-gallon casks of wine, one red and the other white, near the doorway of his palace, the spigots kept open and flowing until the last drop disappeared down the thirsty throats of his fellow citizens.

Prodigality and the desire to excel have always been peculiar to the Creole character, and those traits have persisted in the development of Mexican society. Perhaps we may speak more truly here of a colonial spirit, for there seems to be a definite absence of any notion of saving, much less any wish to pile up riches. All such celebrations presuppose vast expenditures: parades, among them the annual Procession of the Flag, celebrating the anniversary of the fall of Tenochtitlán; the receptions given by the viceroy and other high officials; the birthdays of the saints; the sumptuous meals where wine, very expensive at that time, flowed like water; the upkeep of stables and the support of innumerable servants; the whole taste for luxury. The will of the Creole Suárez de Peralta is conclusive on this point:

> With the arrival of the marquis in Mexico [he is referring to Martín Cortés, the son of the Conquistador, who arrived in 1562] there was no thought of anything but fiestas and galas, and there were more of them held than ever before. Hence many of them ended up with mortgages, and the merchants became the masters of all the gentlemen, for as they ran into debt and were unable to redeem their pledges, they turned over their income [to their creditors], and I believe that to this day [he wrote this in 1580] many estates carry mortgages dating back to that time.

The rich holders of encomiendas of Indians displayed an unbecoming ostentation, and just as Cortés had been the mirror for the Conquistadors in his day, his son Martín was regarded as a model by the slave-owning Creoles. The brilliant retinue that accompanied him everywhere he went aroused envy and admiration. A page followed him on horseback, carrying the base of his lance in a sheath decorated with silk tassels, and it became the established custom for any hidalgo who met him on the street to join his entourage, a practice that inevitably gave rise to serious rivalries. His guards, dressed in red livery and armed with swords, were respected even by the authorities, and on solemn occasions he went about escorted by a small army of arquebusiers.

The period when Martín Cortés was in Mexico City marked the culmination of what we might call the age of chivalry in New Spain. In the portrait that Suárez de Peralta draws of Viceroy Velasco we can see clearly the atmosphere of fiestas and games which surrounded the Creoles: "A most handsome ruler," the historian reflects, "who lacks any kind of interest in or pretense of serving." Every day during his rule, without failing once, his table was liberally set for any and all—"persons who merited a place, to be sure"—who wished to dine in his company. Almost always he had thirty or forty guests who were served a "most delicious meal, of more than twelve courses."

In addition, Velasco was exceedingly fond of the chase. He kept falcons, geese, and cranes, and his master of the hunt, Alonso de Nava, was an important person who was paid an income of two thousand ducats. Another of his servitors, a hidalgo "who cut a very fine figure" and was reputedly the best huntsman in Mexico, was in charge of firearms. At Chapultepec he followed the viceroy and was always ready to hand him an arquebus ready loaded.

"His stables," an expert says, "were worthy of a monarch; and he himself 'a man who sat his horse beautifully.' The merchants did not take part in the jousting games, however wealthy they might be, and the citizen who was honored with an invitation felt he had received the accolade as much as if 'he wore the cloak of a Crusader.' "

In cattle country—where the men went out to the commons to bait the bulls with dogs and leave them mangled on the fields—it was natural that bullfight fans should be in great supply. Velasco used to go to Chapultepec on Sunday, surrounded by a hundred men on horseback, and they would lance the spirited beasts in a bullring he had had built. Later, beneath the canopy of the *ahuehuetas,* the servants would serve up a kingly banquet.

On Sundays racing meets were held, at which constables were barely able to control the spectators. "Silver-mounted harness . . ." Suárez sighs from Spain as he evokes his favorite pastimes; "there is nothing in the world today like what goes on there!" The animated picture of his youth, of the world into which he was born, comes back to life before the exile's eyes, filled with color and movement. He sees the graceful horses race across the meadows; he is dazzled by the glitter of arms and the costumes, and his ears ring with the shouts of the people and the merry music of the hawk bells. When the viceroy rode in the two hardest races, enthusiasm was heightened to the point of delirium. At the peak of his exaltation, Suárez writes: "I swear to God that if the viceroy were to issue an order taking away all the villages and the landed estates, he would be able to console them and make them forget their injuries by having a harness mounted with hawk bells rung in the streets, for that would send them all off into raptures."

To the Creoles, Don Luis de Velasco was the archtype of a good ruler. He knew how to entertain them with such a round of feudal games and pastimes that the Creoles thought of nothing but breeding horses and keeping their harness in trim; they lived happily, dedicated to those "worthy exercises," between jousting and riding for the ring, horse races and bullfights, among their falcons and their mastiffs.

Holy Days, the Hierarchy, and Etiquette

As the sixteenth century advanced, the brilliance of the chivalric festivals waned and the holy days took pride of place. The official establishment of the Inquisition gave a sort of somber pomp to life and modified even the ritual of the public ceremonies. Beginning in 1571, the fires in which heretics writhed were familiar sights, surrounded by soldiers carrying halberds, by monks, and by socially prominent gentlemen.

Even routine performances enjoyed impressive trappings. In the ceremony accompanying the announcement of the auto-da-fé of 1597 where those convicted of heresy by the Inquisition were to be publicly executed, the Inquisitors appeared before the public mounted on luxuriously caparisoned mules and preceded by kettledrums, trumpets, and criers. The magistrate, the members of the city council, and numerous gentlemen followed by servants dressed in costly livery made up the Inquisitors' retinue—a retinue whose splendor could not veil the lugubrious nature of its finale.

On the evening preceding the executions the procession of the Green Cross was customarily held. Bright-colored tapestries, velvet drapery, and banners bearing their owners' coats of arms were hung from the balconies; the altars were dressed with sculptures and paintings and displayed not only the silver vessels but the most precious items too.

In 1597—fifty thousand silent spectators thronged the streets, the windows, and the rooftops—sixty monks from the province, dressed in black and carrying tapers, led the march. A Knight of Saint James in his antique armor grasped the standard of the Holy Office, and fourteen clerical servants flanked him. Eight hundred monks and priests carrying lighted torches preceded the Green Cross, mounted on an ornate base and guarded by twelve Dominicans in chasubles of black damask and velvet, chaplains, and halberdiers. The prelates, the prior of the monastery of Santo Domingo in a black cope that glittered with gold, and the gentlemen of the city closed the march of the suite. Not a sound could be heard except the dolorous psalms chanted by the cathedral choir and the solemn plain chant of the priests making their responses.

The master of ceremonies carried a steel cross, with which he directed the procession's line of march. When it reached the palace where the viceroy waited on a balcony hung with banners, the Knight of Saint James dipped his standard in token of homage, and the Green Cross was placed on the scaffold. The viceroy's pages then emerged from the palace and, after bowing before the stand, they held their torches aloft "in the style of the Court."

Like all sacramental acts, the public ceremonies had a punctilious etiquette. The exaggerated emphasis on honor, in a strictly hierarchical society, provoked spirited encounters every day, while on the other hand the medieval propensity for organizing people into clearly differentiated groups encouraged the founding of religious communities, fraternal organizations, and castes. Monks, priests, and soldiers had not only their dress and their systems of established usage to distinguish them from others but also their exemptions and privileges, which to a certain extent rendered them untouchable. Craftsmen, university professors, and students formed their own groups, and devout men joined together either in sodalities or in one of the many and varied religious institutions of the period.

The presence of the great mass of Indians, who were kept apart from the whites, and the miserable plight of the mestizos also contributed to the creation of a new feudalism. Whereas in Europe the servant belonged to the same world as his master, in spite of his poverty, beatings, and other vexations, in Mexico servant and master were separated by a vast distance, and there was no point that brought them together. The Indian was a dark, exotic creature—there were those who even doubted his sanity; he spoke his own language; he lived in a hut; he hardly ate at all. Since the days of Hernán Cortés the Indian had been seen everywhere, always busy, in the native markets, in the streets, and outside the churches. Covered with a blanket, his face hidden beneath the wide brim of a palm-leaf hat, sitting on the ground like an Oriental, he appeared almost invariably at the side of a well-dressed lady in her velvet farthingale, the encomendero in satin, the court official, or the artisan.

Apart from that bizarre element, the Indian, on whose brown shoulders the white world rested, Mexico's tiny feudal society tended to conduct itself in an aristocratic manner. The place a man was entitled to occupy at table or during a ceremony, the privilege of walking to the left or the right of some personage, the problem of who should precede whom into a drawing room, or what seat he should occupy in the chancel of a church were all matters of serious concern.

In this struggle for precedence, the Inquisition tried to prevail even over the viceroy, and that gave rise to a vast number of decrees aimed at achieving concord. José Toribio Medina wrote: "A common practice among all the tribunals of the Holy Office established in America was to embroil their ministers and delegates in every kind of competition with the authorities on principle, and neither the viceroys nor the ecclestiastical authorities were excepted, even to the archbishops and bishops."

The highly developed *esprit de corps* and the jealous spirit shared by the cavaliers, the ecclesiastics, and the royal officials, which we have attempted to sketch in outline, led them to assign tremendous importance—independent of its economic significance—to the place due them in all ceremonies. The order of precedence at an auto da fé or in the Procession of the Flag corresponded to the watchers' or marchers' positions in society. The hierarchy observed in fiestas thus was the same as that in real life.

The Significance and the Pedigree of the Horse

The horse was an essential element of colonial life in New Spain. Its blood lines were always traced back to the fourteen famous horses in the Conquest that Bernal describes with loving pleasure. We can follow their curvetting through the historical chronicles, beginning with the foaling of Juan Sedeño's mare aboard a ship and the course run by this offspring, later reared by some migratory deer; through the intervention of a rowdy stallion in a diplomatic maneuver of Hernán Cortés; the victorious campaigns against the Indians, in which the horse often rivaled Saint James Apostle; to their deeply mourned deaths.

After helping to win the land, the horse was elevated to a place of honor on the altars, and the Indians carved horses on the façades of the churches. They were so important for the excellent reason that Mexico was a land of broad horizons, of great fiefs, and of long roads stretching between cities and distant ports; and yet there were sharp distinctions drawn among the horses. The laborer's or the merchant's horse was one thing, the cavalier's quite another. The first was a mere beast of burden;

the second, a gentleman's pride and luxury. A gentleman could not conceive of himself without his horse. (Even the terms contain the necessity: *caballo—caballero*.) To go about on the same level with the commoners, to court the ladies on foot, or even to affirm his lineage were all equally unthinkable except as attached to the concept "horseman." The horse was everything. Mounted on one, a gentleman could take part in jousting and catching the ring, he could find his rank in the cavalcades and in the retinues of the powerful, he could travel and pay visits.

More than any other symbol, the horse represented the sensuality of the Renaissance in New Spain. These were Titian's horses, as their descendants would be Rubens' and Delacroix's—freedom of form, the spirit of movement, the joy of living. In the Mexican horse were blended all glorious horses: the breed that Phaeton, the celestial charioteer, drove; the horse Aeneas gave to his father-in-law; the charger of Duke Astolfo, that phoenix of the bridle; the horses of the victorious Alexander and Babieca; and the fiery hippogriff of the baroque age.

Balbuena portayed them in his tercets, pawing the earth and neighing with joy through eternity:

> *Their glory here is such*
> *that we're moved to declare*
> *they must come from the stud farm of Mars.*
>
> *Where the proud chestnut champs his bit*
> *and races faster than air*
> *when he feels the touch of the spur.*
>
> *And the sorrel without blemish,*
> *all spirit and color, bright as a flame,*
> *graceful and docile at touch on the rein.*
>
> *Cool pinto, bright-hued in patches,*
> *gallant and fiery and dapple gray,*
> *and red roan with silver-dewed coat.*
>
> *The black-stippled iron gray,*
> *the mustang all malice and spirit,*
> *the beauty with ash-sprinkled coat.*

Prancing and brave the sloeberry black,
and the fabulous fawn-colored steed,
treacherous piebald, and neatly groomed bay.

All the others, too many to number,
coming to water at crystal springs
and freely to graze on the wide open range.

The ultra-classical horses of Chirico and Picasso would have had no place in New Spain. Horses did not wander there, free and reflective, like persons, nor were they ingenious plastic toys. A horse was a horse, not an abstraction of one. It was the white, delicate horse of Saint Martin in El Greco's painting; the chubby, powerful pony ridden by Prince Baltasar Carlos in the canvas by Velázquez; the mounts of Martín Cortés, of Suárez de Peralta, of Viceroy Velasco; Pedro de Alvarado's racing mare; Cristóbal de Olid's handsome dark chestnut. In short, this was a horse with an erect, nervous head, slender legs, round, lustrous haunches; at the same time, it was also the horse of the carmine velvet horse cloth, the ornamented bridle, the gilded sword, the Renaissance cap trimmed with precious stones and feathers. This courtly horse curvetted and pranced, and when the drumbeat of his pace was accentuated by the spray of pebbles in the street, women's hearts leaped with joy and their pulses kept time to the smooth dance that was coming ever nearer the wrought iron balconies outside their houses.

Horses and gentlemen—caballos and caballeros—in the tournaments and ring games, on the promenades and in the squares, in the fields and in the streets, on the dusty roads, in the processions and the retinues. As Balbuena said,

An everyday sight in those squares
are fine horses in luxurious livery
trimmed with nacre and pearl, jewels and gold.

The Voice and the Silence of Mexico City

Ours was a silent city, unlike the cities of Europe. The nervous vitality of Europe was muted here, and the clamor of Spain and Italy dropped to a lower register. Even the markets proved less noisy in Mexico. At the end of the century, the only sounds were the passing of horses or of a carriage, the ringing of bells, and the town crier's announcements. It was as if the grave nature of the Indians and their Oriental courtesy finally imposed on the Spanish citizens and their children a reserve and composure unknown in the Peninsula. Not only were voices softer in the Indies; the manner of speaking became different too. The Spanish poet Eugenio de Salazar, who was in Mexico from 1581 to 1589, observes in a poem:

> *Grammar must step aside*
> *for a new ingenious boyhood,*
> *and good Latin will doff its doctor's cap*
> *to seemly speech*
> *and pure and proper language*
> *which glows anew in writing.*

For his part, Balbuena said that it is in Mexico

> *where the purest of Spanish is spoken*
> *with the greatest of courtesy,*
> *in the tongue's most beautiful form,*
> *all gracefulness, charm, and wit,*
> *pure and smooth, clear and with gravity.*

From the mass of testimony that has come down to us concerning the speech of the Mexicans, it might be fitting to select that of Juan de Cárdenas because he practiced medicine for many years in New Spain and knew the people well. Doctor Cárdenas chose the following comparison to demonstrate the "acute, transcendant, and delicate" genius of those born in the Indies:

Let us pretend, he suggests, that a Spaniard reared in a village is talking with a Spaniard brought up in the Indies, among farmhands exclusively. How would each rustic behave? Let us listen to the Creole speech: so limpid, courtly, and curious, and with so much preamble, delicacy, and rhetorical style, neither taught nor artificial, but so natural that he seems to have been trained at court and to have spent his life in the company of very well-spoken and discreet people. We notice in the immigrant recently arrived, on the other hand, that because he was not reared among city people, no stick could have a rougher and duller bark than his and, furthermore, that the entire behavior of the one is so different in everything from that of the other—one so dull and the other so keen—that there is no man, however ignorant he may be, who could not see at a glance which is the native of Spain and which was born in the Indies.

Cárdenas adds: "For when they [the Mexicans] undertake to utter a pretty speech, an observation, or a highly polished or pointed piece of reasoning, upon my word, no courtier reared in Madrid or Toledo could compose and polish it better."

He then cites examples. One of his patients, who was attempting to tell Cárdenas how little he feared death so long as he had him for physician, expressed himself in these words: "Let the fates wind the thread of my life as long as it please them, for I shall have Your Grace beside me whenever they see fit to cut it, and he will know how to tie it again." Another who offered him his house and person, in accordance with the Mexican custom, phrased his invitation like this: "May Your Grace use this house as his own, for you know it is the dwelling Your Grace has granted me."

In these examples of graciousness, which Juan de Mairena might have quoted in his teachings, the taste for rhetoric is evident, and it is equally evident that such courteous expressions were second nature to the Mexican, flourishes of a style that already heralded the flowering of the baroque period.

The Spaniard in Mexico lost spontaneity but gained courtesy. Overly harsh sounds were softened, circumlocution was chosen in preference to plain speaking, so that artificiality became the Creole's natural manner of expressing himself. The care he took in speaking, the excessive fear of attracting attention, the overuse of glances, and the reiterated diminutives—all make us think that language was handled like something too dangerous to be used freely.

Movement, Travel, and Adventure

Mobility was also characteristic of that period, a Renaissance zeal for travel and adventure, which made possible not only the Conquest but the colonization of immense regions as well.

Within a short time Pedro de Alvarado will reach Guatemala;

Montejo will be in Yucatán; Nuño de Guzmán will leave a trail of blood through Jalisco; and very soon now Hernán Cortés will undertake not only his disastrous expedition to the Hibueras but, with his habitual resolution and his genius for overcoming insuperable obstacles, will determine to launch ship after ship, seemingly with no success, for the chimerical conquest of the Spice Islands.

The mirages of the Middle Ages still had not entirely faded by the middle of the century. During the reigns of the viceroys Don Antonio de Mendoza and Don Luis de Velasco, a new expedition to Florida was organized; Ibarra and Oñate conquered Chihuahua; Fray Diego de Niza had crossed the desert in the north with visions of Cíbola beckoning him on; and, in 1564, the Philippines were conquered, with Mexican men and resources. That marked the culmination of an entire cycle of extraordinary enterprises. At the opening of the seventeenth century, Balbuena described Mexico as the ideal of the empire in this proud verse:

> *In thee Spain and China meet,*
> *Italy is linked with Japan, and now, ultimately*
> *a world joined by treaty and authority.*

The men of the sixteenth century were not indifferent to the seductive call of the islands. While intolerance and increasingly rigid governmental organization combined to cast a shadow over the life of the Spanish Empire, the far-off Philippines still offered a chance for escape. The Edenic simplicity of the islands, the unique tenderness of the Orient, which Gauguin's canvases and Conrad's novels were to capture centuries later, had a powerful attraction even then, and those vigorous, ruthless men felt it.

At the end of the sixteenth century, the Philippines were, at least in part, what the islands of the Caribbean had been at the end of the fifteenth century. Criminals, soldiers of fortune, failures, the hopeless, and the insane headed for them; they exuded a sour, plebeian atmosphere, and such men were able to live there in an environment of greedy brutality like that which Christopher Columbus' jailbirds had established in the Antilles. "The Spaniards in the Philippines," Murillo Velarde writes, "settled into the archipelago and regarded it as an inn

58

rather than as a permanent home." The transitory character that seemed stamped on everything in New Spain was accentuated in the Philippines, where there were very few families of old settlers. There too the law of the "merchant father, gentleman son, beggar grandson," which ruled in Mexico, was also in effect. "The father," the Philippine historian adds, "amasses a fortune, the son spends it, and the grandson is left a pauper. The greatest amounts of capital are no more stable than the waves of the ocean across which they were amassed."

For the citizens of Mexico, the departure of wagon trains to the port of Acapulco, where the China ships lay at anchor, was always food for curiosity. Exiled monks, soldiers, military prisoners, Creoles with bad records, seamen, traders, and muleteers in charge of the mules and their valuable cargoes of silver made up the caravans.

In the Philippines the native women peddled their bodies. "They regarded virginity as ignominious and license an honor, but they considered it a disgrace to give themselves for nothing." The city of Manila offered gambling dens, exotic eating houses, movable markets, and the Chinese quarter with its perfumes, marbles, porcelains, and silks. Sleight-of-hand artists and astrologers and native or Chinese physicians "who can kill with the same ease as the Spanish doctors" abounded. The monks and the authorities amicably shared the monopoly of trade there. No one played fair, and trickery was so habitual that in New Spain illegality and fraud came to be labeled widely "the tricks of China."

Adventures from Castile, Moorish pirates, European merchants, and a few Mexican Indians—the chronicles mention one Juanes, a native of the Tlatelolco quarter, who died in the islands of spells cast by women vying for his favor—met with heretics and saints in the Antipodes. Even though the doorway to China had not yet been opened by the cannon's persuasive voice, the yellow world of strange sins and easy money made itself felt in Portugal as in New Spain, and in the same way.

A story chosen at random—that of Antonio Díaz de Cáceres, a Jew who had settled in Mexico City—will exemplify the dramatic contrasts offered by the Philippines. In the last decade of the century, this miner turned merchant and seaman fled the tribunal of the Holy Office and crossed the Pacific on board his ship *Nuestra Señora de la Concepción*. He docked at Manila and went on to Macao where he was taken prisoner by the Portuguese, but he was able to file off his chains—a very handy maneuver to which Hernán Cortés owed his luck. He then boarded another ship, was taken prisoner a second time, was brought back to Manila, where he was again imprisoned. But his sufferings did not end there. No sooner had he set foot in Acapulco again than his creditors flung him into prison for the fourth time, and not only did he lose everything he possessed but, destitute and beaten, was forced to appear before the agents of the Holy Office. This voyage of Cáceres', destined to be forgotten like many equally heroic voyages of the sixteenth century, is remembered today by many pious souls because of the following quotation in his ship's log: "Felipe las Casas, fifty pesos." This Felipe, who paid fifty pesos for his passage on the Jew's ship, was an excitable Creole who was destined to win sainthood in Japan. He too was a vivid contrast in his world of contrasts.

Men of the stripe of Antonio Díaz de Cáceres abounded in the Indies. Their struggles against the sea, the authorities, business rivals, the English, the Portuguese, the Chinese, and the Mohammedans, their smuggling, and their other tricks made of them a species now extinct. But, although a good part of the trade with Mexico and across the Pacific was carried on through their exertions, punctuated by petty crime, in all but a few cases their deeds and existence have been lost to history.

Transatlantic Navigation

By the end of the century, Mexico, which had been maintaining a precarious communication with Spain in 1540, had become a center of mercantile exchange that affected a great part of America, Europe, and the distant Orient. It had not been easy to scale the walls of religion and the steep tariffs with which the Spanish crown had encircled its colonial empire. Officially, only the faithful of proved Catholic origin had access to the New World, for the children of recent converts were not admitted, much less Protestants or those suspected of heresy. All who took ship were required to show a royal authorization—the passport of today—and proof of having made their confession and communion. This certificate of good spiritual health—the sixteenth century granted small importance to physical health—was, however, no obstacle to the large numbers of Jews, Flemish, and Germans who stole aboard under the very noses of the royal officers of the House of Commerce, the mates, and the clerical servants of the Holy Office. This stream of foreigners gave New Spain a cosmopolitan tone that was accentuated by the Negroes, more abundant even than the Spaniards, and by a few slaves from Bengal, Malaya, and the Philippines.

Transatlantic navigation produced a mixed bag of sinners and saints, beggars and rich men, the wordly and those who lived unworldly lives, rapt in their own spiritual transports. The raw material of new societies! They crowded together on the wharves, but they never forgot their positions in the hierarchy: the younger son, noble as a king "minus money"; the adventurer with his bundle on his back; the timid friars, the gamblers and rogues, archbishop and viceroy, the lady and the female pickpocket. Aboard ship sounded the psalms of beggars and almoners from the monasteries and sodalities, who carried alms boxes decorated with the images of miracle-working saints, and the cries of the cabin boys announcing dinner: "To table, to table, Señor Capitán, pilot, mates, and shipmates. The table is set, the meat is hot. Water as usual for the Señor Capitán, pilot, mate, and shipmates. Long live the King of Castile, on land and on sea! And who does not come will not eat."

The Virgins of the Conception, of Fair Weather at Sea, and of La Barrameda, together with Saint Clara, Saint Elmo, and Saint Nicholas, were the seamen's patrons, to whom they addressed repeated invocations: "Our Lady of Fair Weather at Sea, succor us and give us good weather, with clear skies and a wind, and we shall say an Ave Maria and an Our Father." They entreated Saint Nicholas thus: "Saint Nicholas, watch over our keel, our tiller, our bridge, our tackle which hangs outside and falls inside; that this and many another voyage may be bettered . . . with good weather at sea, a steady wind, and a good voyage and a safe one."

Among the usual prayers, the *Salve Regina* sung on Saturday afternoons was outstanding for its deep poetic feeling. At the altar the mate would say:

> *Salve, digamos,*
> *que buen viaje hagamos.*

Salve, diremos,
que buen viaje haremos.

A Salve *let us say*
That our voyage may be good.
A Salve *we shall say*
To make our voyage good.

And the crew would answer in chorus: "Hail Mary, Our Lady, the King of Heaven sends you to light our way by night and by day, for you have wrought the marvel of making the green pine tree give birth to a rose, and of that rose to make a fruit that we may be saved and all the world."

Some idea of what a sea voyage to the Indies meant in the sixteenth century is conveyed to us by the diary of Fray Tomás de la Torre, who went to Chiapas with the forty-six Dominican monks of the memorable expedition of Fray Bartolomé de Las Casas.

From February 13 to July 9, 1544, the monks awaited the departure of the fleet of merchant ships from Seville or San Lúcar de Barrameda. On July 20 they landed at Gomera (in the Canary Islands), and on July 31 they put out to sea again. Although the ship docked at Santo Domingo, they sailed on to Campeche, the port of entry nearest to Chiapas, and on January 6, 1545, they landed. All in all, the voyage of our monks lasted almost a year, half of which was spent struggling against bureaucratic formalities.

Such administrative problems as a fleet of wildly dissimilar ships, personal documentation for every passenger, cargo specifications, registries, and delays made Seville a purgatory for every soul who wished to attain the paradise of the Indies. Each passenger had to bring his own bed—a coarse mattress of dog hair that was spread beneath the bridge—and his own food and cooking utensils.

Miles of red tape were needed to launch the merchant fleet, and the delays resulted in the spoilage of food already loaded, the expenses of lodging, and an infinity of nuisances that were overcome only by dint of stubbornness and that Spanish genius for wiggling through or around the bureaucratic stumbling blocks with which those same Spaniards liked to encumber their existence.

At last, the monks were on board their ship. The wind swelled the sails, and the ships put out to sea, looking for the exit passage through the bar. Before long, accidents began to occur. The ship, improperly ballasted, ran aground on the San Lúcar bar and remained there for an entire day while the monks devoted themselves to prayer and the sailors to curses.

Once more afloat, the hardships of sea travel seemed almost more than they could bear. The tar would catch fire; the seamen would grow irritated and shout at them, "Friars here, friars there." They were forced to sleep below deck, where they nearly died of the heat; and the crew made a joke of stepping on them, "not their habits," the cleric explains, "but their beards and mouths," just because they were monks, and to make matters worse, when they were seasick thay had to lie stretched out on the deck "like dead men." "A dirtier and more dismal hospital scene than that one cannot be imagined," writes the monk who had been accustomed to a life of privation in his wretched Salamancan monastery. To those men from far inland, the ship was a narrow prison where the heat—they had taken off their shoes and coarse gowns and would have taken off their scapulars had their rule permitted—sickness, vomiting, the stench of the bilge water that chugged ceaselessly through the pumps, and fear of the French were their daily portion.

They rested for a time on the island of Gomera, and the narrator describes his state of mind on re-embarking: "We have acquired such a terror of the ship that we have been thinking we are our own murderers."

No sooner had the voyage recommenced than they collapsed again on their mattresses. The lice ate them alive; they could not wash their clothing in sea water; their salted food created a terrible thirst, which the two liters of water that was distributed daily was not enough to quench. The rich drank wine, and water was the commodity of a shameful trade.

The seamen were astonished at the good weather that prevailed, and said repeatedly that God could not have sent them better. Some of the crew thought it was no natural wind, but one raised by angels blowing on the sails; the Spaniards who had been to the New World already believed that the peril undergone by the ship on the San Lúcar bar could be traced to the sins of the Dominicans but more especially of the bishop, Las Casas, who was destroying the Indies. But a Franciscan claimed the monks could be thanked for the good weather and that the ship would have made headway even without sail as long as they were aboard.

The softness of night air—Columbus was surprised not to hear the song of the nightingale—the sky atwinkle with stars, and the phosphorescence of the sea sweetened the hardships of sailing. The monks sang hymns and psalms, and the seamen sang ballads to the accompaniment of their guitars. Greed slept, and hatred too, "for when there is calm and health, love lifts the heart to God in goodly measure."

The calms, when the ship lay idle for days, with slatting sails, followed by a north wind; the joy of the first islands in the Caribbean—"If I were the discoverer of that isle," the friar says with a sigh, "I would doubtless think it an earthly paradise for its great beauty"; the funerals for those who had died on board—all contribute to the picture of a normal transatlantic voyage. Not infrequently plagues or storms turned those ships into real ghost vessels, coffin ships carrying a company of dead men tossed by the waves of the indifferent sea.

For America, navigation was an essential phase of life. Everything good and everything bad that came to New Spain landed with the merchant fleets at Vera Cruz. The ship would bring news, change, the governor, the archbishop, the visitador, the Inquisitor, iron, mercury, books, wine, and, above all, paper—paper bearing a seal—the thick, crackling written sheets that contained the orders, the decrees, the legal settlements, the family letters, that brought power or ruin or good fortune.

Medicine, Disease, and Death

Disease, the practice of medicine, and death constitute one of the darkest and gloomiest aspects of the sixteenth century. In 1522, the year the Conquest was completed, Hernán Cortés begged Emperor Charles V not to grant the clergy, lawyers, and doctors authorization to come to Mexico. His fears were justified as time went by. The clergy lacked a high moral sense, and their conduct contrasted painfully with that of the first evangelistic monks. The lawyers not only seized power over the colony but ultimately they boldly overthrew the Conquistadors. The doctors, for their part, were so rapacious that Motolinia expressed himself vehemently to this effect:

In Mexico, when some citizen falls ill and, after lying twenty days in bed, dies, all the property he owns will be needed to pay the druggist and the doctor, so that barely enough will be left for his burial. . . . I heard a married man, a wise man, say that if either he or his wife should be taken sick, and if death was a certainty, the husband was to kill the wife, and the wife the husband, and they would try to have themselves both buried in any cemetery, whatsoever, rather than be left poor, alone, and in debt.

Many Spaniards contracted mortal illnesses on their way across the Atlantic and died lamentable deaths when barely arrived in New Spain. Two of the five members of the first Audiencia, Counselors Parada and Maldonado, died of a "pain in the side" thirteen days after disembarking in Vera Cruz, and Counselor Jaraba, one of the three judges appointed by Philip II in 1564 to inquire into the circumstances of a Creole rebellion, died in mid-ocean on his way to the colony, and Dr. Carillo died at sea on his way back to his own country.

During the time that Hernán Cortés was governor of Mexico, death came successively to Governor Francisco de Garay, eldest of the thirteen Augustinian monks who had come with Fray Tomás Ortiz; Visitador Luis Ponce de León; and Counselor Marcos de Aguilar, the Inquisitorial delegate who succeeded Ponce as governor of the colony. Undoubtedly Aguilar was the most seriously ill; he was fed either by a wet nurse whom he brought from Spain or by a herd of goats, without any distinction.

According to the stories of Cortés' enemies which were divulged later, Garay died from eating a dish of herbs and eggs; Ponce from a dish of custard; and Counselor Aguilar from a rasher of Flemish bacon which he ate when he grew tired of the mournful bleating of his goats. Among these deaths, all attributed to Cortés, Counselor Ponce's was especially dramatic. Despite an overwhelming sleepiness that overpowered him—the "drowsiness" to which Bernal Díaz del Castillo alludes—the dying man managed to communicate a terrible fear of death.

The physicians Don Pedro López and Don Cristóbal de Ojeda attended him. The latter was a doctor of few scruples who altered his diagnoses to suit himself. When the illness had obviously become critical, however, he did not hesitate to call in a native healer, in much the same way that Moorish healers were summoned in Spain when the ministrations of Spanish doctors failed. Though nearly dead, Ponce, who was dying far from his native land and in the prime of life, summoned the energy to grasp his staff of office in fevered, unsteady hands and deliver it, before his enemies, to Counselor Marcos de Aguilar.

From time to time the records of juridical proceedings in that period tear aside the veil that covers the dying moments of some of the more exalted invalids. The groans of pain breaking the silence of the night, the premonitory symptoms of the final dissolution—coma, incontinence, and vomiting—remind us of man's weakness and helplessness in the face of death. The pompous diagnoses set down in Latin—Ponce was pronounced ill of an *emitritea sincope humorosa*—merely proclaim the ignorance of those solemn graduates of the College of King's Physicians. They almost invariably prescribed blood-lettings and purges, a practice they were to follow until the time of the *Placebo Sarniento,* and even though officially they could charge only half a peso per visit, according to a municipal court ordinance of 1536, honorariums considerably enriched the medical men, as the magnificent residence of Dr. Pedro López, whom Cervantes de Salazar mentions in his second dialogue, would prove. The plague, scourge of Europe, origin of the dance of death and the plundering of victims (according to historians of the Middle Ages) inevitably showed its sinister face in New Spain. It first attacked the Indians and, combined with the hardship of the mines and the slavery of the encomiendas, their number was impressively reduced. Father Sahagún, working alone, buried more than ten thousand residents of the Tlatelolco quarter; and, in 1545, Motolinia tells us that it would often happen, as an Indian was going to work, that "his soul and his body both quitted him, and he lay stretched out at the door of his hut." During these great epidemics, corpses covered the streets and there were not enough hands to bury the dead. "Many perished of hunger, and others from grief."

Judging by what Dr. Juan de Cárdenas wrote about the scourge of syphilis, it was as widespread an illness in Mexico as in Italy under the Borgias. Cárdenas, whose mania for investigating origins has left us many lengthy descriptions of unimaginable nonsense, attributed the extraordinary spread of the *morbo galicus* to the warm, damp climate of the Indies, though he was not unaware that its transmission generally accompanied the practice of certain acts which he designated as "filthy, stupid, and unchaste." A doctor of our day would be astonished at the disrespectful freedom with which Cárdenas refers to his patients and his colleagues. According to his cynical statements, men wore velvet patches on their faces to cover the ravages of syphilitic chancres, and a lump at the temple or the lack of a bone in the forehead were so common that they passed unnoticed. Be that as it may, to keep mentioning "sores" in the mouth, "little ulcers" in the joints, or the mottled color of the skin—all symptoms common to the majority of the citizens—would make a story with no end. "It is a definite, verified fact," Cárdenas declares, "that nowhere in the world is there a province or a kingdom where this illness afflicts more people, nor where more mercury, china root, and sarsparilla are consumed, or more polychrest, septentrionaline, or *Colchicum variegatum* syrups are swallowed." The incredible prevalence of syphilis, called the "fruit of the earth"—an evil that was neither secret nor shameful—certainly made Mexico a paradise for doctors and druggists. In the sixteenth century a saying ran through the Indies that had the quality of a time-honored proverb: "There is no honored man who does not have a certain touch or trace of this chronic indisposition."

Religion competed with the doctors and the native healers and offered its powerful resources to the sick. Public prayers for help arose, vows and promises were made, and holy images and relics were brought to the bedside of the dying in an attempt to drive away death. Philip II, from whom all authority emanated, was the first not only to sanction these customs but to furnish his subjects with an example of what faith in supernatural resources could accomplish when the skill of medical men had failed. On the night of April 19, 1562, his son, Prince Don Carlos, fell down a stairway on his way to some amorous adventure and fractured his skull. Nine doctors, Spain's most famous, held fifty successive consultations, none of which kept the stricken heir from growing alarmingly worse. While his son lay ill, the king wrote letters to the monks of the famous monasteries, "begging them to implore the favor of our Lord God, as should be done and as we are accustomed to doing in all our affairs, and the intercession of His Holy Mother, praying them to restore my son to health." Processions were held with long lines of flagellants; the queen prayed ceaselessly on her knees "in her private chapel," and "Princess Juana went barefoot on a very cold night to the convent of Our Lady of Consolation to pray for the life of the prince."

On May 9 the prince lay on his bed, looking like a corpse. As a last resort, the doctors had authorized a Moorish healer, called El Pinterete, to apply two salves of his own composition, in vain. At nightfall an impressive scene took place outside the palace. Several monks, followed by a crowd of townspeople, came marching, the coffin holding the mummy of Fray Diego de Alcalá, a Franciscan lay brother, on their shoulders. He had been dead for more than a hundred years, and miraculous cures and acts of humility performed during his lifetime—he had never hesitated to lick the sores of the incurably ill— had won him the halo of a saint. The doors were opened to the funereal procession, the stinking mummy was placed on the sick man's bed, and the broken, motionless head of the prince was covered with the cloth that had been wrapped around Fray Diego's skull.

Philip had left Alcalá that night on his way to Madrid to arrange the funeral services for his son. On the following day, the prince came out of his coma—it would have been better for him to have died then—and soon recovered his health. "Neither Don Carlos nor King Philip ever doubted that the cure was due to an authentic miracle." The Spanish crown subsequently made the canonization of Fray Diego a matter of state.

We must not let the circumstances of this miracle mislead us about Philip II's attitudes toward materia medica. He encouraged scientific knowledge, insofar as he was able, and tried to safeguard the public health by decreeing that physicians were to be under the control of the government. One of his personal physicians, Dr. Francisco Hernández, made a tour of New Spain on an official mission to collect animals, plants, and minerals. No danger could deter him. He traveled throughout the tropical region, the high plateau, and across the peaks of mountain ranges, enduring hunger, fatigue, and serious hardship—he was followed always by his herbariums and valuable collections. Hernández might have made his fortune practicing medicine, but he scornfully rejected that possibility and devoted himself to scientific investigation. Icazbalceta says: "He had the efficacy of medicines tested by ordering their use in the hospitals, and by virtue of his title of royal physician he could call upon the professors of science then in the city to make similar experiments and to communicate their results to him."

Flavorsome personalities were plentiful even in the peaceful world of medicine. Juan de Unza, a Basque of noble origin who had killed a man in circumstances unknown to us, sought sanctuary in a hospital in Extremadura and became an excellent surgeon; eager to pay for his crime by martyrdom, he came to Mexico where he adopted the habit of a lay brother in the monastery of San Francisco. Here his marvelous cures earned him a wide reputation. He was obsessed by the desire to return good for evil, and whenever one of his patients died he scourged himself unmercifully.

On a slightly less melodramatic plane, we meet the Augustinian friar Agustín Farfán, author of the *Breve tratado de medicina* (*Brief Treatise on Medicine*), the first work of its kind published in New Spain; and Dr. Juan de la Fuente, a great credit to his profession. During the terrible plague of 1576–77, Fuente acted as adviser to his colleagues, made them hold consultations, and eventually performed an autopsy on an Indian victim of the epidemic.

We always find three figures surrounding important deathbeds—history does not care to concern itself with the humble—the doctor, the monk, and the scribe. Of the three, the churchman was the most important, because, of course, the ordering of the affairs of the world and the body was less important than ordering the affairs of the soul. The mournful reminder that we are dust and unto dust we shall return and the gloomy maxim *sic transit gloria mundi* rang constantly in the ears of the people, with all their terrible force. Death, trampling underfoot pontifical tiaras and royal scepters or wearing the crown that conquered invincible monarchs, was the powerful shadow that loomed across the world. In those days the dead were not hustled efficiently away, as they are today, by undertakers with an eye on profit. Rather, they were extolled as examples of the end to which all things must come. This feeling about death was carried even to the point of entering into the mystery of the tomb. In the paintings that hung in churches and monasteries, the actual decomposition of the flesh was emphasized. Skulls and crossbones alternated with portraits of women in a cruel kind of X-ray image, half showing their earthly beauty clothed in silks and jewels, and the other half the skeleton upon which all that glory rested. The rose, the symbol of ephemeral beauty, was always on their lips, and it was the motif dearest to the poets.

This familiarity with death, plus the consoling certainty that the descent into the grave would be surrounded by the firmest assurance of the ascent to glory, softened to some extent the agony of dying. A fixed belief in another life, eternal punishment or eternal reward, filled the future with the concrete realities of hell and heaven. No financial sacrifice was too great if it could assure heavenly joy. The wills of the period provide for an immense number of Masses, public atonements, and public prayers, which testify unequivocally to fear of the temporary flames of purgatory and, with much greater cause, of the eternal fires of hell, which lay heavy on the guilty consciences of our forefathers.

A man's death was undeniably more important than his birth. It was not a confused performance involving walking on tiptoe and taking off hats, but a transcendent event, a glorification, and it behooved a man to meditate on it and prostrate himself on the ground. A man had ceased to be; the bells were busy making public his transfiguration, filling the city with their brazen tones. Tapers were burning in the church beside the solemn catafalque, the priest at the altar was chanting the office for the dead, and the congregation was shuddering and offering up ardent prayers for the salvation of a stranger. Their piety would be repaid, for when their turn came, other citizens, also strangers, would pray for their souls. "I saw myself as you see yourself; as you see me, so shall you see yourself" was the reminder usually placed at the feet of the remains of the deceased faithful.

Colonial Culture

The cultural atmosphere was authentic, with deep, rich motivations. Hernán Cortés, the first actual governor of the colony, the members of the second Audiencia, which included Don Vasco de Quiroga himself, and in a special way the first viceroys, plus many humble friars and church dignitaries, were all keenly interested in maintaining and consolidating the elements that were essential to the spiritual life of Madrid. Spain was then at her zenith. Her aspiration to world hegemony was strong and, in a great degree, was united to an apostolic zeal to make all men Catholic. Her ambition for wealth was combined with her thirst for glory into so strong a fighting spirit that the saints and the soldiers dispensed sermons and slashes alike on the way through Flanders, Italy, Mexico, Peru, or China. What such faith and heroism accomplished seems utterly miraculous. In less than fifty years, a few thousand madmen discovered oceans, volcanoes, forests, and immense rivers; they sailed around the world and took possession of a continent, thus establishing the greatest colonial empire in European history. When the Spanish theologians had given new force to Catholicism, and the *Tercios* had become a fabulous infantry fighting on another front, there appeared in the Indies warrior-colonists, builders of cities, and chroniclers of their own exploits.

The labors of creation, always directed toward practical ends, had as one of their main objectives satisfying the needs of the churches and monasteries, which in the early days were announced with unarguable urgency. "The founding of countless villages," George Kubler writes, "was the duty and the rare privilege of the first settlers in Mexico." The thick towers of the houses, their battlements, and their nail-studded doors established at the outset a feudal, gloomy, and warlike type of city living, which was gradually softened by the graceful work of the silversmiths, the beautiful fountains, and the squares with their cool arcades.

Religious construction work flourished alongside the civil. Franciscans, Dominicans, and Augustinians competed among themselves to multiply their cloisters in town and country. Even though many of the primitive structures have been destroyed or have undergone radical alterations, ruins still survive in such impressive number as to give us a clear idea of their passion for building. The towers, façades, and arches of the churches and the cloistered walks and colonnades of the monasteries gave the cities of New Spain their unmistakably religious physiognomy, and at the same time, with their buttresses and battlements, they introduced an essentially feudal note throughout the country that is visible in our own day.

This world of stone, built for the most part by Spanish monks who were architectural amateurs, this offshoot of Western Europe grafted onto an entire continent, differs in many ways from the religious architecture of the Spanish peninsula despite the similarities. The Indian, although only a collaborator on the builder's plans, introduced a new sensibility, a deliberate deviation from the various accepted modes, and breathed onto the stone his strange, fresh style.

However important it may be, the modification in style due to native builders is less than the modification in the dynamics of our religious architecture, because this relates to the characteristic style of colonial culture. In less than fifty years, according to the acute observation of José Moreno Villa, the sculpture in New Spain—as revealed in the stonework of capitals, crosses, baptismal fonts, figures, and elaborate ornamentation—re-created in Mexico the styles of the Romanesque, Gothic, and Renaissance, and blended forms that Europe had evolved during four hundred years. "The arts or artistic modes," Moreno Villa concludes, "are in full spate here, and by that I mean they do not obey an internal evolutionary process, as in Europe." Indeed, this phenomenon is not confined to architecture, but rather marks the entire colonial culture of the sixteenth century. If the native craftsman, with his patent artistic sensitivity, could turn himself into a medieval or Renaissance stonecutter, then it should not be any more difficult for the Creole poet to write medieval couplets with one hand and Petrarchan sonnets with the other.

The Magical Universe of Books

The bookshop, with its shelves bulging with volumes and its erudite proprietor, was unknown in the sixteenth century. Yet a great deal of reading was done, as can be proved by the quantity of books imported and the number of dealers in the book trade. What were the settlers in New Spain reading in the sixteenth century? We may cite two important documents of 1576 that will give us a satisfactory answer. The first mentions a local purchase of 341 volumes, and the second the acquisition of 1,190 books imported from Spain. The fact that these purchases were made by dealers in the city of Mexico and not by institutions or private buyers helps us to form some idea of the literary tastes and the technical needs of the colony.

Both lists—the first is dated June 22 and the second December 2—were composed largely, as is to be expected, of "theological books, manuals, or religious writings." The presence of twenty Bibles published in France or Antwerp and of numerous copies of the works of Erasmus, considered a dangerous heretic in 1571, demonstrates that (in spite of the Counter Reformation) some degree of freedom did exist in the circulation of banned books.

Among the other works mentioned in the two lists, medicine, jurisprudence, and philosophy hold preferential place. Ancient materia medica, one book by the Greek Dioscorides, and a pharmaceutical treatise by Juan Mesue, physician to the fabulous Haroun-al-Raschid, stood side by side with modern works by Charles V's and Philip II's physicians. In philosophy, the all-powerful Aristotle rubbed shoulders with Vives and Fray Alonso de la Veracruz, and in jurisprudence the theoretical works of older writers ranked alongside the works of contemporaries, even with law digests for the Indies.

Although a brief sweep of one collection of books cannot cover the extremely complex panorama of a culture at its zenith, as the Spanish was, this scanning may suffice for us to trace with broad general strokes the tastes and tendencies that influenced readers in New Spain. Unquestionably, by mid-century the culture had become considerably refined. Books on chivalry, which had so delighted the generation of the Conquistadors, had given way to a new and more demanding kind of reading.

Poetry was preferred; but then poets had been the favorites in Mexico from the beginning of the colony. Vergil is champion with thirty-three copies of his work in Latin and thirty-four in Spanish; Martial has twenty-five; but Ovid's spicy *De amatoria*—another book that might logically be supposed to be in the limbo of the Inquisition's Index—has the distinction of appearing on both lists.

The prose writers were also circulated widely, with Cicero heading the list—his letters appear twenty-one times, and his *De Oficiis* twenty-six. Books of Lucan, Martial, Seneca, Sallust, Justinian, and Julius Caesar were also active in the trade, thereby justifying Menéndez y Pelayo's opinion, that: "Mexico City was beginning to acquire the name of the Athens of the New World," and even matching the exaggerated and optimistic view of the Creole or mestizo monk Diego de Valadés in his *Rhetorica christiana,* that "we may easily come to equal the Greeks."

The book market in New Spain provided its customers with contemporary Spanish authors as well as the classics. The "newcomers" of the period, the books most in vogue—the best sellers of the sixteenth century—as listed in 1576, reflect essentially two well-defined characteristics of Mexican society: a fondness for realism and sensuality, as combined in *La Celestina,* and an enjoyment of the apologue, fully satisfied in the *Golden Book* of Marcus Aurelius. Both were favorite works of that century. Such a period, given to moralizing and to finding hackneyed lessons and examples in everything, might well have chosen as its outstanding work the *Tragicomedy of Calixto and Melibea.*

3

Humanism versus Avarice

A STRUGGLE WITHOUT A VICTORY

Sin boldly.   Luther

The ideals of justice and liberty that are the common patrimony of all men, and the peculiar characteristic of the Spanish Humanists, deeply influenced Mexican life in the sixteenth century, more as a practical attitude than as a literary style. Between the Graeco-Latin culture of the Renaissance and Las Casas, between Zumárraga and Erasmus, between Don Vasco de Quiroga and Thomas More lie deep differences, even though they all shared in the same spiritual environment.

Except for Cervantes de Salazar, the Humanists who came to Mexico reveal themselves to us as energetic men of action. They were at work in a New World; they had before them a reality *sui generis,* and they were inspired with a sacred mission, to which they dedicated themselves with all their strength.

Consider the ideas of the most notable of American Humanists, Fray Bartolomé de Las Casas, the bishop of Chiapas. As the literary historian Menéndez y Pelayo said: "They were few, and made fast to his spirit with the tenacity of nails; his nature was violent and very stern; his temper irascible and choleric; his doctrinal fanaticism immovable and rude; his language hyperbolic and intemperate, a mingling of pedantry and brutal insults."

How many ideas should an apostle command? The ideas of Las Casas tended to champion the stumbling dignity of man and to insist that justice be implanted in the Indies and understood as "the goal and the supreme norm of all human society and all legitimate authority." Hence it was natural that his few ideas should be carried in his soul; and even fastened there with nails. He alone was daring enough to take upon himself the responsibility for the Indians, and he did it in the very days when the white men set their dogs on them, worked them to death, and branded their faces with the iron of slavery. He had nothing in common with his opponent Ginés de Sepúlveda, the soother of consciences, nor with the theologians who had forged their law from theory. They wrote in their libraries, by the warmth of their fires, while Las Casas met the slavers face to face, took their insults and the stones they flung at him, suffered hunger and the heat and burden of the day, crossed the ocean many times even in his old age, and wrote and spoke like a man possessed—"I have written on many sheets of paper, more than two thousand, in Latin and in Spanish"—and he never quailed before the task of telling kings to their faces that they would be charged with the sins of the Conquest.

How could he be other than violent and harsh, irascible and choleric, this man who witnessed the destruction of the Indians in the Caribbean with the bitter and despairing certainty of his own helplessness? He embodied the moral conscience of the Spanish Empire in the Indies, and this cross, which he accepted willingly, brought down on him the hatred of the Scribes and Pharisees of his time and of ours. Even Motolinia, himself a sincere defender of the Indians, wrote to Charles V:

I marvel that Your Majesty and the members of your councils have been able to suffer for so long such a heavy-handed man, restless and tactless, turbulent and litigious, so strenuous, so ill-bred, so insulting, so mischievous, and so completely without serenity that Your Majesty ought to lock him up in a monastery before he can cause greater evil.

"When Francisco de Vitoria, Domingo de Soto, and José Acuña adopted the teachings of Las Casas," Gallegos Rocafull remarks, "it lost its aggressiveness and fire, but gained in exchange vigorous solidity and a serene depth; so much so that it became the embodiment of the Spanish idea of the empire," which Vitoria expressed as "service to humanity, fraternity among peoples, obedience to plans, a rule of justice, the victory of human social living."

A very noticeable hiatus lies between this high-minded concept of imperial policy and the reality of the Indies. Neither the code of human rights elaborated by the theologians nor the incessant stream of royal decrees benefiting the Indians succeeded in modifying to any noteworthy degree the condition of the natives, upon whom the economic structure of the empire rested. The fine words that sanctified the rule of justice and human brotherhood in the Indies were engraved as on the façade of a temple, while injustice and exploitation reigned within. Las Casas did not succeed, could not succeed, in rescuing the Indians from slavery; but his struggle for social justice did at least manage to encourage multitudes by opening before them the prospect of future freedom. His work, aimed at defining with terrible clarity the distance separating a fine plan from its realization, left the dark side of the Conquest and Spanish colonization without any possible moral justification. This is the reason why he was so hated. Hispanicists speak of his exaggerations, as though his crime were one of statistics; but after four centuries the best proof of the truth of his denunciation is the situation of extreme poverty and destitution which is still the common lot of millions of American Indians.

What does it matter that Spain's enemies made full use of Fray Bartolomé de Las Casas' accusations? What matters is that a Spanish monk formulated them in the midst of a storm of passion and self-interest, both red and white, and that the best of the Spaniards were on his side. Whatever Spain's detractors may have said later lacks life and authentic feeling. It is only fair to recognize—and we do not know whether it is a national vice or a national virtue—that the Spanish have criticized themselves mercilessly and repeatedly, as no other people has done, in the sixteenth century as in all centuries. Hatred of injustice and slander is a Spanish form of love, and Fray Bartolomé de Las Casas had that love to a heroic degree that has no other example in the world.

Zumárraga: The Contradiction of His Time

Despite his fondness for Erasmus, Zumárraga does not appear to have been endowed with those traits traditionally assigned to the Humanist. The first bishop of Mexico was a monk of the Middle Ages, to judge by the picture we have of his life. Charles V, who knew him incidentally in his humble retreat at Abrojo, entrusted to him the mission of exterminating the witches of Navarre, the first task he carried to completion outside the cloister. Later he was appointed Bishop of Mexico, Protector of the Indians, and Apostolic Inquisitor, three rather vague and open-ended titles which, as he expressed it, he took "for his cross and martyrdom."

The situation facing Zumárraga in Mexico exceeded every previous calculation. Nuño de Guzmán, who had brought twenty ships filled with Indians from his seat of government on the Pánuco for the purpose of selling them in the islands of the Caribbean, boasted of his high office as president of the Audiencia. The list of crimes committed by this same Guzmán, by the oidores, the agent Salazar, and Inspector Chirinos—each of them governor in his turn—sounds incredible. Although an official could not own Indians legally as slaves, the members of the Audiencia did in fact have all the Indians at their disposal. The Indians built the Spaniards' houses, mills, and villas without receiving a cent for their work; the Spaniards stripped the Indians of their property, their water, and their lands, by means of ridiculous contracts, and then oppressed them with heavy levies and tributes; they sold offices and appointments; they kept slaves in the gold-mining placers, and led them like cattle to the Pánuco. Some of the natives, driven mad, committed suicide or refused to have children by their wives. The rape of beautiful Indian women, even those who were living in houses of correction, was the order of the day. Prostitutes shared the armchairs of the council with the oidores.

Zumárraga was not even an ordained bishop—he had sailed before receiving the necessary papal bull—but he rose bravely to the defense of the Indians, knowing that he must deal with the hatred of the Dominicans, who were on the side of the Audiencia, and lacking any organized body of clergy to support him. García Icazbalceta says:

> The president and the oidores ordered the town crier to proclaim that no Spaniard must go to the aid of the protector in matters concerning the Indians, nor must the Indians take their complaints to him, under pain of being hanged. That announcement by the crier struck such fear into everyone that no one dared to talk with the archbishop any more than with an excommunicated man.

There was no check on violence. A priest who undertook to plead with the judges was driven from the pulpit with blows, and when the authorities violated by force the conventual right of asylum in order to avenge themselves on two poor devils, Zumárraga did not hesitate to place himself at the head of a mutiny. He tore down the doors of the Casas Reales, he answered with anger the insults hurled at him by the oidores, and he escaped death only because a lance thrust aimed at him by Delgadillo passed beneath his arm.

After the Audiencia had recessed, Zumárraga was able to assume his episcopal duties with more calm. We discover at that moment with some surprise that a Humanist is concealed beneath the monk's habit. The thesis of his *Doctrina breve muy provechosa* (*Brief Useful Catechism*) (1543–44), inspired by the *Paraclasis* of Erasmus, is repeated with minor variations and in abbreviated form at the conclusion of the other *Doctrina* published by his order about 1546, which indicates that Zumárraga dared to launch an Erasmian program of Christianization ten years after Erasmus had died, and when his books, vanished, like his high-placed defenders, from Spain, were the objects of implacable Inquisitorial persecution.

In both *Doctrinas,* the first bishop of Mexico affirmed the need for translating the Gospel into all the languages in the world, and for making it known to all. He placed the living word of Christ, taught with simplicity and especially by personal example, above the superstitions of the people and the works of the theologians. "Would you like me, brother, to tell you what I feel? I cannot understand the reason why we wish to make the wisdom of Jesus Christ incomprehensible through the writings of men instead of learning it from the mouth of Jesus Christ himself." To him, Christ was the only teacher, the greatest and truest of theologians. He trusted more in prayer than in debate and condemned all pedantry, for "[the word of God] is shown better through living a good life than through arguing well, and is learned better by divine inspiration than by school work."

The contradictions in Zumárraga's soul were manifold. In the catechism which he sent to press in 1546—an almost literal copy of the *Suma de doctrina cristiana* by Doctor Constantino—he makes no mention of the Virgin, purgatory, or indulgences. Bataillon writes:

> It might be suspected that to the intrepid "evangelists" who undertook to Christianize the Indians, anything that might encourage the worship of the Virgin and the saints, as practiced by the "old Christians," contains the risk of confusing that worship with the earlier idolatry and of obfuscating the fundamental, which is obedience to the law of God, knowledge of sin, and redemption through the blood of Christ.

Despite his significant omissions, and at peril of confusing idolatries, Zumárraga's name is linked to the appearance of the Virgin of Guadalupe, the miracle most deeply expressive of the religious spirit of Mexico. And this was not the only flaw evident in Zumárraga's Erasmianism. He conscientiously carried out his duty as Inquisitor, notwithstanding the fact that the Dutch philosopher had condemned the use of violence to impose Catholicism and destroy heresy. "While in Mexico," García Icazbalceta emphasizes, "he seized a sorcerer named Océlotl and exiled him to Spain for being dangerous." He often saw the devil lurking behind the native codes of law and the native idols, for which reason he resorted to the purifying stake; and his authority culminated in the death of the chief of Texcoco, which was handled in such a way as to bring him a reprimand even from the Spanish Inquisitors.

Zumárraga's loathing for every whiff of heresy did not conflict with his pure affection for the Indians and their culture. We owe to the bishop not only Mexico's first printing press and, in part, its university but also the idea for the Colegio de Santiago Tlatelolco. The touching sight of native children devoted to study and craftmanship in the huge convent of San Francisco under the tutelage of Fray Pedro de Gante inspired in Zumárraga the desire to "establish for them a secondary school where they could broaden their studies and eventually serve as teachers." The old monk conceived everything on a grand scale. To Charles V he wrote: "The thing that most occupies my mind, that my will is most fixed upon, and my small strength fighting for, is that in this city and in this diocese there be a secondary school for Indian boys, who may at least learn grammar, and a large convent to which a goodly number of the young Indian girls may be admitted by right."

He offered his library and a village he owned to defray the expense of bringing fruit trees by ship from Spain. These trees were to be planted in the orchards of the secondary schools in order to help people to forget "the desire for Castile, for they cry for her fruits more than for any other thing."

With the help of the emperor and the viceroy, Don Antonio de Mendoza, the colegio was ready to open its doors in 1536. Among the men who taught at Tlatelolco were Fray Andrés de Olmos, who had come to Mexico with Zumárraga—a writer, linguist, and "evangelist to remote and savage peoples for forty-three years"; Fray Juan Gaona, a famous theologian, "as humble as he is wise"; the French monk Juan Focher, with a doctorate from the University of Paris; and Fray Bernardino de Sahagún. The last-named monk—who was so handsome in his youth that his superiors had hidden him, in order to deprive him of the chance to be ruined—was the moving spirit of the colegio for many long years. He brought together an unsurpassed group of Latinists, interpreters, illuminators, and native compositors who worked on his *Historia general de las cosas de Nueva España*. The poverty of the colegio, which marked even its days of greatest splendor, and the "envy and passions" to which Viceroy Mendoza was to allude later, did not hinder the training of many Indians, among them the famous orator and Latinist Antonio Valeriano, Diego de Grado, Mateo Severino, and the rector Martín Jacobita.

The fighting spirit of Saint Paul, which God denied Erasmus, a man of letters, was granted to Zumárraga, a man of action. Even though he was himself a monk, he closed his ears to monkish attacks on his guiding spirit (perhaps because he thought them just) and tried to bring to the New World the word of God restored to its original purity. Perhaps he was a long way from classic Humanism as Erasmus understood it, even though he made some of the Dutchman's reforming ideas his own and, like him, was no champion of saints, relics, superstitions, and the pomp of ecclesiastical ceremonies. He dreamed of leading a new evangelical church that would take the Gospel as its guide; he did not realize—or if he did, he thought it unimportant—that what he considered the truth and the salvation of the Christian world, the movement that inspired Spain to her finest hour, was condemned and persecuted with blood and fire by his own people: the monks, the clergy, and the Inquisitors, its most exalted representatives. In this struggle between reason and secular tradition, between evangelical doctrine and the fossilized hierarchy of the Church, he was vanquished. The historical change in Spain made the realization of his ideals impossible. Monkishness carried the day; the pomp of religious ceremonies increased; violence and superstition triumphed. And in the end, those feudal elements also prevailed in Zumárraga's soul; fundamentally, he lacked the tolerance and the warm understanding which the Humanist should possess to the highest degree. In the grip of his time, he encouraged superstitions, for he was a monk always respectful of his order; above all, he was a Spanish madman, which is to say a madman different from other madmen. He was close to eighty years old when he decided to go to China to preach the Gospel with his friend Fray Domingo de Betanzos and thus leave his diocese unoccupied.

The ecclesiastical authorities rejected his absurd petition. Fighting to the last, he died in bed, at nine o'clock on the morning of Sunday, June 3, 1548. An hour earlier he had said, to those who were standing around him: "Ah, Fathers! How different it is for a man to find himself at the point of death than to talk about it!" His last words echoed in the little cell: "In manos tuas, Domine, commendo spiritum meum" ("Into thy hands, O Lord, I commend my spirit"). Soon the tolling bells announcing the vacant see filled the silence of the archepiscopal palace.

The detractors of the Colegio de Tlatelolco tell of the resistance it encountered during Zumárraga's lifetime. The writer Jerónimo López reported the following incident to Charles V. A priest who visited there in 1541 found himself surrounded by clamorous Indian students. So many questions about matters of faith and the sacred Scriptures assailed him "that he felt overwhelmed, put his hands over his ears, and said that the place was hell and those in it disciples of Satan."

López invidiously specifies that the friars were not content to teach the Indians how to "read, write, mark up books, play the flute, the cheremía, the trumpet, and the keyboard, and become musicians," but that they had made the greater mistake of teaching them grammar and the sciences. Indians should know the Our Father, the Ave Maria, the Credo, the Salve, the Ten Commandments, "and no more." "It was a good thing for them to know doctrine," the disgruntled scribe concludes, "but reading and writing are harmful as the devil." Of what use was Latin to the Indians who, however, according to him, were able to speak with the eloquence of a Cicero? Assuredly, "it was of no use to them except to enable them to recognize which priests were idiots when they were saying Masses and performing the divine offices, and to laugh at them and belittle them, and also to permit them to notice whether or not they were saying something nonsensical in Latin while they were preaching or lecturing." Obviously, study was of no use to them, except that it made them "more crafty."

A Man "Alive in Christ"

In 1535, two oidores, accompanied by a scribe, attested to a pitiful sight seen very frequently in the city of Mexico. A group of Indians, who had been purchased in New Galicia, were awaiting the hour when they would be sold as slaves. Men, women, even children of three or four months, showed on their faces the "brand they say is the king's, almost as big as the children's cheeks"; "and we saw all this and more," comments one of the oidores, Don Vasco de Quiroga, "for some of them were sick men and women, almost at the point of death."

They asked their owners: "What crime had those women and suckling babes committed to cause them to be branded like that?" Their owners answered only: "We have hauled them out of the caves in the mountains where they had hidden in flight from the Spaniards."

"The sheep flee from the wolves," Don Vasco wrote later to the Council of the Indies. "The Indians keep running away and trying to defend themselves from the inordinate affronts, assaults, and injuries" which they receive, "with the weapon of the rabbit, which is to flee to the woods and crags." To run away is not the same thing as to rise up in arms. Only "we, blinded by greed, give the name of rebellion to natural self-defense, because it suits our own private interests to do so."

But the Indians of New Galicia were not the only ones to suffer. In many other parts of the country "free and innocent" Indians had been enslaved by the "Christians,"

. . . and worse than slaves, even worse than those condemned to the mines; they brand them in the face . . . the initials of their names are written on all those whom they buy and sell again and again, one from another, passing them from hand to hand; there are some who bear three or four initials . . . so that a man's face, which was created in the image of God, has become as a piece of paper in this country, through our sins, not as fools, but as men greedy for money, which is worse and more damaging.

They demanded beautiful Indian girls "by the dozen and half dozen"; they bartered Indian men—"I don't know what devilish kind of barter that is"—not to indoctrinate or to instruct them but to work them to death. Yes, the "Christians" did all that, "the evil and greedy Christians."

At the conclusion of his report, Don Vasco adds:

The natives are not on our side; they are like the birds at sight of the net; they shrink from us, frightened and fluttering, and they run away from us and our works and the nets we spread for them for the purpose of capturing them and turning them to our use by any means whatsoever, fair or foul, to their total destruction and ravishment.

Don Vasco de Quiroga is perhaps the most attractive figure among the early Mexican Humanists, a man with the charity, the practical realism, and the fertile imagination of the great apostles. The ugly sin of intolerance never swayed him from his essential balance. After holding an official position in the Audiencia, he moved on easily to the archdiocese of Michoacán. "They yanked me out of the magistracy," he writes, "and placed me at the rudder of the priesthood for my sins . . . and so it happened that before I had learned, I began to teach." He was one of those men who labored to achieve the global ambition of his time and of his country, to whom "the principal function [of Charles V] was to see that all nations would profess the same orthodox faith, and that the entire world would be converted to the worship of the one true God and become a single flock with a single shepherd."

He began with what was natural to the Indians—communal agriculture and craftsmanship—and transformed More's Utopia into a reality by founding the hospices of Santa Fé and Michoacán: a new idea, applied to a new society, in a New World. The words "yours and mine," a universal source of discord, were forbidden inside his Utopia. The working day was six hours long; the fruits of the agreeable communal labor were distributed "according to each one's needs for himself and his family." The members made their own clothing of cotton and wool, "white, clean, and decent"; the officers of the hospice were democratically elected; the children learned agriculture at play; and everyone was taught the word of God and good manners. Quiroga advises: "You will be well served by keeping a guard over your tongue, so that living thus, in such concert and good order, free from both need and evil idleness, and from greed and disorder, you will show yourselves thankful for the gifts of Our Lord God, and save your souls to boot."

Like Zumárraga, Don Vasco often spoke of founding "a new and primal church." He was one of the men "truly dead to the world, alive in Christ," who taught, according to the ideal of Erasmus, "the word of God sincerely among the savage peoples." He believed that the Europeans had fallen a long way from their ancient simplicity and good and had finally landed in an iron age, while the Indians "were still in their golden age." He set out to build the City of God in Mexico, alone and unaided. The olive trees he planted still stand in Tzintzuntzan, on a patch of red earth overlooking the silver limpidity of the lake. The lacquers of Pátzcuaro, the hammered copper of Santa María, the ceramics of Patamban, the musical instruments of Paracho—all these we owe to him. The foot that spins the potter's wheel, the hand that glides across the weaver's loom, remind us today of his teachings. The city built in the sixteenth century which was dedicated to the ideal of communal living, an ideal that has come down from Plato, lives on in his name, which is echoed with reverence by all the Indians of Michoacán.

Humanism in the Secondary Schools

The Humanism of those men, more "pious and saintly" than educated, as Zumárraga wished them to be, died with them. Theirs was an ideal of human dignity so lofty and so pure that it could not thrive in the feudal world it had fought. The greed of the encomendero and the crown official strangled it in its cradle, but the real cause of its failure lay in its excision by the Christian world. Spain tried to stamp out heresy and impose by force what she believed to be for mankind's salvation. Joaquín Xirau describes "the moment when Luis de León, Juan de la Cruz, and the archbishop of Toledo are about to be imprisoned and when the followers of Luis Vives, the Valdeses, Thomas More, Erasmus . . . shall fill the dungeons or be burned in the public squares."

A story which is all the more interesting because it has to do with a mestizo is that of Fray Diego de Valadés, "the first Mexican who succeeded in having a book published in Europe." He had been enrolled at the customary tender age in the huge monastery of San Francisco, where he had the opportunity to work side by side with Fray Pedro de Gante. He lived with the Indians for thirty years—"thanks be to God!"—and served as preacher and confessor in three languages, Mexican, Tarascan, and Otomí, for more than twenty-two. He performed the duties of Solicitor for the Order of Franciscans Minor before the Holy See, and his *Rhetorica christiana* was published in Perusa in 1597. In the words of Méndez Plancarte, it was "a huge treatise that merits long and careful study not only for its literary quality but also for its historical content with reference to the ancient rites and customs of the Indians of Mexico."

Despite the small amount of study so far given him, the figure of Fray Diego de Valadés reveals the unquestionable "Humanistic saturation" of our sixteenth century. In addition to being a missionary, an engraver, and an expert in indigenous languages, he was a man of "the greatest Graeco-Latin erudition," a writer who "handles Latin with skill and elegance," and an ardent student of Plato.

His mind, a just combination of the qualities of the intellectual and the man of action, was an authentic product of the Humanistic movement, which enabled him to overcome the obstacles faced from birth by a mestizo of his time. Once, in the house of a public official of the king, he dared to tell a certain nobleman who was denigrating the Indians: "I truly think that the itch to speak evil of the Indians is the mark of those who see the situation from above and not from near at hand. Or, to put it better, it arises from the fact that they see the subject with prejudiced and not very Christian eyes."

Facing away from Life

The arrival of the Jesuits in the last quarter of the century brought an increase in Humanistic studies. Latin plays were performed, and literary groups and competitions were held. Child prodigies who could speak Latin and recite the *Aeneid* at the age of ten were exhibited in the Colegio de San Pedro y San Pablo like little monsters worthy of the highest praise. When the New Spanish literature had come to a rolling boil, an inordinate number of Latin poems, odes, and topical epigrams splashed out of the common pot. All this somewhat bogus production, which had nothing whatever to do with life, added a new colonial element to the complex panorama of the culture. Its obvious artificiality not only did nothing to help the search for expression, it interposed an obstacle. The Spaniard born in America was surrounded from the beginning by elements and motivations conceived in another setting, and his mind could not resolve the conflicts between experience and applied culture. There was no catalyst that could fuse it all and give him a new sense of the arbitrary blending of Classicism, Renaissance, and Catholic feudalism with the cultural elements of Spain and Italy —indeed nothing that the studious Creole could force himself to swallow in a single spoonful.

On the other hand, the social disorganization of the colony, the final divorce of imported culture from the demands of American reality, insured that there would be little originality in the literary expression of New Spain. Nothing is produced by spontaneous generation in the realm of the spirit. The creation of individual forms is the fruit of an organic development, of a true culture that pervades and enriches the life of a people. Between Apollo, the symbol of Greece, and Coatlicue, the Mexican symbol that by that time was well buried and stigmatized—between the Italy of the Renaissance, with its spirit of harmony, and Spanish feudalism nourished on the sentiment of its people—yawned abysses that only the passage of the centuries and the slow, painful birth of a national life could close.

4

The World of Light

We grew afraid to say that there was pain and glory forever in what we were reading. It often happened that we spent much time discussing this; and we liked to say many times, forever, and ever, and ever.

Santa Teresa de Jesús

By and large, throughout the sixteenth century, man rested peacefully on the cushion of his faith. His world was not, like ours, an empty world with a blind, unalterable course, but a world firmly based on religious beliefs. Above all else, man was preoccupied with the salvation of his soul and with the fate that awaited him after death, a state of infinite joy or sorrow with no boundaries and no change, a place eternal and everlasting. Good and evil warred incessantly in his soul—the weaknesses of the flesh and earthly joys versus the desire to be saved and whatever made him conscious of living in sin—a rending conflict that only his mature years would settle; when a man was young, his demoniacal forces held sway, and only at the end, when passion was spent, could the celestial hosts prevail. Accordingly, the life of the Spaniard is revealed to us clearly divided between a longing for pleasure—a truly evil frenzy—and the insatiable desire to order his accounts with God and win for himself a place in heaven through prayer and sacrifice. In good measure, this preoccupation was reflected in the large numbers of convents and monasteries, churches, and religious establishments, and in the liberal alms that poured from the purses of aging sinners—all of which contributed to the strength of the clergy and the religious aspect of the period. If today we live in a changing universe, the inhabitants of the colony were submerged in a stable medium, which forced them to continual reflection on a group of unchanging subjects. Their essential preoccupations were sin, death, hell, purgatory, Christ's passion, and the shrewd vigilance of the devil.

Furthermore, no one could hold himself aloof from the religious passion that burned in the Spaniards. That was the time of great saints and devout kings, when wars and conquests were undertaken in the name of God. A desire for martyrdom and extreme sacrifice, for redeeming men through divine love, for dedication to contemplation and to serving the Divine were emotions experienced in common by Columbus, Hernán Cortés, and Saint Ignatius of Loyola, by the seaman, the soldier, and the humblest friar of that century.

That zeal, shared by all the Conquistadors, for accomplishing great deeds and winning vast regions with no heed to danger and sacrifice, also inspired the missionary monks. These two bands of militia—Christ's and the king's—marched side by side and worked together through one country and one community of men. Each was typical of the character of Spain in her historic moment so wholeheartedly, so naturally, that when the hand that brandished the sword first faltered, the hand that grasped the crucifix began to weaken too, and both became infected with corruption and decadence.

The pages of monastic chronicles give off a strong odor of sanctity. Exhausting travels for the conversion of savage tribes, extremes of fatigue and harassment were joyously undertaken, because to those monks life was an incumbrance that was depriving them of the beatific vision, and martyrdom was the best road to freedom. Anything might be expected of men who would die in order not to die. Their love of danger, their scorn for wealth, and their authentic Christian charity led them to achieve wildly heroic deeds on a scale disproportionate to their numbers and their physical strength.

The Indians were not content to live in the shallows of this stream. Even though they were barred from membership in the religious orders, many of them took vows of chastity and relinquished their slaves to lead the life of the saints. The old tree trunk may blossom occasionally with the little flowers of Saint Francis. A young native noble, inspired by the life of the saint of Assisi, which he had read in the language of his own people, gave his goods to the poor, put on a sackcloth, and begged for the monk's habit. It was not granted him, but he did succeed in living a devout life in a corner of the large monastery of San Francisco.

The faith of the Indians was new and touching. In the diary of Comisario Alonso Ponce, we read:

He saw so much devotion in the Indians that he considered his labors on land and sea well rewarded, for he found in those poor little creatures as fervent a devotion as in the true Christians of the original Church, and the sight of them marching in a procession, or on their knees weeping and begging to be blessed, offering bouquets and garlands of sweet-scented flowers, bread and fruit, eggs and hens, according to what they could give from their poverty, was something to praise God for.

During one night he spent in Tlaxcala, the natives, dressed in white, raced their horses with lighted torches in their hands, "all with the strangest piety and gaiety."

The feudalism of the sixteenth century accentuated the intensity of the religious life. It was not unusual to see in the streets people who were being punished by the Holy Office, wearing the garments of penitents and begging to obtain the money needed to ransom their habits, or to see hanging on cathedral walls, like grim warnings, cardboard coronets with the devil painted on them worn by those who had been sentenced to death and executed and by those who had served their term and were free.

Each aspect of life had its antithesis. A large measure of the precious metals extracted from the mines was poured into the churches and monasteries of the colony. Saint Dominic alone was given, among other treasures, a candelabrum of silver with three hundred tapers and a hundred oil cups, valued at four hundred thousand ducats. The jewel-encrusted images, the utensils of worship, and the priests' vestments comprised a world of splendor that bore no relation to the cripples and beggars waiting in doorways for paupers' soup from the monastery, which was served from an immense copper kettle by two filthy lay brothers, or to the barefoot Indians, clad in rags, who sat on the ground and filled the naves of the churches with their mournful psalms.

Apart from that, however, religion was the one point of unity and concord where the stratified social classes could meet without harm to one another. The hallowed glow of the altars and the splendor of the church ritual were shared by rich and poor, by white and Indians alike. Inequality ended at the church door, and it was not important whether the nobleman had a pew in the chancel or not. The disparate members of the congregation were united in their single desire for redemption.

The material riches and the unlimited spiritual power of the Church might have managed to establish the shining City of God in New Spain had it not been for the devil, operative in the New World as he had been in medieval Europe. His grinning face unleashed nightmares in the dark nights of the city; his soft paws, armed with claws, his bat wings covered with scales were always in motion to destroy the sinner. Man felt his presence; he knew that the devil walked at his side, was his enforced companion throughout his lifetime, and that he was being drawn ceaselessly down toward the abyss of unspeakable seductions; yet the conviction that his fate was in the hands of a demon ready to wreak havoc upon him gave man the strength to refuse to be dragged outside the perimeter of the light, of the world redeemed by the blood of Christ.

The Universal Charity of Bernardino Álvarez

Bernardino Álvarez represented in the Indies a characteristically Spanish type, that of the adventurer turned saint whose image Mateo Alemán sketches in *El pícaro Guzmán de Alfarache*. A life like his may be divided down the center like an orange; one half belongs to the devil and the other to God. In the first, the sinner yields to the legions that drag his soul toward the caverns of hell; in the other, he enlists in the choir of angels and ascends with them, amid clouds and beating wings, to the dazzling throne of the Most High.

At twenty, the age of all good immigrants who trust in their swords and their fists more than their dull enforced studies of Latin, he enlisted as a soldier and went to the north of New Spain where, according to his biographer, Don Juan Díaz de Arce, the war was "very brutal." About 1534, the year of his arrival in Mexico, a career at arms lacked attractions. The cycle of the great conquests had been closed, and it was not possible even to join in those lighthearted, easy forays against the Indians of the Caribbean—Indians who had only their naked bellies as bucklers.

In the wilderness, Bernardino ate a soldier's rations, yawned away the tedium of the garrisons, constructed of logs and mud, and occasionally guarded a mule train loaded with silver. His battles were confined to chasing invisible Indians; from time to time a man in the small detachment would fall to the ground with an arrow through his windpipe. Was that living? Bernardino soon grew tired of that life and went back to the city of Mexico, which was "very rich" at the end of the sixteenth century. There, everything changed at once for him. He lived amid a crowd of spongers and strumpets in squalid lodgings, gambling incessantly, not above cheating and brawling.

Juan Díaz de Arce tells this part of the patriarch's story with obvious repugnance. The hero of his apologia, in defiance of any visible auguries of future sainthood, had sunk so low as to captain a band of highwaymen, and however hard his biographer may try to smooth over the rough spots, even to the point of characterizing the adventures of that period as "naughty pranks," justice was less indulgent and the twelve bandits were flung into prison and condemned "to sail for the voyages of discovery in China." "It seemed to Bernardino and his companions," writes Arce in his sententious manner, "that though China might be a proving ground for brave men, they could probably have exercised their valor in New Spain without sailing that far." Conclusion? Escape. Of the twelve, three were apprehended, turned over to justice, and hanged without more ado. Meanwhile Bernardino Alvarez sought refuge in the house of a woman "not of Jericho but of the Necaltitlán quarter," who kept him hidden for several days, brought him news of his hunters, and finally provided him with money, arms, and a horse. Bernardino took the road to Acapulco, sailed on a ship bound for Peru, and finally reappeared in New Spain after a long absence. He was not the same man. He had left a beardless youth, poor, and on the run from justice, and returned bearded, serious, and wealthy. As he was to explain later, the money—amounting to more than thirty thousand pesos —was "a gift from God," that is, it was not won with marked cards, or by the sword, but by trading with the Indians of the Andes, from hot Callao to cold Cuzco where the Spanish arcades and roof tiles rise above the cut stone of the Inca palaces.

The trader, hoping for a reconciliation with his family, wrote to his mother and sent her a thousand pesos. The old lady needed nothing; she had money enough, and life had ceased to offer her much—she wanted to die in peace, devoting herself to prayer in the serene country seat of Utrera. The old lady's letter, full of advice and suggestions, came like the bolt of lightning that toppled Saul from his horse. When Bernardino had finished reading it, he had already set off on the road to goodness. He could have built himself a house, drunk wine from silver goblets, and dressed in brocade; but instead of enjoying his wealth, the *indiano* had his hair cut off, chose a penitential belt and sackcloth, and became a servant in the hospital of the Purísima Concepción, founded by Hernán Cortés. He spent ten long years caring for the sick, the poor, and the imprisoned. That kind of expiation would have been enough for any ordinary penitent. The hospital and the prison show the other face of society. There were half-mad Indians, naked mestizos, and the lowest of thieves. One lifetime could not begin to remedy so many ills. But Bernardino Alvarez, with the zeal of his epoch, offered his brimming charity to all the needy. He had seen that when the sick were discharged from the hospital, they either died in the streets or, lacking the strength to work, were doomed to suffer bitter privations. With the aim of solving the problem, he built the hospital of the Convalecientes with what was left of his fortune plus whatever money he was given as alms. But what about the aged, who had no one to care for them? And destitute children? And incapacitated clergymen? And the insane, called the innocents, who had no asylum? Bernardino thought about them all, and bought a broad tract of land not far from the church of San Hipólito; there he labored as a mason, went out begging for help, fed the poor, watched at the bedside of the sick, and taught the children their first lessons.

The Croesus of the sixteenth century, Don Alonso de Villaseca, promised him a hundred thousand pesos if Bernardino would name him patron of his asylum. Bernardino answered: "God is the patron of this work. He will provide the wherewithal to support its living stones. This work shall have no patron but God."

He was to be seen often in the streets of the city, going from door to door, followed by two insane patients carrying a basket. "For the love of God, give to the living stones of Christ," he would say. Donations poured in: bread, money, old clothes, blankets, shoes. Everything multiplied in his hands. He founded a new hospital and inn for the needy immigrants of Jalapa; a mule train would bring them to Mexico City to rescue them from the unhealthful climate of Vera Cruz, and they were cared for until they could be admitted to the San Hipólito Hospital, where an *Ecce homo* was carved above the main door with this phrase: *Dominus providevit* (the Lord will provide). For a long time there was an inscription on the outer wall that served to define the spirit of the asylum: "In this general hospital all who are in any way needy will be succored."

On August 12, 1584, Bernardino Alvarez, the repentant sinner, died at the age of seventy, after half a century in the Indies. His fervent intention had been to "succor all the poor in the world." All that he left are his hands—large, strong, nervous hands—folded with visible effort in the attitude of prayer. A symbol of his life, those hands had worked in two different fields. In the first—the field of darkness—they had reached out, armed and greedy, for cards, wine, women, and the tender bodies of victims. In the second—the field of light—the same hands had stretched, tireless and protective, over the heads of the sick, the mad, and the helpless. Voluntarily relinquishing violence and sensuality, he left his piety and his love of mankind as the memorials of a universal charity, which was to be his eternal salvation.

The Servant of God, Gregorio López

In the northern wilderness of New Spain, a strange figure appeared one day in 1562 before Captain Pedro Carrillo de Ávila, owner of an estate near Zacatecas. It was a young man of "gentle mien," barefoot, and clothed in a prickly hair shirt held in at the waist by a cord. He asked for some land so that he might live withdrawn from the world, and, as the land was precisely what was most abundant in the north, the captain gladly acceded to the precocious anchorite's request.

With the help of the Indians, the young man built himself a hut. He slept on the floor, with a board for his mattress, and ate no meat but only corn and fruit that he raised in a garden or was brought to him by the Chichimecas. He avoided any contact with the Spaniards and never went to Mass; nor did he wear scapulars nor any other token of a devout man. Soldiers, from time to time crossing the desert in pursuit of native warriors, took him for a madman or a heretic and mocked him, saying, "Brother, you smell to me like a dead man."

Almost no references to his life in Spain can be found. At the age of ten he lived the life of an anchorite in the mountains of Navarre—mysticism, like music, is a gift of childhood; at twelve he was a page to Philip II; and at twenty he was a visiting monk in several famous monasteries. His later destiny was revealed to him in the convent of Nuestra Señora de Guadalupe, and he sailed for New Spain. He had barely stepped off the ship in Vera Cruz when he distributed his clothes among the poor—"the desire for wealth of those born here had no attraction for him"—and he spent an entire week on bread and water in Luis Zapata's house. Many years later, after Gregorio López had acquired renown as a saint, Zapata, then settled in Taxco, wrote him this letter:

It must be twenty-nine or thirty years ago, when I was living in Tacuba Street in Mexico City, that a gentle soul came from Spain and lodged in my house, dressed in cast-off clothes. Upon my word, he fasted on bread and water during that Lenten season, and called himself Gregorio López. They tell me Your Mercy also calls himself by that name. Please be kind enough to write me if that man is Your Mercy and to commend me to God.

Gregorio answered in his fashion: "I am he whom Your Mercy says, and I shall do as you command me."

He himself surrounded his early life with impenetrable mystery. His biographer, Father Losa, priest of the Cathedral of Mexico City, says that he was born in Madrid and was baptized in the parish church of San Gil, attached to the royal fort. In his lifetime, which also was a time devoted to mysteries and poetical fancies, a legend grew up that has survived to our day without losing its freshness. That young anchorite, who might have dropped from heaven, was none other than Prince Don Carlos, the hapless son of Philip II, whom everyone supposed dead.

The background with which his contemporaries anointed him befitted Gregorio López' strange nature. To borrow the words of Esdrás, which he sometimes quoted, his goal was the "City, configuration of Glory, where no one may enter but by labors and dangers." The road he took was one of solitude, of unflinching confrontation with temptation. The cold horror of his struggle gleams through the first years of his stay in the north, where he wrestled hand to hand with the devil, and the Evil One's bellowing could be heard plainly over the howling of the coyotes in the stark nights on the open plains.

He was above all a man who yearned for solitude, a true lone wolf; yet what is surprising about him is his reason, his plain common sense, his self-reliance. He was not visited by angels or granted the grace of ecstasy; nor did he walk the beaten path of sanctity—only his own path; and though he built walls of isolation between his struggles with the devil and other men, his life was that of a man eternally persecuted.

Fray Domingo de Salazar, a holy man who figures in all contemporary accounts, implored López to adopt the habit of the Dominicans after his seven years in the desert, and succeeded in persuading him to join the monastery in Mexico City. Gregorio needed to buy a new sackcloth garment for that purpose, and since "he never begged nor asked for anything," he worked on a ranch until he had earned the price, then set out to travel the long and dangerous journey on foot.

The brotherhood of Saint Dominic received him with open arms, but Gregorio was still convinced that his vocation demanded solitude, and he soon left the monastery. This flight did not imply a renunciation of life in the world, for he had been a stranger in the world since childhood. By his own admission, a confession that to some degree provides the key to his life, "he had never been a child in his habits." Like Saint Benedict—the prototype of medieval *senectus*—Gregorio López was an old man while still in his cradle. A deep serenity, a yearning to stand aside from men, and a grave and silent temperament, natural to some old people, were his essential traits in Spain as in Mexico.

Although he belonged to a discursive and polemical period, he never spoke except to answer a question, and when a certain friar suggested that he discuss a theme from the Scriptures, he replied "that he did not argue, nor did he know anything but what God had given him to understand." He trimmed and measured his words so carefully that he never used one too many or one too few. "He did not exaggerate, nor did he overpraise." He would listen to those who had been granted the gift of words, and he said to his biographer: "Father Losa, I see that many people talk well. Let us work well."

He had no great opinion of himself. A bishop who visited him considered him a "witless madman." "And no wonder," he added to support his harsh judgment, "for he never wants to speak unless he is questioned, and so, by not speaking, he gives no indication of what he is."

When the bishop's opinion of him was told to Gregorio López, he made this comment, "I would think the same thing if I were to meet a man of my own stripe."

He feared the acquaintance of men, and fled from them as often as he could, but men pursued him. He brought persecution upon himself by staying away from Mass, by owning no holy images, and by taking no part in official devotions. He came to La Huasteca, Atlixco, the Sanctuary of Our Lady of Refuge, the hospital of Huaxtepec, founded by Bernardino Alvarez, and San Agustín de las Cuevas, in turn, and left them all, beset by his search for a new refuge. He was called heretic, Lutheran, and Jew. The Inquisition sent its agents after him; some monks—"not the most learned"—thought that his wisdom, out of keeping with his youth, was the work of the devil; and Archbishop Moya de Contreras submitted him to several tests, from which he emerged victorious. "After Satan had exerted all his power to blacken the life and fame of this great servant of God," said the bishop of Guadalajara, "he emerged purified and resplendent, like gold from the crucible." Father Losa, one of the men sent by Moya de Contreras, left his parish to follow the hermit, and the Jesuit Alonso Sánchez confided to his biographer: "Upon my word, sir, compared with this man, I have not even begun to learn my spiritual ABC's." He was believed to have the gift of knowledge through the grace of God, but in point of fact he read a good deal. Losa remarks: "He was exceedingly fond of books, and he searched for them continuously. He was always borrowing books, and no matter how large the volumes were, he would read and return them in three or four days. His manner of reading was unusual, something more than natural, like angelic comprehension."

There was no real mystery about the rapidity with which he read. The anchorite himself confessed to Fray Jerónimo de Ocampo that "he read only the opening summary of the chapters, and if he found in some chapter heading a doctrine that was new to him, he would read it; if he was familiar with the material, he would pass on."

He knew Latin without ever having studied it in school, astronomy, history—he is the author of a *Cronología universal*—geography, and astrology. He was an accomplished calligrapher and so well versed in theology that Archbishop-Viceroy Don Pedro Moya de Contreras remarked after consulting him on an abstruse problem, "I never realized he knew so much."

Gregorio López never enjoyed good health. In La Huasteca he had a stomach ailment—the illness of the mystics—and in Huaxtepec, where he wrote his *Tratado de medicina o Secreto de las plantas medicinales de la Nueva España* (*Treatise on Medicine, or the Secrets of the Medicinal Plants of New Spain*), he suffered from a wasting fever, "diagnosed very late," which caused him severe and constant pain.

On May 22, 1589, he retired to the small house that had been built by Don Vasco de Quiroga, not far from his Hospital of Santa Fe, and he never left it. Father Losa, his companion in seclusion, has left us a detailed account of the life Gregorio led there. He opened his window at dawn, washed his face and hands, and read his Bible for a quarter of an hour. Even though he knew it almost by heart, he never stopped studying it; not long before his death he said to the old priest from the cathedral, with regret: "It has been ten days since I have read the Bible, and I cannot remember having failed to read in it for so long a time since I began to live in solitude." Then he would close the holy book and sink into his habitual meditations. At eleven o'clock he went out, carrying his water jar, ate, and as evening fell he went back to his cell. The strange circumstance that from his earliest days as an anchorite he had slept only two or three hours and spent the rest of the night awake in the darkness interested Father Losa, who once asked him what he did all night, without being able to read. "My interior exercise," the hermit replied, "does not depend upon this material light, but on the spiritual light which never fails me by night or by day."

All efforts to penetrate the great secret of his ecstasies came to naught. The bishop of the Philippines, Fray Domingo de Salazar, once tried to ascertain the nature of his inexplicable meditations. Gregorio answered, in one of his short, enigmatic phrases, "Loving God and my neighbor."

"Upon my word," exclaimed the irritated bishop, "you said those very words to me in Amaxac twenty-five years ago."

"I have always said that," Gregorio answered impassively, "even though there is a difference between the work of then and now."

The dual life of Gregorio and the mystical raptures that isolated him from his surroundings were a source of concern to his contemporaries. During his stay in the hospital at Huaxtepec, Brother Esteban de Herrera asserted that often when he went to call the visitor to a meal he would find him sitting, standing, or kneeling, lost in himself. When his attention was caught, Gregorio would ask, "What do you wish?" but some time would pass before he would awaken and follow him, saying "Blessed be God!" He was so wrapped up in his inner life that only once did he notice the countryside, with its rivers and forests. Losa, the man who witnessed close at hand the impenetrable mystery of his raptures, wrote that he was unable to say whether Gregorio "was lost in prayer . . . meditation, or contemplation, or whether it concerned melancholy or happy things."

He was the most retiring of men, but his fame spread throughout New Spain. High officials, men of letters, ecclesiastical dignitaries, the viceroy himself, Don Luis de Valasco II— all flocked to see him and to beg his advice.

The viceroy's letters brought forth submissive replies like this one, which his biographer has preserved: "I shall do what is commanded in this matter." Yet his relations with the viceroy evidently were broken off, on the anchorite's insistence that the viceroy refrain from visiting him. To the many who expatiated to him on the theme of their human afflictions, he would say only, "Dawn will come and we shall wax strong."

After fifty-four years on earth, thirty of them spent in solitude, July 20, 1596, dawned at last for Gregorio López. He rejected minor conventions to the end. As he lay dying, he was asked if he would like the candles lit so that he could see in the darkness. He answered: "All is light; there is no darkness; it is high noon to me." In his last agonies, this man illuminated by grace thrust aside the light that Goethe would beg for in his dying moments. An engraving made in Rome in 1740, at the time of his beatification, shows this *Servi Dei Primi Anchoretae* of the West Indies being borne upward by angels. He is kneeling upon a rock, dressed in a soutane, and a rosary—which he never held—dangles from his waist. The print is of a man whose ascent ended on one of the lower rungs of the celestial ladder, a secondary figure to whom the glory of the saints did not belong.

Gregorio López should not be portrayed surrounded by angels in the pomp of baroque Rome evoked by the engraving. An old oleo in our museum of history shows him as he ought to be, standing alone, wearing a garment of black sackcloth, like a Turkish caftan, which stands like a shadow against the darkness of the background. His arms are crossed, he stands erect, and his bearing is delicate but somehow substantial; he seems to be waiting, with icy resolution, for the imminent onslaught of the devil. His forehead, his nose, the cheekbones made more prominent by his sunken cheeks, are framed by his hair, his mustache with drooping ends, and his beard. His somber eyes, heavy with shadows, complete the picture of the enormous dignity, the stern mysticism, of this strange man. In a land in love with rhetoric he remained true to the motto of his life: *Secretum, meum mibi.*

Felipe de Jesús, the Creole Saint

Felipe de Jesús came from an ordinary Creole background. His father, Alonso las Casas, a minor Castilian hidalgo and the poorest of the poor, was walking through Seville one day, longing to go to the Indies, when by chance he met Antonia Rodríguez, the daughter of a tailor who lived in narrow Tintores Street where gossips tore reputations into shreds and tossed the shreds about among the balconies. On November 5, 1570, Las Casas married the girl in the sacristy of the Metropolitan Church, and a part of their honeymoon was spent at sea, on a ship that pitched excessively, whether riding with bare poles or under full sail.

Once settled in Mexico, the couple prospered. Alonso combined his honorary and far from lucrative post of censor to the Holy Office with the richly rewarding job of merchant and purveyor to ships in the China trade. He was commonly to be seen along the road between the city of Mexico and the port of Acapulco, on horseback, followed by herds of domestic animals and their drovers. He dispatched the plate ships, lent money, and dealt in colonial products from the freighters coming from Peru and Guatemala, as well as in fragile porcelains, silks, marble, and spices from Tidoro, Ophir, and Macao.

Felipe, his son, fitted well into this atmosphere, half Oriental and half Indian, which was the usual environment of the Mexican from the high plateau who did not live with the sea at his back. His family was distinguished for its extreme piety. One of his brothers was a Franciscan monk; another an Augustinian who died in the Philippines, struck down by arrows; two of his sisters were nuns; and Felipe himself entered the monastery of Santa Barbara in his home town at the age of sixteen.

Soon after entering, he was tempted by the devil. Doubtless it was a devil invented by the baroque biographers of the eighteenth century, for it used a hackneyed device: the novice was warned against pride, the devil's own sin, the sin of Lucifer and Adam—in short, the sin of feeling like God. This devil whispered the following puerile admonition in Felipe's ear: "You are indeed proud to consider yourself worthy to wear that sackcloth. Do you think you are capable of wearing the habit when so many great and saintly men have never donned it? This presumption of yours will destroy you, and you will be damned through your great pride."

It is possible that the temptation—shades of Saint Anthony!—took a much less religious form, since it was offered to an adolescent. Here was Felipe, wearing coarse sackcloth, praying around the clock and living in wretched poverty, while Creoles his own age, decked out in silks and plumes, amused themselves by going to the festivals and showing off their horses before the windows of the town belles. That contrast, perhaps, decided him. He simply hung the sackcloth on a nail in his dreary cell—the Kingdom of Heaven is full of the repentant—and went back to the paternal rooftree.

After leaving the monastery, Felipe apprenticed himself to a silversmith. Like Periquillo Sarniento, the model for Creoles, he tried everything his surroundings could offer, but at bottom he was not interested in the religious life, in silversmithing, or in any modest position. What did interest him were love affairs, horsemanship, and amusement. His mother was the only one in the family who had any faith in the handsome lad. Her unreasoned faith led her to believe blindly in her son and to pray that the heavenly powers might deign to crown his naughty, charming head with the halo of sainthood.

A Negro serving maid—her name is lost to history—who was fond of soliloquizing and moral reflections, was openly pessimistic about any possibility of converting the boy. This servant would often pause in front of a dried-up fig tree that grew in the center of the patio, one of those relics that families will keep, like old dogs, in memory of bygone services, and say aloud: "Little Felipe a saint? Yes, when the fig tree turns green again, when the fig tree turns green."

The father, who believed neither that Felipe would mend his ways nor that the fig tree would be resurrected, made up his mind to pack him off to China. "Go on, son. Go and trade in the islands, where you can make your fortune and enjoy it with God's blessing and ours." The merchant's decision had a sound basis. The Philippines were the ideal stage for demonstrating the strengths and the weakness of a man's soul, as the islands of the Caribbean had been a hundred years earlier. A good man would suffer a sea change that made him a saint; a bad man would become a devil, a soldier a hero, and an adventurer a millionaire, not to the lazy rhythms of normality, but all at once and forever.

Felipillo's story was like an obscure minor novel about young immigrants, from 1590 (the date of his disembarkation in Cavite) to 1593. "Manila," the best and most liberal of his biographers confesses, "was the best place in the world for a bachelor of twenty"; better than Cuba and Panama with their African women, and better than Mexico with its mulatto girls glittering in brocades and pearls. Tagalog girls, half-naked Cambodian women, Chinese women wise in ancient sins, and Arab women of powerful and abiding sensuality made up that *mundo carnalis,* the mysterious and forbidden continent of lust, where perfume, license, and ecstasy reigned under an aegis unknown to the great Catholic cities of the Indies.

Not a word, not a trace can be found of Felipe during those years—nothing that has not been painstakingly erased by his pious biographers. The trail of his life vanishes in Manila, to emerge again, with no transition, in the image of a kneeling, weeping penitent in the convent of Santa María de los Angeles, who sobs to a Franciscan monk: "Father, I beg you to receive me into your order; I am prepared to suffer

all the trials and adversities it may please God to send me for my sins."
On May 22, 1594, he took his solemn vows and donned the rough
sackcloth that had irritated him so much in Puebla. The Franciscan
chronicles tell us of a little novice who spent the small hours listening to
the chanting of the monks in the choir or waiting on his sick brothers
with humility and joy.

When the news of the conversion reached his father, Alonso las Casas,
he prevailed upon his friends the Inquisitors to give Felipe leave to
exercise his ministry in Mexico. Permission was granted, and our
wandering Creole sailed from Cavite on July 12, 1596, aboard the
galleon *San Felipe,* whether of his own free will or not, we do not
know.

Until the moment when he began his crossing of the Pacific, his life
had been a normal one. No one was surprised that a restless Creole
youth should go off to the Philippines, nor that he should try to save his
soul after repenting of his sins by becoming a monk. Although it may
seem incredible to us today, in those days the Pacific Ocean was to
Mexico something like the Mediterranean, and colonial society was
filled with adventurers and penitent sinners. Only a truly resounding
conquest or an exceptional sacrifice could bring fame to anyone. Felipe's
indecisiveness, his adventures, more private than public, his short and
simple life as a monk, the almost complete anonymity in which his
youth had been spent—none of them auguries that would explain a
sudden, violent method of winning sainthood—were left behind him in
Manila, forgotten, and his biographers have labored mightily to portray
his fate from the hour he set foot on the deck of the *San Felipe* as the
splendid, forsaken, doleful one of the martyrs and the chosen of God.

After a few days of sailing, the calm ocean began to frown. The ship
was overloaded—she carried a million and a half pesos worth of
merchandise—and she began to wallow in the heavy seas. The seamen
and monks, knowing the ship had been blown off course in the darkness
and forced to listen to the screaming of the wind, came out of one
typhoon only to plunge into another, "with death in its eye." One of the
Franciscans on the galleon, the famous Juan Pobre, dreamed one night
that the crew were all condemned to die except for the cabin boys and
galley slaves, and the next day, standing on the upper deck, he delivered
a prophetic sermon. "God's wrath can be appeased only by penance,"

declared the holy man, and, making an example of himself, he raised his habit and scourged himself cruelly in the sight of everyone. On September 18 the typhoon split the sails, and carried away the shrouds, the masts, forecastle, and galley.

On the 19th, the weather moderated and the men were able to look at one another. "They could scarcely recognize their companions, or even themselves, according to those who were still on their feet."

But the ship encountered still more storms. On October 5, the vision of a great heavenly cross seemed to loom above the Japanese coast, so the captain, Don Martín de Landecho, decided to seek shelter in the port of Urando. At first everything went well. Governor Chokosabe of the province ordered the badly damaged San Felipe towed in, paid an official call on the ship's company with full Oriental pomp, and ordered the cargo unloaded and deposited on the wharf in the care of his own guards. Later, however, he confiscated it, alleging that he could not return the merchandise without due authorization by the Emperor Taico Sama.

A series of terrible disasters had recently struck Japan. Earthquakes had razed her cities, and one had destroyed Taico Sama's palace, his collection of paintings, and his salons "trimmed with gold." Seventy of his wives were killed in the earthquake, but the emperor leaped out of bed naked and escaped. A historian says: "The luckless man remained as if in shock and in such a state of melancholia that no one ventured to look him in the face; but he was not moved on that account to recognize the hand of God, which had struck him such hard blows in order to awaken him from the deep lethargy of paganism."

All these portents, which historians of the Philippines interpreted as a warning of imminent tragedy, were associated in Taico Sama's mind with the suspicions aroused by seeing Christianity enter his empire.

Nagasaki, where representatives from Spain and Portugal had settled, was already the most active evangelical enter of the Far East. The Jesuits, armed with an apostolic brief from Pope Gregory XIII granting them a missionary monopoly, had succeeded in converting eight thousand Japanese, and they enjoyed some status in the court; Pedro Martínez, a member of the Company of Jesus, was the bishop. Meanwhile they fought tooth and nail with the Franciscans, who were trying to enter that fertile field. They used all available weapons; the bishop had even ordered Japanese converts not to attend the Franciscan churches under pain of excommunication, and he proclaimed publicly

that our religious men were vile and low; that they knew neither courtesy nor policy, and that their life was that of paupers; that they smelled bad and went around covered with grime; and that they had neither salons nor reception rooms, nor furniture fit for receiving gentlemen and dignitaries, and other slanders of the kind. . . .

Captain Landecho, in Urando, was in despair. He had appointed Fray Juan Pobre, the Augustinian Juan Tamayo, and Felipe de Jesús to act as delegates to the emperor and arrange for the return of the cargo; meanwhile he pressed Governor Chokosabe most undiplomatically and threatened him with the vengeance of the king of Spain, whom he always called, with obvious complacency, "the most powerful lord in the world." When he was informed of the captain's language, Taico Sama—who believed he was a descendant of the gods and absolute master of the universe—did not deign even to receive Landecho's envoys. Felipe and a Japanese acolyte, Tomás Cozaqui, went on from Osaka to Kyoto and sought shelter in the small Franciscan monastery of Santa María de los Angeles.

On December 8 the comisario, Fray Pedro Bautista, his monks, and the Japanese Christians were imprisoned inside the monastery. Because Felipe had been acting in the capacity of ambassador, they offered him his freedom, but he refused it proudly with these words: "God does not wish that my brothers be prisoners and I go free; let it be the same with me as with them."

On December 30, the officer Xinaboxo appeared, with an order to conduct the Christians to prison. He found the community saying vespers in the choir of the church. The comisario, a pious man who held an exalted view of his mission, showed great fortitude. As the soldiers put chains on the men they chanted the *Te Deum Laudamus* and the *Te Deum Confitemur* before the altar of the church, and as they went out they sang the beautiful hymn *O Gloriosa Domine*.

In prison they found Fray Martín de la Ascensión, from the Osaka monastery, three Japanese of the third order of Franciscans, and three

Jesuits, captured the night before. They were all taken to the headsman's block, and their left ears were cut off. As he was being mutilated, Felipe exclaimed joyfully: "Now I bear the mark of Christ. Even should the tyrant order me to be set free, I would not accept it." The boy Cozaqui picked up his bloody ear off the ground and, holding it high, he shouted to the headsman: "Cut some more; take your fill of Christians' blood!"

Their way of the cross from Kyoto to Nagasaki lasted thirty days —thirty mortal days of suffering and persecution. They were traveling in the dead of winter, barefoot and in ragged habits, nearly perishing of hunger and cold. The people heaped insults on them, stoned them, and spat upon them; when one of them fell in the snow, the guards would beat him to his feet and the peasants would call the fallen man a beast and stuff his mouth with frozen grass. Fray Pedro Bautista gave courage to the faltering men: "Take heart, brothers, this is the royal road that fills the thrones in heaven." A soldier marched ahead of the small group of martyrs, carrying the imperial sentence written on a flagstaff:

Whereas these men did come from Luzon with the title of ambassadors, and did stay in Kyoto, preaching the law of the Christians, which I forbade many years ago, I hereby decree that they shall be punished, together with the Japanese who have accepted their rule. And therefore I command that these twenty-four men be crucified in Nagasaki. And again I make the said prohibition for the future, and I hereby make that known to all; and I order that it be done accordingly. And if any man dare to defy this decree, he and all his generation shall be punished. The first year of Keycho, on the tenth day of the eleventh moon.

On the day that the sentence was to be carried out in Nagasaki, the priests Rodríguez and Passio heard the confessions of the twenty-six condemned men—two had been added along the way—and accompanied them to a wheatfield on a hill where the crosses had been erected. The Japanese cross was different from the Christian; the man to be executed was placed on a central transverse beam and held suspended by five rings. Two of the rings held his feet apart at the ends of a beam, two confined his arms, and the fifth closed around the victim's neck. As soon as Felipe saw the cross that had been assigned to him, he ran toward it saying: "Oh, happy ship! Oh, lucky galleon *San Felipe!* You were lost, so Felipe could win. Oh, lost, but no loss to me, only the greatest of gains."

This ingenious play on words, somewhat unseemly in a martyr, might be taken for a joint posterior effort on the part of his biographers if we did not know the Creoles' taste for preciosity. Felipe showed that he was touchingly true to his native idiom in the solemn moment when he was about to die for his faith, surrounded by a swarm of infidels. Forced, elaborate diction had come as second nature to him; he had taken it with him to Japan, and the dramatic circumstances of his martyrdom could not change him.

As his cross was being set into the ground, the young novice slipped and hung suspended by his neck. He was strangling, his legs were skinned, and he realized he was about to faint. This would detract from the value of his martyrdom, and he begged to be set upright. The executioner then struck his lance into his right side and ran it through to the left shoulder. Felipe could say only, "Jesus, Jesus, Jesus," when a second lance was buried in his left side and emerged through the opposite shoulder. When he was dead he was given a third lance thrust, this time through the neck, and his body hung from the cross, pierced by two slender and symmetrical lances, like a figure in a gilded cathedral chapel.

Meanwhile the Jesuit confessors were at work in the wheatfield, giving aid to the dying, and the bishop, under house arrest, witnessed the scene from a window as he gave his blessings.

On February 13, 1597, on the very day that Felipe's head hung like a lily above the Nagasaki wheatfield, the Negro maid in his family's house went into the patio and found the dry branches of the fig tree covered with tender, velvety leaves. She startled the household with her cries of joy: "Señora, the fig tree has come to life again! Little Saint Felipe! Felipillo the saint!"

At that moment began Felipe's glorious career, the one figure whom Mexico has been able to place high on the altar. Like Cuauhtémoc, our greatest lay hero, this hero of the Church represents a denouement. A far from common martyrdom plucked him from anonymity and granted him admission to the exalted company he now enjoys in heaven. He is a Mexican, a Creole, a native of the city, and the patron saint of silversmiths, the aristocrat of the national guilds. He has been beloved by the devout for centuries because he was young, handsome, of the same nationality as they, and because he behaved in foreign lands like the best of the saints. He is the invention of a people in need of affirmations, and they do not call him merely Saint Felipe, but by the pet name of Felipillo Santo (Little Saint Felipe); they weave legends around him and deck him in a garment of hopes and dreams despite the efforts of his biographers to strip him of it. Now he is mummified by the vulgarities of the Church, but a poet of this century, worried about Mexico's future, rescued Felipillo from the commercial, ejaculatory prayers that almost buried him, with this odd verse, left at the foot of the baroque altar in his cathedral:

> *Te dará frente al higo y al obús.*
> *un higo San Felipe de Jesús.*

> *In front of the fig tree and the cannon,*
> *San Felipe de Jesús, I shall give you a fig.*

5

The World of Darkness

Soon after America was discovered and made a part of the Christian world came the horrifying realization that it was by no means the idyllic and virginal land extolled by Christopher Columbus, where man wandered innocent and naked in a state of nature through a smiling paradise. For the devil was waiting for the Spaniards on the farther shore of the *Mare Tenebrosum,* hitherto veiled from Western curiosity. And to think they had believed themselves to be leaving that unmistakable personage behind them, mired in his struggle to thwart the establishment of the Kingdom of God in their own ancient cities! Perhaps no secret revealed by the discovery of America was more important or more disturbing; since the day of the original sin Satan had held absolute sway in person not over a people only or a nation, but over that entire world.

Sahagún, a monk who came to this abomination of desolation as a very young man, filled the monastery of Santiago with his lamentations.

"What is this, my Lord God?" he cries to heaven, wringing his hands. "How hast Thou permitted that enemy of mankind to rule at will, and for so long, over this sad and helpless nation where he has spread his poison and his darkness with complete freedom, and with none to say him nay?"

"A people in the power of Satan!" A whole people, all of nature, permeated, contaminated, almost converted into a demonic substance.

The devil was Tezcatlipoca—the black god who blends with the shadows of night—by his limp ye shall know him. He was Huitzilo-pochtli, god of war, and he was Tláloc, in the flowing water, the water from the clouds, the water that descends to earth and the water carried by creeks and rivers. He was also the inventor of fishnets and pottery, and tamer of the wild maize. He was present in women who died in childbirth, mocking their husbands. He had a pact with the kings, sorcerers, and medicine men, and he had invented cannibalism, with its cruel and sumptuous rites, its songs, and dances. The Indian tribes showed his brand on their flesh, the symbol of demonic possession, and not even the newborn escaped this stamp of his dominion.

No feudal knight, no missionary monk could ever have imagained a land riper for adventure and crusade than the land of Mexico. The warrior—God's instrument—rises in his stirrups and charges into the teeming forest of heresy. Each two-handed blow of his sword strikes a devil to earth, each lance thrust exterminates a vile sinner, for "the total expiation of the Indian's guilt, due punishment for his sins, can be achieved only by the destruction of his civilization and the death of his gods. Indeed it seems," Luis Villoro remarks, "that the whole meaning of American history must have been that waiting for God to take it fully into account, for the sake of his universal design."

Once the Conquest—the first and necessary prelude to conversion —had been successfully achieved, with the help of Providence, the field was left to the missionaries. And the harvest of souls was al-most too great for the number of reapers. Hitching up their robes and grasping the crucifix in one hand and the Gospel in the other, that tiny host of soldiers of Christ went among the dense crowd of pagans, to drench their dark, vanquished heads with a full measure of holy water and exorcism. The results of that apostolic fervor were soon visible. The courtyards of the monasteries were thronged with zealous converts, and the Indians, as part of the program of indoctrination, took upon themselves the destruction of their own temples. Sahagún tells us naïvely how the neophytes fell upon their pagan compatriots and lovingly cudgeled them into heaven.

But the intoxication of their victory, unprecedented in the annals of

Christianity, did not blind the wider missionaries to the realization that, in spite of all their efforts to combat him, the devil retained a considerable portion of his old power. Beneath the touching outward semblance of a new faith, the Indians' religious sentiments remained unalterable, and the cord by which the devil had bound them was still unbroken. Idols were found side by side with Catholic images in shameless defiance; or, when public worship of them was made impossible, the builders of the altars hid their gods inside them, often at the very spot where the transubstantiation of matter into the body and blood of Christ took place. The hymns that accompanied the bloody pagan rites, those gloomy hymns taught by the devil, still resounded in Spanish ears, inextricably blended with the ceremonies of the Church; and at the slightest pretext the old, exhausting dances exploded into life with a frenetic display of feathers and jewels. Now and again "the blue mantle of the Virgin became a cloak for Tonantzin, the Chihuacóatl mother of the gods; the wrinkles of Tocitzin were venerated in those visible on the face of Saint Ann; and the cape of the chaste evangelist, cast on Tepochtli, their great Tezcatlipoca, was still adored."

Countless idols were destroyed every day, but in most of the villages the Indians tried to save them by hiding them in their houses or carrying them into the woods. Some Indians traveled with their gods carefully swathed in blankets, and we know of a merchant who owned a very great one which he never unwrapped "because he said that whoever should unwrap it would die." The grip of the old creed was stubborn. That passionate devotion to the gods, that atmosphere of implacable sacrifice and incessant vigilance, that instinctive association of the deity with the phenomena of nature, could only be exacerbated by the persecution and cruelty unleashed by the Spaniards.

In one way or another the Indians kept alive the worship of their gods, and protected their sorcerers and medicine men. The sorcerers lived naked in mysterious caves and fed on plants and herbs. They practiced chastity "and wore a tonsure on their heads, in the style of the monks." The medicine men practiced their profession openly, without persecution. They could be seen every day in the markets surrounded by their herbs, their dried birds, their amulets, and the potions with which they could bring about death or madness.

No one of the race of the conquerors was ever witness to the barbarous

Walpurgisnacht which took place in the depths of the mountains. Then the idols were put back in the ruins of their temples. The warriors performed their dances, concealed behind masks of animals and demons, the chirimía moaned and the teponaxtle bellowed its hoarse notes as the hand of the priest reached for the heart in the victim's open chest and a clamor of rejoicing shook the faithful crouching in the shadows.

The ancient ceremonies ended before the light of morning. A torch of resin burning near the ruins, an offering, some cotton cloth stained with blood, papers traced over with hieroglyphs—these were the only visible signs of this subterranean current of idolatry, which the Spaniards' vigilance could not check. Ordinances designed to abolish the surviving pagan rites proved useless. In 1546 any Indian who refused to enter the Catholic faith was horsewhipped, his head was shaved, and he was not permitted to hold office or title in his village. Anyone who would affix to his children's clothing or hair "names, devices, or symbols to indicate he was offering or commending them to demons" was punished with a hundred lashes, as was anyone who adored the sun, the moon, stones, or papers. These measures could not have been very efficacious, since two centuries later, the Inquisition enjoined the Indians in the following edict:

Destroy the idols, cast them to earth, burn, raze, and make an end to all the places where they were, wipe out the sites, woods, and cliffs whereon they were placed, cover over and close with stone and mud the holes wherein they were hidden so that their very memory may not come to your minds; make no sacrifice to the demon, or seek advice of the magi, the enchanters, the malevolent sorcerers or diviners; have no dealings or friendship with them; nor shall you hide them, but bring them forth and accuse them; even though they be your own fathers, mothers, children, brothers, husbands, or wives; do not listen to or believe those who wish to deceive you, even though you see them perform acts that seem to you miracles; for in truth they are not, but are instead the snares of the devil to draw you away from the faith.

The Martyrs of the Old Religions

Outstanding among the martyrs of the old religions was Don Carlos Ometochtzin, the lord, or to put it the Mexican tongue, the *chichime-catecutli* of Texcoco. Don Carlos, son of Netzahualpilli and grandson of

Netzehualcóyotl, the poet king, was a member of that tiny group of indigenous high nobility in whom the virtues of a whole people were refined into pure gold. All the little we know about him—from such testimony by Indians as history collects almost in spite of itself—bears the mark of authenticity and greatness. His antagonist was not a soldier, but the bishop Juan de Zumárraga. The conflict may be summed up briefly: an Indian accused Don Carlos of worshiping the god Tláloc; Zumárraga intervened, and due process was set in motion. During the trial Don Carlos brought to light many interesting details of the religious double life practiced by the Indians. When there was no rain in his realm, the lord of Texcoco went with his people to a mountain consecrated of old to Tláloc and made offerings and sacrifices to him. The familiars of the Holy Office found two idol temples hidden in his palace; and, as if these exhibits were not enough to damn him, evidence was presented showing that he was not only a heretic but a rebel too, an enemy of the religious and political forces of the empire, and that he used intolerable language in speaking of the Spaniards. "Who are these people," he would say, "who destroy and disturb and live off us, whom we carry on our backs and who keep us in subjection?" Such an Indian could not be allowed to live in the colony. He was sentenced to be burned alive in the Plaza Mayor, and the sentence was carried out on Sunday, November 30, 1539. His death scandalized even the Spanish Inquisitors. It was ordained that in the future the Holy Office was not to proceed against the recently converted Indians, and the Inquisitor General wrote a letter "reprimanding the most illustrious Señor Zumárraga for putting an Indian chief on trial and sentencing him to death for idolatrous practices."

Generally speaking, the Indians were damned, and it did not matter much whether they belonged to Christianity or to their primitive religion. Those who spent their lives in the company of the devil and identified themselves with him to such a degree that they seemed almost to be made of his very substance—such creatures were guilty of a sin so grave that the mere intention of rescuing them from their diabolic surroundings and opening to them the gates of eternal salvation was enough to obligate them absolutely to their redeemers. And so it was that the Spaniard's aspiration to live off the labor of his slaves found a religious justification which, in the end, transcended social relations and the regime of the encomienda. Whichever it was—a world of slaves suspected of heresy or a world redeemed and overflowing with abundant gratitude—it was still a realm of darkness, unforgivable and monstrous, that had been set side by side with the white world full of light, confidence, and the graces natural to a privileged community.

The Jews in New Spain

At the end of the sixteenth century, a large number of converted Jews, most of whom had come from Portugal, fled the Inquisition's bonfires which had been fanned by the religious zeal of Philip II, to take up residence in Peru and New Spain, thereby laying the ground for religious conflict on a much higher plane than that which the peculiar nature of our Indians had instigated from the beginning.

One of the most notable Jews in the group that arrived in Mexico was Don Luis de Carvajal, called El Viejo, (the Old Man). He, too, was of Portuguese origin; he had served as a treasurer in Cape Verde while very young, although later he had transferred his allegiance to Spain and settled in Seville, that antechamber open to the dazzling Promised Land. The little we know of his family background helps us to understand him. His uncle, Don Duarte de León, had held the office of governor of Guinea, and his father-in-law had been a slave factor who dealt in Negroes from Santo Domingo. One brother, a prominent Jesuit, died in the flower of his youth, and another, a priest, came to an obscure end in Oaxaca. Clergymen, slavers, or soldiers of fortune doubling as merchants—they were all given to laying ambitious plans and working hard to carry them out. They were people with the energy of giants, but none ever entirely overcame the resentment and distrust which they inspired. However hard they might try, they never managed to make people forget that they were crypto-Jews or the descendants of Jews.

The life of El Viejo Carvajal was one of constant frustration. Himself a sincere Catholic, he married an intransigent Jewess, Doña Guiomar de Rivera; but not even she was able to bring him back to his old religion. On the other hand, he could not persuade her to his new beliefs. When

Carvajal decided to go to the Indies in 1566 on a ship with a cargo of wine, after a ruinous business venture, Doña Guiomar firmly refused to follow him.

In Mexico, Carvajal plunged into business, exploring, and—principally—fighting. In Pánuco, the center of his military operations, he captured the pirates led by the Englishman Hawkins, pacified the regions of Jalapa and La Huasteca—Viceroy Don Martín Enríquez said, "He tried harder to make a peace treaty with the Indians than to drink their blood"—and finally discovered the New Kingdom of León and started out to conquer it. In 1578 he went back to Spain, and the following year a royal decree gave him the title of governor and captain of the New Kingdom of León. He was also authorized to take with him a hundred settlers, "without requiring them to prove that they were old Christians, as the law provides."

As the governor was making ready for his return voyage, he found himself almost entirely alone. His increasing estrangement from his wife led him to think of his sister Francisca Núñez de Carvajal, who lived in Benavente. He managed to persuade her and her husband, a poor trader named Francisco Rodríguez de Matos, to go with him to the Indies, taking their numerous offspring. These were Baltasar, the eldest son; Gaspar, a Dominican monk; Luis de Carvajal, who was to inherit the office of governor at his uncle's death; Doña Isabel, the widow of a certain Gabriel Herrera; Catalina, Mariana, and Leonor, three unmarried girls; and Anica and Miguel, still very young children. Even though they had not had the opportunity to practice their religion in Spain, with the exception of the monk this family were all of the Jewish faith, a strange circumstance in view of the proved Catholicism of Carvajal. There were many Jews too among the settlers he brought to the colony, some of them as distinguished as the scholarly Antonio de Morales, a famous rabbi and physician.

While El Viejo went ahead with his conquests, the family of Rodríguez Matos settled down in the Pánuco. This new Jerusalem was actually for them "a barren desert inhabited by many mosquitoes and very hot, where they lived quite poorly" to the extent that the women went barefoot.

The governor soon realized that his relatives were thoroughgoing, dangerous fanatics. Doña Isabel, "considered something of a saint owing to her strict, even exaggerated, observance of the Mosaic law" and inspired by an insatiable zeal for proselytizing, committed major acts of imprudence; and Luis, El Mozo (the Boy), was also dedicated to an extreme mysticism.

A short time after they had come to live in the Pánuco, Rodríguez Matos took his son Luis to Mexico City with him to sell a certain number of Indian slaves. The city's large Jewish community received the newcomers enthusiastically. (We cannot know how far this race of intelligent and enterprising men might have succeeded in influencing the colony if they had been able to consolidate their position and to prosper.) Between the 1570's and the 1590's, they were found mingling with the rich merchants on San Agustín Street, with the jewelers on San Francisco, with the mining men of Taxco, Pachuca, and Zacatecas, and with the China traders. The majority of them piously performed their duties as Catholics, but in their own homes they kept the Sabbath, sang the Old Testament psalms and the prayers for the dead, washed and wrapped their dead in new winding sheets, and avenged the religious intolerance surrounding them by burying images in the doorways of their places of business or sewing pieces of cloth on which Christ on the Cross was painted into the lining of cushions. Such irrational acts of defiance would bring savage punishment if they were discovered, but at times even a farcical note was struck. Word has come down to us of a Jew who ran about disconsolately looking for refuge when he heard the viaticum bell, so that he would not have to render public homage to his hated enemy.

Old Rodríguez Matos, who was not made for rustic life, spent six months ill in the house of a relative, went to confession, and took communion, with apparent piety—the Jews were permitted to feign Christianity—but in private he exhorted Luis to remain true to his own faith, and before dying he begged him, "Son, wash this body of mine, so I need not go into the earth dirty like this."

Back in the Pánuco, Luis devoutly read the Bible which a priest had sold him for six pesos. This Bible was his one treasure, his comfort, the fount from which he thirstily drank the water of divine wisdom, for the soul of the Jew, like that of the Christian, required its nourishment, its "provender" (the traveler's term he used in his *Autobiography* even more than his body.

One afternoon when Luis was in the corridor of his house, he read the following verse from Genesis:

He that is born in thy house, and he that is bought with thy money, must needs be circumcised; and my covenant shall be in your flesh for an everlasting covenant. And the uncircumcised man-child whose flesh of his foreskin is not circumcised, that soul shall be cut off from his people; he hath broken my covenant.

Luis left the book open at that passage, took a pair of scissors "with dull blades," and went to a ravine where he circumcised himself. A year later, when he was out searching for a stolen horse, he lost his way in mountains inhabited by Chichimeca Indians; after many vicissitudes he was rescued, as it seemed to him, by some miracle. The book of Esdras, copied in his own hand, which he was carrying concealed in his doublet, had brought him through his adventures unharmed, and the circumcision performed in such a painful fashion was throughout his brief life a "stout shield against lust and an aid to chastity," as he put it.

In those early days, Jehovah was not too proud to step into the lives of his chosen people with some handsome and timely gift. One day the house of Luis' mother was assailed by the barbarous music of native flageolets and Spanish trumpets. When the door was opened, Antonio Díaz de Cáceres and Jorge de Almeida, two wealthy Jews, appeared before Doña Francisca's astonished eyes—Luis was away in León—surrounded by a splendid retinue. They dismounted from their horses and respectfully requested the hands of the barefoot Doña Leonor and Doña Catalina.

The marriages were performed with Fray Gaspar officiating, and the family shifted its hearth to Mexico City. Doña Francisca, dressed in her best and riding a mule, was in the retinue that followed the principals. Old ladies ran to her and asked: "Señora, what was the good prayer you said? What saint did you make your patron?" But the mother took care to guard her tongue—so well that Jehovah caressed his luxuriant beard as he smiled above the tropical forest. What a day of confusion and of hope for the mothers in El Panúco with unmarried daughters!

Prison, Dreams, and Torture

When Luis left the "grim and hilly prison" of the desert, he found that his sisters, "who had laid aside their worn-out sackcloth," were dressed in silk and velvet. Doña Francisca and her unmarried daughters were still living in poverty, however, because they had definitely broken with the governor, "although when he went out of their residence they were properly clothed, they were living in great need."

Carvajal El Mozo worked at times as scribe for a merchant—he was an excellent calligrapher—and at times in his brothers-in-laws' mines, but he never failed to practice his religion with great piety. He and his brother Baltasar—"they loved each other like water and earth"—used to visit a crippled Jew for whom the scholar Morales had translated the Book of Deuteronomy. They met in improvised synagogues to chant psalms and listen to the word of God, and they scrupulously observed the feast days and the fasts. El Mozo was always the soul of such activities. His whole life was in reading his Bible and composing canticles and poems. His dreams were full of faith and religious fervor. From time to time, when he would awaken from his mystical trances, his eyes would open to reality. In a city that had sworn publicly and solemnly to persecute heretics like mad dogs, a city full of spies and vigilant enemies, the slightest indiscretion—and they had been guilty of many—might ruin them. Constant dissimulation, added to the fact that they dared not even put on clean clothes on the Sabbath or cut off a chicken's head without risk to their lives, eventually made their stay in the Indies hateful to them, and they decided to move with their families to Rome, where the Pope in return for an annual tribute permitted the Jews to practice the religion of Moses without any restrictions.

Luis and Gaspar made up their minds to move on to Italy and to take their brother the Dominican with them in order to convert him in good time to Judaism. Some notion of the heedless fanaticism that ruled this family is conveyed by the scene that took place in a cell of the monastery of Santo Domingo, where they marshaled all their naïve and puerile arguments to make the monk see that the Catholic religion was not the true one, to their brother's terror and confusion. He knew that his brothers were guilty of mortal sin, but he was not able to dissuade them from their error, nor could he bring himself to denouce them to his superiors as he was in duty bound to do.

Meanwhile, Luis' fears had been realized. Captain Felipe Núñez, to whom Doña Isabel had preached Judaism in the Pánuco, denounced Luis to the Inquisition, and at the same time Luis de Carvajal El Viejo was taken to the royal prison because of a lawsuit involving a question of jurisdiction which he had brought before the viceroy.

First the imprudent widow was taken prisoner, and then her mother, Doña Francisca, one night as they were readying supper. A platoon of guards, constables, porters, and scribes from the Holy Office burst into the house. When the old lady had heard the order for her arrest, she took her cloak "with meekness" as Luis wrote in his *Autobiography,* "and weeping for her work and praising the Lord God, she was carried off by those ministers of damnation, the executioners of our lives, to darkest prison." The daughters, also weeping, screamed, "Where are you taking us? For the love of God, have pity on us!"

Not long after, the whole Carvajal family, even the two young children, Miguelito and Anica, were taken into custody by the officers of the Inquisition.

Luis was not to be left alone there. A spy for the Inquisitors shared his cell, a barefoot old recluse from Valencia province named Francisco Ruiz de Luna, whom the Holy Office had brought to judgment for performing the offices of priest under falsified documents. The young Jew, carried away by his fervor, succeeded in converting his cellmate to the Mosaic law so firmly that many years after the old monk had been reconverted he was arrested again in Havana, charged with Judaism, and brought back to Mexico where he was sentenced to ten years as a galley slave, two hundred lashes, public ignominy in the churches, prison, and perpetual exile.

The darkness of the dungeon kindled Luis dreams. On one occasion he saw his father, the old merchant whose body he had washed and wrapped in a winding sheet after placing a coin in its mouth. The father no longer wore the earth-stained garments of the Pánuco woods, but was garbed in a white alb decorated with little gold bells. He held out his hand for Luis to kiss, embraced him, and said, "Come here, my son, and rest from all your labors."

In another of his visions a crystal flask appeared before him filled with the nectar of divine wisdom; he heard the voice of the Lord say to Solomon: "Take a spoon, fill it with this liquor, and give it to this boy to drink." When Luis had drunk from that flask, a marvelous feeling of goodness arose within him. From that moment he relinquished the name Luis de Carvajal and expressively renamed himself José Lumbroso (Joseph the Enghlightened). Dreams were his release, his only escape from bitter reality; for Luis' faith, his ardent and sensitive spirit bore no relation to the weakness and timidity of his flesh. He had a positive horror of torture, of being put to the question; and the torments to which he saw his family condemned exacerbated to the point of madness his fear of undergoing the horror of a trial by the Inquisition.

He made a small hole in the door of his cell with the aid of some mutton bones, and one morning he saw his mother going to the torture chamber, accompanied by the warden and the executioner. He could do nothing to help her. For long hours he stood by the door and listened to her screams. Imagining her torment, he felt in his own flesh all the steps of that terrible Calvary through which she was being taken.

What was happening to his mother corresponded very closely to her son's picture of it. At eight in the morning the clerk began to read the sentence, after invoking the name of Christ:

Christi Nomine Invocato. We are mindful of the ordinances and the merits of this case, the evidence and suspicions that arise in it against the said Francisca Núñez de Carvajal, upon whom it is our duty to pronounce judgment. We do hereby sentence her to be put to the question by torture concerning the impairments sworn to in this case, which will be brought out by putting her to the test and by her confessions, for as long a time as it may be our will. . . .

"I have already said," Doña Francisca replied, "that I have honestly believed in the Law of Moses, and this is the truth. Gentlemen, have pity on me and my orphaned children, for whom I feel more concern than I do for my own life. For the love of God, do not shame me!"

Doña Francisca was a woman who had known nothing but hardship during her whole life. When she was nine years old her parents had betrothed her to Rodríguez Matos, and their marriage was consummated when she was twelve. Surrounded by danger, struggling constantly against poverty, she had grown old before her time, without any consolations except the traditional ones of the Jews: her selfless love for her family and the practice of her religion. When the test came, the moment when the threat that had always hung over her head fatally confronted her, she tried to defend herself and her own by refusing to give details, although she confessed her faith because she had been born a Jew and she had never seen any reason for ceasing to be one.

In the face of her refusal, the chief torturer was brought in at half past eight—that was a part of the judicial routine—and she was ordered to take off her clothes.

"Kill me!" screamed the outraged mother. "Garrote me, but do not strip me naked and shame me; I would rather die a thousand deaths. Behold, I am a woman, a decent widow, and never in the world ought such a thing to be allowed, especially among those who themselves profess holiness. I have already told you I believe in the Law of Moses and not in that of Jesus Christ. There is nothing more I can say, nor do I know anything more except that I am a wretched, inconsolable widow, with children who will cry to God."

The chief torturer and his assistants pulled off her clothes while the clerk admonished her: "As you revere God, tell the truth. Tell the truth unless you wish to put yourself through much trial and jeopardy."

"This is sheer iniquity," the old woman exclaimed. "Sheer evil! This will go for the remission of my sins."

She was stretched forcibly on the rack, and her arms and legs were tied while the clerk intoned, "Tell the truth, tell the truth."

"You know that I have told the truth and that you are taking a mother from her children. I never believed that such cruelty could be used against a poor woman. I commend my soul and offer up this martyrdom to Him who, as I read in the *Mirror of Consolation,* adored the Maccabees." The chief torturer gave a turn to the roller, and the ropes cut into her flesh.

The thick, official parchment on which this event was recorded still repeats to us the screams that escaped from her mouth—repeats them with the fidelity and precision of a sound track playing back the protests of the elemental and pathetic flesh. A poor, naked old woman, she writhed and howled with pain, stretched out before a group of men seated in full dignity on velvet-covered chairs. "Oh, oh!" she screamed. "Such cruelty! So much! I am dying!"

At the second turn, the clerk still repeated, "Tell the truth, tell the truth."

"I have confessed everything, and they refuse to believe me. I am dying, I am dead! Let me die and have it over! Oh, they are pulling me apart and destroying my life! Oh my God, I can suffer no more, but however much I suffer, I must say the same thing!"

"Tell the truth, tell the truth."

"I have already told you I believed in and worshiped the Word of Moses and not of Jesus Christ. Have mercy on me! I have told the whole truth. I am dying! I am dying—oh, I am dying!"

At the fourth turn, the woman was completely undone.

"Tell the truth, tell the truth."

"I can suffer no more. This poor mother has been destroyed for her children."

"Tell the truth, tell the truth."

"For the love of God, my lords, pity me in this martyrdom!" Here the torturer gave a fifth turn to the roller. "I am dying!"

"You are again admonished to tell the truth and give no cause to continue the torture at such great risk to your life, for you might spare yourself much suffering and martyrdom. Tell the truth out of reverence for God, repent, and have pity on yourself."

The old Jewess had become incoherent and delirious. "I have nothing to say, but to bear witness . . . and God does not want me to say that, nor will I say it. I do not know . . . Blessed be He, for they treat me with such cruelty, unheard of toward a woman."

"Tell the truth, tell the truth."

"I do not know what to say," she cried, raising herself, "except that I came forth from my mother in sadness, my lot has been misfortune, and my old age is sad."

The torturer went on stretching her, in vain, for her agony had exhausted her. Naked, covered with blood, vanquished, she knelt on the floor and sobbed out the story of her life, but was given the strength to "conceal some things that might be to the disadvantage of her children."

Shortly before noon the trial was recessed, but it was resumed at two in the afternoon. The prospect of renewed torture and the suffering she had already undergone had undermined her resistance. The tenderness of a mother, the love for her religion—everything that had been the core of her life—had crumbled. She gave up and denounced her children, betraying her family and herself.

Luis later wrote in his *Autobiography:* "On that day of surpassing bitterness and affliction, I heard my beloved mother's moans of agony as she was being tortured, and there was nothing I could do but to commend her to Jehovah."

Freedom, Prison Again, and the Comfort of Letters

At the closing of the Carvajal trial, the Inquisitors showed a little clemency. During the auto-da-fé held in the cathedral on February 24, 1590, Doña Francisca, Isabel, Leonor, Catalina, and Luis became reconciled to the Church by "publicly abjuring their errors." They put on the yellow woolen garments of penitents who had been tried by the Inquisition, with the red cross of Saint Andrew conspicuous on them, and held lighted tapers in their hands.

Luis, sentenced to life imprisonment in that habit, was taken first to the San Hipólito hospital for convalescents, where he worked as a servant. After a year he was permitted to transfer to the convent of Santa Cruz de Tlatelolco, where he taught Latin to the Indians. Thanks to the efforts of Almeida (his brother-in-law), Luis' mother and sisters, who were to have been cloistered in different nunneries, were allowed to live together in a house in the same quarter of Tlatelolco, where they were under the guardianship of Fray Pedro de Oroz, warden of the convent of Santa Cruz.

Life began to smile upon them again. They were happy to be reunited and to resume in secret the practice of Mosaic religion. But the pain Luis had suffered at the hands of the Inquisition, far from teaching him to be more cautious, seemed to have given new strength to his messianic spirit. No sooner had he won the confidence of the convent warden than he obtained a key to the library where, scorning even the minor precautions, he not only devoured the books on sacred subjects but copied several chapters from the Old Testament in his beautiful handwriting and carried them around with him always. Instead of causing him annoyance, the penitential garment earned him money; he would wander through the streets of the city and along the roads, begging alms to purchase his eventual freedom. Even after he had amassed the stipulated fee he continued to exploit his plight until September, 1594, when the writ that would free him and his family, obtained by his brother-in-law Almeida, arrived from Spain.

Each small advantage that Luis gained increased his imprudence. He practiced Jewish law scrupulously in his home; he never flagged in his evangelical efforts, begun with such success in prison, and he often visited orthodox Jews. Then a new sorrow was visited on the family. His sister Leonor finally lost her mind. During her seizures she would hurl religious images into the street or lean over the balcony to insult passersby, until the family was forced to keep her tied to her bed. In that dark period of religious mania, the figure of Justa Méndez, a beautiful Jewess who attended the Mosaic rites with her mother, cast the light of a tender love on Luis' tormented and fanatic soul.

As was to be expected, the Inquisition's prosecutor Marcos de Bohór-quez officially accused Luis of being a recidivist to Judaism on February 1, 1595, and, since he was a man already reconverted, that meant the stake.

During the course of the new legal proceeding, his mystical exaltation increased. He believed he was one of the chosen and talked with enthusiasm of his forthcoming martyrdom. The somewhat craven figure of the first trial, who had seized any available recourse in order to go free, had vanished. This time Luis appears to have faced his judges courageously and defended his beliefs with quotations from the Old Testament and "numerous and apposite arguments." He showed too an extreme repugnance for falsehood so that the charges he made against himself went far beyond the extremely serious accusations already brought against him by the prosecutor.

But despite this extraordinary attitude of the prisoner, the Inquisition forced him to share his cell with another spy, this time a repulsive priest named Luis Díaz, who had managed by the use of influence to get himself ordained. He had been saying Mass without license, and he made himself out to be a comisario of the Holy Office as a cover-up for various acts of theft and violence. He was at bottom nothing but a despicable drunkard. The prisoners, who were aware of his base role, spat in his face and insulted him, but Luis de Carvajal, who considered himself God's instrument, tried to convert him by "opening his own heart." His candor knew no limits. He realized that Díaz "was an inveterate drunkard, a man who haunted the taverns, and so incontinent he would even soil his garments"—vices that were repellent to a man of settled temperance like himself. Yet Carvajal went so far as to show Díaz where he had hidden his *Autobiography* and his extracts from the Bible. He confided to him the names of many practicing Jews, and, what is worse, he told him of "the filthy desecrations that he and other Jews had practiced with the crucifix."

The prolonged fasts to which Luis had subjected himself (he buried a large portion of the meals that were brought him because they contained forbidden food items); his nights of devotional vigil filled with ecstasies and mystical visions; his enforced intimacy in a small, dark cell with criminals and pederasts; and, above all, the terror the Inquisition aroused in him (the mere sight of the cruel Alonso de Peralta made him tremble); the interrogations and the torture—all ended by unhinging his mind. Because he was unable to bear physical pain, he denounced members of his family and a host of acquaintances, and attempted suicide by throwing himself from one of the galleries into the patio of the Inquisition.

Such weaknesses, lamentable in a man who believed himself to be a prophet and the chosen of the Lord—he announced the coming of the Messiah in the year 1600, and imagined he had been called to beget Him when he fell in love with Justa Méndez—alternated with gestures of courage, inspired by the love he professed for his family. He sent them touching messages, written with the point of a pin on avocado shells, on sweets, and on fruit. In one of them he urged Doña Leonor to "have the patience of Job. My heart's souls, visit Adonai our Lord. Glory to God, I have patience; I am in chains for my God."

This message, also addressed to Doña Leonor, was carefully hidden inside a banana peel: "My angel, rejoice, rejoice, for the journey to paradise is better than the one from Castile. Blessed be the bread you eat and the water you drink, and the ground you walk upon, and the womb that bore you, for it will not be long before we shall share the sacred religion of the angels. Oh, what beautiful gardens, what music and feasting await us!"

None of these missives reached its destination. The Inquisitors, who were informed of all this, ordered him supplied with paper, pen, and ink, and the warden of the prison complied under pretext of having Luis write some memoranda of orders for him. The simple youth, still gullible, wrote to Leonor, "Rachel of my heart, my Lord Adonai has bidden me to console you, and he has given me this paper and ink." Later, when the Inquisitors decided to build their case upon the correspondence, Luis was still able to send admirable letters to his family and to be sure they would be received.

He wrote to his mother:

Ah, mother of my soul, may Adonai be with you! Ah, my beloved flock that has been so scattered, may the almighty God defend you! Ah, mother of my life, may Adonai comfort you! Ah, sisters of my life, may the father of orphans protect you! Ah, mother of my heart, may the Lord God see your affliction and walk beside you and save you and shed His holy blessing on all your fruit! Ah, my wounded people, may the Lord of the world heal you! Ah, my prisoners, may Tobias set you free from oppression and sin, from dungeons and hell! Amen. Amen. Amen. Amen. Amen. Amen. Amen.

To poor Anica he wrote:

My Ana, blessing of my eyes, soul of my heart, may our Almighty God and Lord visit you and all your blessed companions, and give you strength, as the constant cries of this sinner and his tears entreat. Through His miracle, ink and this bit of paper have come into my hands so I might write to you. Although all of you are absent from my sight, owing to my sins, you are ever present in the eyes of my soul and heart. Most of all, you—my wounded one, my little orphan, the gift of my God—may His mercy protect you. My life, they have seized me by the direct will of my God for the good of my soul and by the accusation of good Lucena. You, my angels, were accused on suspicion alone. If you in your innocence are punished here, take that as an unmistakable sign that my Lord God, your Heavenly Father, holds you not in abhorrence, but in great love. Be glad and rejoice, blessed child, for this is the way to Paradise, and glory awaits you. All the saints have passed this way, and now they rejoice in it. Oh, what beautiful necklaces of gold and pearls of Ophir thy Lord God will command to be hung around that suffering neck, my martyr! Oh, what handsome gold chains! Oh, what jewels to repay you for your sufferings! Now, now, my innocent child, have patience, for I bring you tidings of great joy!

After promising his little sister, whom he had also denounced to the Inquisitors, music, silks and rich dresses, vines and fountains of perfumed water, he ends his letter thus: "Rejoice, now, rejoice! Joy! Joy! Joy! Joy! Lay aside your cares and sighs, for my Lord God has revealed His great wonders to me here! I commend you to Him, my angels. He will visit you and save you. Amen."

The Auto-Da-Fé

The voice of the preacher, who struck the shining edge of his pulpit with unrythmical gestures, resounded in the enormous square. When the sermon was finished, a Dominican, straining his voice, read a long oath of allegiance to the faith, in which a complicated strategy for the extermination of heresy was outlined. The friar completed the reading, then added: "In unison: 'We promise and swear it.'"

The crowd replied in a vast, muffled echo, "We promise and swear it." "If you do thus," the Dominican summed up, "Our Lord, whose cause this is, will help you in this world of the body and in the other world of the soul where you will remain longer; and if you do the contrary, that which God does not wish, He will call you to account for it dearly, as rebels who knowingly took His holy name in vain. In unison: 'Amen.'"

When all was silent again, the man whose duty it was to read the sentences which had been passed on the numerous prisoners climbed to one of the side pulpits. From beneath the awning that sheltered the grandstand came his monotonous voice, like the insistent buzzing of a hornet. The viceroy, Don Gaspar de Zúñiga y Acevedo, Count of Monterrey, was seated in his chair of walnut wood—he was the only person who used two velvet cushions, one in the chair and another to rest his feet on—and was trying to overcome his drowsiness by running his glance over the sumptuous and variegated spectacle.

To his left, in the place of honor behind a table covered with a black velvet throw embroidered in gold, sat the Inquisitors; at the ends of the table, the six members of the Audiencia who represented the secular arm. The viceroy studied the decorations of burnished silver on the portable writing case, and the impassive face of the Chief Inquisitor, half hidden behind the standard of the faith which was held by the prosecutor of the Holy Office, between two knights in their splendid Crusaders' mantles. His eyes paused next on the face of the clerk of the court and on the small chest placed within reach of the clerk's hand, from which he took the sentences. The golden chains and the burnished swords of the nobles glittered. The Franciscans, the Dominicans, the Augustinians, and the Jesuits stood out in big blue, white, and black patches. From above he could spot the strange, somewhat Oriental birettas of garnet velvet worn by the rector and the doctors of the university, afloat among the familiar blend of tonsures, shaved heads, monkish beards, and courtiers' mustaches.

The assembly, a wholly masculine throng whose strong odor of sweat mingled with the scent of incense, in the shaded section and the toneless voice of the reader bored Don Gaspar de Zúñiga and increased his drowsiness. Again he made an effort to banish it; he fixed his attention on the pyramidal staging where the condemned stood motionless in their gaudy penitential robes and peaked caps: Negroes, Jews, Spaniards, Portuguese; old witches, weeping and terrified; stoical slaves; the vigorous form of Manuel Lucena, the apostate who had borne the worst tortures without opening his lips; and the serene face of Justa Méndez. Luis was there too with his hands tied, twitching nervously as though the sharp tridents of the devils on his robe pricked him, and the painted flames really blazed out through his wide and feverish eyes.

His long trial almost over, the blasphemous and recidivist Jew had turned out to be the most singular character in the whole auto-da-fé, the most impassioned figure in New Spain. In a sense his body was already dead, and—theoretically at least—his soul had passed by some sinister sleight-of-hand into the clutch of the devil. If the Church wanted to avoid showing an unthinkable weakness of spiritual resources in the face of the omnipotent strength being demonstrated by the Prince of Shadow, Luis must be snatched from the claws of the demon. Accordingly, from the moment his second trial began, the monks had undertaken the task of saving him, but without much hope of success. The Dominicans, powerless, had called on the wisest theologians for help; public prayers had been said in the churches for the triumph of religion. There was no resource the clergy had not employed to rescue him from hell, once it was clearly impossible to spare him the earthly flames to which the secular arm of justice would irrevocably condemn him.

Luis' vigor was inexhaustible. After surviving an attempt at suicide and many prolonged refinements of torture, he had witnessed, the evening before, the rehearsal of his own death; now, facing the avid eyes of the curious, he seemed to have been confirmed in his devilish spirit of rebellion. Seated in the center of the condemned, indifferent to the enumeration of the charges, he never ceased exhorting his mother and his sisters, already converted to Christianity, to die in the Mosaic faith. Finally, the Inquisitors ordered a gag placed in his mouth. Even then, though he was forced to be silent, the obstinate Jew elbowed the cross away from the members of his family each time they approached it, and kept quiet only when the reading of Justa Méndez's sentence began. Then he freed himself of his gag by a great effort, and entreated the guards who were standing behind him, "Let me hear the sentence of that fortunate and blessed damsel."

The pathos of the scene increased when his turn came. Each time the reader pronounced his name, Luis de Carvajal stood motionless as though it had nothing to do with him; only when he heard the name José Lumbroso, the Enlightened, would he stand erect and answer, with joyful wholeheartedness. The list of his crimes rang in the silence of the square, freezing the spectators with terror.

Everyone present was in the grip of religious frenzy. Three robust servants had to hold Luis quiet to keep him from bending his knees each time the reader mentioned the God of Israel, and even then the heretic struggled with them and his eyes were filled with tears.

In that open duel between God and the devil, Satan seemed to have carried off the honors, even after the reading of the sentence. Luis returned to his place on the stand quite unmoved, and it was obvious even to the least concerned of the witnesses that he was ineluctably damned unless at the last moment some instrument of grace should reveal its hidden power. Unnoticed among the many monks, priests, and friars stood Fray Alonso de Contreras, an obscure Dominican to whom we owe the account of the incredible events that were to take place after Luis had left the platform. Fray Alonso had had no intention of attending the auto-da-fé and did not ask permission of his superiors, as many other Dominicans had; but a letter from the prosecutor, Marcos de Bohórquez, appointing him a member of the tribunal, obliged him at the last moment to attend. Once on the stand, he left the excellent place assigned to him for another not so good but which had the advantage of placing him where he could move quickly into the street. This enabled him to follow Luis closely on his way to the stake and to attach himself to him tenaciously, as though impelled by some unknown force.

The face of the condemned man was full of pride and courage. They placed him on a horse with a pack saddle—"the worst brute of all," writes Fray Alonso, "so restless and unmanageable that I do not know why they kept it unless purposely to cause the culprit greater woe"—and the march began. It was not easy for anyone to keep close to Carvajal or to make himself heard. All these tears and pleas of the official confessor, the Dominican monk Jerónimo Rubión, had failed, and when one of the friars, on an irrational impulse that would lead only to new acts of irreverence, approached Luis and held out the green cross for him to kiss, Luis spat on it and rejected it with angry words. "You'd force me, then, damn you! Is there some law that requires this? The Inquisition ought to haul you away and punish you severely, for you deserve it more than I do."

Even though the recidivist's horse had stepped on Fray Alonso for the second time, he was carried along by a design that he was to make clear only later. Despite his pain, he judged the time was ripe to ask, "Luis, do you know what the Inquisition and the Holy Office are?"

Luis replied in Latin, *"Consilium impiorum et cathedra pestilentiae."* ("A council of the impious and a chair of pestilence.")

The monks were appalled. Luis then addressed the Dominican directly for the first time: "Is there a greater torture in the world than to be a man with his hands manacled, so surrounded by mad dogs?"

The monk immediately rejoined: "David, acting with divine propriety in the person of Christ, said that he complied with his arrest, and bowed to the councils and authorities which the high priests and the Pharisees had arrayed against him, those truly vicious and powerful dogs that thirsted for his life. You must take Christ as your example of forbearance and cling to his divine goodness and sanctity."

"Father," the Jew answered, "I love Christ and have a real respect for him, but Christ is not God."

This sacrilegious statement provoked a storm of outrage. Infuriated spectators broke through the line of halberdiers, approached the heretic, and spat in his face. When calm was restored, in the center of the pressing, straining crowd, in the heat and the dust, Fray Alonso and Luis began a half-Latin, half-Spanish debate on the topic of Christ's divinity.

Just then a small monk slipped through and placed himself "almost under the scapular" of the Dominican. Startled, Fray Alonso asked him, "What is your wish?"

"I've come," said the little monk arrogantly, "to argue with this heretic."

"We are already engaged in that, and I'd thank you to leave me alone."

Luckily, the polemicist went away as unexpectedly as he had appeared, and Fray Alonso returned to the debate. But soon the procession came to a halt before the magistrate's tribunal, situated at the corner of Merchants' Gate and Plateros Street. There the magistrate notified the prisoner that he had been sentenced to be burned alive, and added the following warning:

Señor Chief Constable, let it be known to the public that this is a major excommunication and that therefore no one but his designated confessor may go with this heretic; it is your duty to enforce this rule and to drive away all others with blows of the truncheon, even though they be struck down.

That was final. Fray Alonso was about to turn away in discouragement when the magistrate caught his eye, winked, and indicated that he was to remain at the Jew's side. Plateros Street must have looked to him then like an endless way of the Cross as they went into it exchanging exhortations and Bibical quotations.

Fray Alonso was accustomed to carrying on arguments inside his monastery, surrounded by friendly adversaries and a large supply of learned volumes, but certainly not to extemporaneous debate with an enemy of his religion, an astute man who knew the Bible well and who, in addition, was mounted on a horse, while he had to go on foot, jostled by the crowd and blinded by sweat and dust. Half fainting with fatigue, he stopped to mop his face; when he tried to take his place again he found a large, portly monk walking next to the Jew's intractable mount. The monk was speaking indiscreet words to the condemned man:

"Remember me, Luis? I gave you alms and some food one day, remember?"

The portly monk was injecting a note of low comedy into the desperate struggle; he distracted the prisoner, thereby jeopardizing the dialogue just begun. But before long it became evident that God was decisively on Fray Alonso's side. Luis' horse—again his horse!—balked, and at that point the intruder tried to control him with a smart slap on the belly, like an experienced horse trainer: "Steady, you limb of Satan!"

The Dominican ran to his side.

"Father, are you a priest?"

"Yes, for many a long year," the monk answered.

"Then how can you do anything as irregular as this?"

The procession had reached the point where the Good Friday penitents usually placed the image of Christ. There the intruding monk, fearful of punishment, vanished in a crowd. At the same time, our Dominican was granted an inspiration—another sign of divine favor. He said urgently to the constable guarding the prisoners, "I beg you, for the sake of our Lord, to call a halt so that I can say a word here."

The constable acquiesced, and the procession stopped. Instantly the Dominican was surrounded by citizens and dumfounded clergy. Expectancy had reached its highest pitch. In a day of overwhelming emotion, this struggle between God and the devil had acquired, in everyone's eyes, a force affecting their very existence. Now all were seized by the feeling that things were about to reach an unexpected climax.

After commending himself fervently to the Virgin, the monk addressed the prisoner, with every appearance of having lost his mind: "Luis, I want to say only one word to you, which I believe will persuade you, through the virtue of Jesus Christ; if not, I promise you I'll turn back and not harass you any more. Listen to me, now. There is this very clear text by Christ in the Divine Scriptures: *"Spiritus oris nostri, Christus Dominus, captus est in pecatis nostris cue diximus, in umbra tua vivemus inter gentes.* Tell me, what does that pertain to?"

"Where is that?" asked the Jew, wonderingly.

Not at all sure of what he was saying, the monk replied, "In the prophet Jeremiah."

Carvajal burst out laughing. "That prophet is the one I venerate most of all, because I am descended from him. I believe he spoke better than the rest, and I am in him, as I now declare. I have not read that in his book, nor has any human being ever told me of it."

The Dominican realized with delight that "the wall of that adamantine heart" had been breached. Ecstatic, delirious with joy, his words rang in the silence, broken only by the sputtering of the torches: "Now as you take pride in being noble, do one noble thing. Give me your word that if I give you the exact text from the prophet, which you will be satisfied is the word of Jesus Christ, our Saviour, and as it is understood there, you will be converted to His faith and to the Holy Church."

Luis asked the monk to repeat the text to him, and after he had heard it again, he exclaimed determinedly: "Yes, I give you my word. *Vincet qui vincit.*"

The Dominican had wagered everything on a letter. Properly speaking, he had not raised a question of faith so much as one of Biblical erudition. The phrase might be in Jeremiah, in which case the contest would end happily. But the chances were equally great that it might not be, to the consummate defeat of the Church and the Dominican's everlasting ignominy.

Fray Alonso, beside himself, called upon the people present to witness Carvajal's promise. He begged them to say an Our Father and an Ave Maria, and in a loud voice he requested a Bible, which was brought to him on the spot. Then our monk, forced to move along beside Luis, began to look in the long book of Jeremiah for the text that was to work the desired miracle; but he could not find it. He was a man transported. His habit was torn; dust got in his eyes and covered the pages as he scanned them; a constable's horse stepped on him again; the monks grumbled at his imprudence, because it might work a serious injury to the faith of the populace; and, as if this concatenation of circumstances were not enough to annihilate him, Luis de Carvajal was rocking in his saddle as he went along, laughing triumphantly at his easy victory.

Fray Alonso closed the useless Bible and, at the peak of his exaltation, he shouted for a concordance. He was trying to ward off defeat, hoping that some unforeseen event would offer him an escape from the trap into which his unreflecting apostolic zeal had impelled him, for it was obvious that there was not a single onlooker in San Francisco Street, churchman or layman, who would have with him a reference book usually found only in the monastery libraries. Then what everyone thought impossible happened. For no apparent reason, the procession had stopped in front of the house of Dr. Alonso Muñoz. He was a first cousin of the Dominican, and because he chanced to be at his own door and not in the Plaza Mayor or near the pyre, as might have been expected, he heard Fray Alonso's plea, rushed into his house, and plucked from among the books in his library a copy of the concordance. Then he forced his way through the crowd and placed it in the hands of his distraught cousin, who opened it with fear and trembling. There, under the word *Spiritus,* in the fourth chapter of the Lamentations of Jeremiah, was the text he sought, the key that would open the gates of Paradise to the blasphemer. Fray Alonso's heart leaped with joy—"he seemed to have been resuscitated"—and holding out the Bible to Luis he said, with relish in his triumph: "Read, my son."

Luis read slowly. When he had finished, he murmured meekly, with lowered eyes:

I keep my word, and surrender and yield to our Holy Mother the Catholic Church. And I do truly admit that the prophet Jeremiah spoke here of Jesus Christ God and Man, the spirit and soul of all the faithful, consecrated in every man, prisoner and captive, who was scourged and died for us, in whose shadow, which is His grace, we Jews shall be able to bow our heads and to merit the benefit of His sacraments among the Gentiles, through which we shall gain life eternal. I do so confess. Give me the crucifix.

As they stood waiting, the horse "repaid the monk's efforts" by giving him a painful butt on the temple. Why him, and not the onlookers or the soldiers who were nearest? Why had that brute not chosen the official confessor, who was walking on its other side? The answer was plain. The devil had tried to block the salvation of the Jew at any cost. Now that he had been foiled, and forced to give up his prey, he entered into the beast and avenged himself on the catechist by dealing him such a blow that his victim later remarked, "I don't know but that it was a slap in the face given me by the devil."

Carvajal's mystical vein was now flowing through other channels—we must not belittle Fray Alonso's victory by attributing it to Luis' fear of the stake. Weeping and sighing, he covered the crucifix with kisses and said to the Dominican: "Oh, my guardian angel, restorer of my soul! Who put those words into your mouth? Who showed you that? Here is the fountain, Lord, here the water with which I shall be washed, and my soul shall be whiter than snow."

"Luis, my son," the friar exhorted him, "in order to be washed clean you must confess your sins. Call them to your memory. From here to the spot where you are to die, I shall give you time to make a good examination of all the sins you can remember, for I shall stand by you until death."

Luis no longer made any reply to the many who were following him and importuning him. With lowered eyes he repeatedly kissed the corpus and recited, *"Dilectus meus mibi et ego illi,"* all the way to the funeral pyre. As he got down from his horse he still had heart to quip, interrupting the flow of his religious passion: "I hope, O Lord, that my ears will soon be rewarded in Glory for receiving Thy word so lovingly; and that these bones that the devil has so fruitlessly crushed—even to placing me on this horse that has not spared me a single ache—will straightaway be given ease when my soul goes to rejoice in Thee."

They were at the San Hipólito execution ground, a wide stone platform above which the garrote stakes and the scaffolds stood out in the yellow flare of hundreds of torches. There the principal members of that strange family of fanatics were reunited after a long separation: Luis, the old mother Doña Francisca, and her three daughters Doña Isabel, Doña Catalina, and Doña Leonor. The bones of old Rodríguez Matos were there too among those of other dead heretics which had been taken from their tombs and piled on wretched mortuary stands. Effigies of the absent ones stood up among the many living recidivists and heretics. The past and the present, the quick and the dead—all that portion of colonial society whose sinister relations with the world of darkness had been exposed and condemned—were playing their final roles on the funereal proscenium.

The entire population played its role flawlessly, as actors in an audience assembled to witness the triumph of the Church and the temporary annihilation of the devil, in this final episode of a dramatic struggle. The crowd filled the grandstand constructed for the purpose, and flowed onto the causeway, keeping a precarious balance at the water's edge. Some hung in clusters from the trees.

Luis was the center of this drama. He had requested the chief constable's permission to say good-bye to his mother. Embracing her old legs, he said to her in his impassioned manner: "My mother, until now mother of a hard and stubborn sinner, but now mother of a son converted to the faith of Christ through His love and charity, I beg your forgiveness and blessing."

Fray Alonso had not deserted his convert. He led him to the garrote stake and covered him with his cloak. Then, their two tear-stained faces close together, Luis began his confession: "By the sign of the Holy Cross on which our Lord Jesus Christ died . . . I, Luis de Carvajal, the greatest of sinners . . ."

At the conclusion of the confession, which the Dominican called "the briefest, clearest, most complete, and most truthful he had ever heard in his life," he gave the "Boy," at his request, the penance of "your death and your sufferings." And in order to give Luis' soul the firmest assurances of winning heaven, he withheld none of the spiritual resources that could possibly be exploited in such a situation. Fray Alonso regretted that he had not brought with him the papal bull of the Crusade, but on the other hand he offered twenty Masses—which he actually said on the following day in the monastery of Santo Domingo—and, lest the celestial gates still fail to open with the desired promptness, a priest held up before Luis a holy image which could gain him a plenary indulgence if he said three times, "Blessed be the passion of our Lord Jesus Christ." At Luis' express request the crowd recited an Our Father with him, and with every invocation a dutiful "Amen!" rose from thousands of throats over the murmur of the prayers and lamentations of the condemned.

Fray Alonso, exhausted with joy and bathed in tears, fell on his knees before the new convert and said good-bye, praying Luis that he would not forget him in heaven. That conversion was the masterpiece of his life. By the force of his reasoning, he had succeeded in crushing the arrogant head of the serpent; now that Luis, cleansed of his sins, was about to die in cruel torment, the friar felt that with the destruction of this man, who was bound to him by a chain of such extraordinary events, the tangible proof of his incredible victory would also be destroyed.

Luis was made fast to the garrote by a ring of iron placed around his neck. He intoned the words of reconciliation at the top of his voice until the Dominican, pitying him for his effort, ordered him to stop. After two turns of the screw, he still had strength to ask that a Credo be said. He was wringing his hands—the executioner strangled him with great difficulty, because he was so limp—and Fray Alonso, in the last act that history records of him, fixed the cross in his rigid fingers. His mother and his friend Lucena were already dead. Within a few moments, his elder sister died and the old lady Paiba hung with her white hair falling over her contorted face.

At the very moment when the flames from the pyres paled the light of the torches, the Grand Inquisitor in the plaza absolved those who had abjured their heresies. The solemn plain chant was heard coming from the chapel of the cathedral, and the procession, including the prisoners who had not been turned over to the secular authorities, returned to the Inquisition building, lighting the way with thousands of torches and lanterns and carrying the crosses, not draped in mourning as they had been early in the day but hung with scarlet velvet and twined with flowers.

Some days later the sentences on the reconciled heretics were carried out. They went to their deaths mounted on horses, with the hangmen scourging their naked backs, and the servants of the Holy Office exhorted them as they had in 1574 when Hawkins' pirates were punished. This time, however, the populace refused its role of silent spectator, and insulted the prisoners by throwing garbage and all kinds of filth at them. A week later, the viceroy, the officials, and the hidalgos paraded through the streets in festive garb as an act of thanksgiving.

The Inevitable Epilogue

The most spectacular religious drama of the sixteenth century, which General Don Vicente Riva Palacio, among others, employed as the subject of one of his popular pamphlets, would be incomplete without some reference to the final destiny that Fate held in reserve for the remaining principals. Luis de Carvajal El Viejo is in the front rank of those who must be dealt with. The unwitting author of his family's extravagant misfortunes died in prison of melancholy and despair, despite his useless titles of captain general and governor of the New

Kingdom of León, which he had founded. His labors as a Conquistador and colonizer, his estates and the mines he established through sheer tenacity in the wilderness, had brought him neither joy nor satisfaction.

All that history retains of this luckless man—the police arrested him with three reales in his pocket—are his two most striking features: a rough beard and two burning eyes.

The poor madwoman Doña Mariana, who used to hurl images through the windows of her house, had barely recovered her reason when she was brought to trial on a new count and was executed on March 25, 1601, at the San Hipólito stake. But the greatest suffering was reserved for little Anica. Her long, unhappy life finally made her a saint in the eyes of the Jews. But in Catholic eyes she was a deeply dangerous woman who had frequent relations with the devil, according to the testimony of a certain Father Bocanegra, who swore on oath during her trial that he had seen the devil visit her cell, in the guise of a little Negro boy. Naturally, she was condemned to the stake; the sentence was carried out in the Grand Auto-da-Fé on April 11, 1649, when she was sixty-seven years old. The erudite Don José Medina wrote: "Death must have come as a rest for the wretched old woman, for—to say nothing of other serious illnesses—she was suffering from a cancer of the breast so deep that her internal organs could almost be seen."

Because of the influence he could bring to bear, the wealthy Antonio Díaz de Cáceres was sentenced only to pay a fine of a thousand ducats toward the expenses of the Holy Office, notwithstanding his clearly proved Judaism. In the case of the other brother-in-law, Jorge de Almeida, the Inquisition had to be content with burning him in effigy *in absentia* after confiscating his property.

Fray Gaspar is perhaps the most to be pitied, even though the ban of excommunication against him was lifted and his ecclesiastical rights were restored. It was his fate to suffer in his own flesh the religious drama that divided the world into two irreconcilable camps. He denounced his mother; he saw his father's bones burned and, as he himself said, he kept picturing him burning in hell; he witnessed the torture and execution of his own people, only to find himself stigmatized and banished from his community. His story was a cruel and unusual one, even for the sixteenth century.

Baltasar, the eldest brother, and Miguelito, the youngest son of the Carvajals, were the only ones to escape the persecution of the Inquisition. After a great many adventures they found a safe refuge in Catholic Italy. Baltasar married a rich Jewish girl and lived in Pisa, surrounded by his children. Miguel became a learned rabbi and officiated at a temple in ancient Salonika.

These two fortunate exceptions were not enough, however, to restore balance to the scales of justice after they had tipped so heavily to the side of the Catholics against the Jews. Jehovah, a deity plainly in a state of decadence—unable even to mitigate the sufferings of his chosen by one of those terrifying acts with which he used to crush the pride of the Pharaohs—did, however, ultimately wreak a minor vengeance which helped somewhat to repair the damaged machinery of divine justice. The supreme council of the Inquisition ordered an examination of Alonso de Peralta, that cruel official whose mere presence made Luis de Carvajal tremble with fear, and he was found guilty of thirty-two fully proved crimes. "He had made contracts as if he were a merchant," in defiance of the active ban against such trade, and had taken advantage of his position to buy and sell. He had had the audacity to imprison Lucas Padilla for remarking to the warden of the secret prisons that Peralta "should not keep a public dry-goods shop," and behaved so arrogantly that the prisoners were made to kneel in his presence. Neither did the prosecutor, Marcos de Bohórquez, whose sole aim in office was to enrich himself, escape. This corrupt official, owner of several landed estates, had "disobeyed the council's order to sell his property and had accepted bribes in a shameless manner."

6

The Spaniard

CONQUEROR AND CONQUERED

To determine at what point the Spaniard becomes a Mexican is a puzzle worthy of Zeno, as hard to solve through the written word as it was later at the presentation of diplomatic claims. Alfonso Reyes

A span of fifty years stretches between the young, raw, violent era of the Conquest and the publication of the *Historia verdadera* by the veteran Bernal Díaz del Castillo. In other words, a long lifetime went by between his pen sketches and the events they record. As he writes, Bernal's view is blocked by tombs, but this does not discourage him from recounting the events of a remote past as if they were happening on the very day he sets them down. Neither age, nor the bitter presence of death, nor his relative poverty could quench the vital optimism of this remarkable soldier and historian. Certainly he had a clear sense of mission, for in speaking, in his marvelous Chapter 205, of "the valorous captains and the strong and vigorous soldiers" who went to Mexico with Hernán Cortés, he gives thanks to God and the Virgin for preserving his life through so many perils "so that now our heroic deeds may be revealed and seen clearly, and what those men were . . . who won this part of the New World, and that the honor due all of them does not depend upon a single captain."

Influenced by Gómara, one of the best prose writers of his day, Bernal regrets not having the master touch of Apelles, Berruguete, Michelangelo, or Gil de Siloe, in order to sculpture and to paint the features and gestures of his comrades as they live in his memory. His frequent use of devices like this, appropriate to a student of rhetoric, help us to measure the distance that separates the work of a man of the people who, thanks to the time he lived in, was able to take part in the making of history, from the work of a learned man who wrote what he had heard about the exploits of a group of adventurers in a region of the world unknown to him. To Gómara, the Spanish soldier is a symbol, an abstraction, a dark, anonymous shadow, with the brilliant Cortés looming over him. To Bernal, he is Jerónimo Mejía, known as Rapapelo, the Scalper, "because he himself said he was the grandson of a Mejía who was a great thief in the time when Don Juan was king." He is the Sevillian Tarifa Manos Blancas (White Hands), who earned his nickname because "he was no good for war or when it came to work, but only to talk about past things." And he is Pedro de Solís, Tras la Puerta (Behind the Door), who owed his nickname to his habit "of looking at those who went by in the street without letting himself be seen"; or he is his brother, named Solís, él de la Huerta (the Solís with the Orchard) "because he had a very fine orchard and got a good income from it"; or perhaps he is the one they called Sayo de Seda (Silk Coat) because "he loved to wear silk."

Very few of the five hundred men who left Cuba to accomplish the Conquest of Mexico made a fortune, and the fate reserved for their captains was seldom a pleasant one. Pedro de Alvarado, second in command to Cortés, was made a Knight Commander of Saint James and governor of Guatemala, but he met an abrupt end beneath a horse that fell on him during battle. The brave Captain Gonzalo de Sandoval, considered Cortés' right arm, a man innocent of letters "except for the very plain ones," died of a strange illness in the port of Palos after returning to his own country. The giant Cristóbal de Olid, whom Cortés called "a Hector in the fray," was stabbed with a dagger at supper, and later accused of treason to the king and beheaded. Juan Velázquez de León, a relative of the governor of Cuba, died on the Noche Triste, pierced by arrows on a bridge that had been cut off by the Aztecs. Cristóbal de Olea, a rugged and peaceful man, twice saved the life of Cortés, once in Xochimilco after the Mexican squadrons had pulled the captain general off his horse, El Romo, and again in the ambush that Cuauhtémoc had laid for Cortés during the siege of Tenochtitlán. The Indian chiefs, obedient to their rule of warfare that enemies must be taken alive so they could be sacrificed later, had captured Cortés, who was wounded. But in the confusion of battle Olea, surrounded by dead bodies strewn over the pavement, made a final effort; he flung himself against the men who had seized his captain. It was a savage struggle. The maddened Aztecs held onto Cortés while Olea, covered with blood, fought them with his terrible sword until the chieftains yielded. "And so," Bernal concludes, "his life was saved, and Cristóbal de Olea was left there dead for having saved it."

Juan de Escalante, captain of the Villa Rica, died at the hands of the Indians in Almería, and Diego de Ordaz, a former majordomo to Governor Diego Velázquez, who was the first man to climb Popocatépetl, the volcano sacred to Anáhuac, fell in distant Marañón after winning the title of Knight Commander of Saint James. The other captains, those who "died of their deaths"—the dirty, grim death of the civilian and not the fine death of the soldier—were worth little more than a brief obituary note from Bernal, except for Sandoval. Francisco de Montejo, governor and adelantado of Yucatán, died in Castile; Pedro de Ircio—all words, no deeds—flickered out of life as obscurely as he had lived; Alonso de Ávila died in Yucatán; Francisco de Luga, Andrés de Tapia, Juan Jaramillo, and Luis Marín serenely breathed their last in their home, with neither grief nor glory.

The Reason and Unreason of Fame

Some of Cortés' soldiers were able to wrench open the doors of history, but for quite various reasons. Maldonado, a youth from Medellín; Captain Andrés de Monjaraz; the good soldier Juan del Puerto; Rodrigo Rangel, a prominent personage; and the artilleryman Francisco de Orozco—were all assured of immortality because the wounds they sustained in battle summoned them to the field of the pen, as Don Luis de Góngora remarked with good churchly sense.

Juan Pérez, Juárez the Elder, and the valiant Escobar merited two lines in Bernal's heroic roll call for other reasons. The first killed his wife, known only by her *nom de guerre* of La Vaquera (the Cowgirl), a vulgar enough designation, for the historian did not take the trouble to find out her real name. The second also got rid of his wife, regaining his freedom by the use of what Bernal describes as a stone for grinding corn (what we know by the familiar name of the hand metate). And the third paid on the scaffold for the crime of raping a maiden and "for being an incorrigible troublemaker."

Bernal rescued others from anonymity because he was fascinated by some outstanding personal peculiarity. In this group we must point to the "very dapper" Francisco de Saucede, a former footman to the admiral of Castile, whom his comrades nicknamed the Courtier; to a certain Espinosa, known as the Blesser, because whenever he exaggerated some event in his reports, he would add the phrase "with the good blessing"; and a member of the Order of Saint John who lost his name but kept throughout the centuries the nickname of the Blow-Hard, which his conceit had won him; and to Alonso Ruiz, known in spite of his great height as the Kid, the name under which he invariably appears in the chronicles.

Among the few tough and spirited old men who fought in the wars, Solís Casquete (the Shell), the brother of the other Solises, stands out. He earned his nickname because "he rather disliked questions." Another was an anonymous crossbowman who was a great card player, and still another was the father of Orteguilla, a boy who could speak Nahuatl and was a page of the Emperor Moctezuma. These last two old men and the boy met the same fate—all three died captives of the Indians.

Bernal himself destroys the proud, often reiterated claim that the majority of the Conquistadors were "hijosdalgos" (sons of someone). The beings he paints are men who have not yet shed their smell of earth and onions; they are still very close to the poor village, the lonely farmhouse, the vegetable patch, and the kitchen hung with strings of garlic where the talk was of unearthly visitations, of far-off wars, and of miracle-working saints. One can almost see their callused hands and hear their mule bells, their country songs, and their nicknames.

The historian must never forget the vain men, the elegantes, or the one-eyed, the crippled, and the maimed. To those men, nourished on romances and books on chivalry, a fighting spirit was of such passionate interest that they could remark upon their comrades' criminal exploits without bitterness and even with marked benevolence. They loved glory, money, and courage, but at the same time they were greedy and brutal, and they lusted after women. When the time had come to cast up their accounts and collect what they believed was due them, they were capable of spending half a century writing memoirs of the services they had rendered to the Crown.

They had a peasant's sly humor, and a peasant's highly trained hearing and eyesight. And they can describe with equal pleasure the star on the forehead of Cortés's horse, the curly hair of González de Sandoval, or the ashy color of a corpse whose features his own children had eventually forgotten.

Bernal Díaz in Quest of His Past

As the old man writes, the dead gather around his desk. Some come to him limping, others with their faces laid open by a sword-slash or with an empty eye socket. They wear their ragged hats, their battered breastplates, their faded doublets, their medals, and their arms. Before him glitters the diamond Hernán Cortés used to wear on his finger and Alvarado's gold chain. But the astonishing thing about these ghosts from the past, mere specters of the forgotten heroic age, is that their voices have not lost the old ring. For a youth, Gonzalo de Sandoval had a voice "not very clear, but somewhat startling, and he lisped at times"; the voice of Velázquez de León "was loud and thick and he fumbled his words a little"; Diego de Ordaz could not pronounce some words correctly, and half the time he stuttered; Pedro de Ircio was "very talkative, too much so; he was always telling stories about Don Pedro Girón and the Count of Ureña, and for that they used to call him an unsung Agrajes" (a character in *Amadis of Gaul*). The conversation of Alonso de Ávila was vivid, clear, and well reasoned; Narváez, the tragic figure who loomed large in the Conquest, was noted for a "very deep voice, as though it issued from a cave."

Bernal remembers especially the singers and the musicians who accompanied the army, as might be expected from a historian with such a sensitive ear. He mentions Benito de Bejel, who played the drums and the tabor in Italy and New Spain; Morón, a great musician but an average soldier; Ortiz, who played the viola and danced; and Porras, a red-haired singer who died, like so many others, as a captive of the Indians.

A goodly number of the men who filed past his writing desk could be described as people without office or benefice: brawlers and boudoir adventurers, fugitives from Spanish justice, gamblers, failed students, clowns, astrologers, jugglers, and soldiers who renounced their encomiendas and became monks or hermits, after taking their fair share of Indians.

Those whom Bernal left unmentioned, because they had not distinguished themselves in either peace or war—a large number of the soldiers who came with Pánfilo de Narváez or in later expeditions—are ordinary people: blacksmiths, carpenters, seamen, cabin boys, servants of great houses, field workers, or common professional soldiers who never had a chance to fire the crossbow or the arquebus—those tools with which they earned a hard living, in Bernal's sight.

When the time of battle was over, the booty was divided—a handful of gold weighed on dishonest scales. We can see the men in the camp at Coyoacán risking it at cards by torchlight. In a sense, the official life of the colony begins with an orgy of eating, while the soldiers dance to the music of the flute and drum, reel drunkenly between the tables, or chase women through the trees in the orchard. As they dream on the grass, with belts loosened, of roast geese and turkeys flying by, of pastries and capons within reach of sweaty hands, while the idle lance still covered with blood rests beside them, they look like a genre painting by Peter Breughel. But to his rendering of a European paradise are added the peculiarities of the New World, the encomienda and its slaves, the garments of brocade and satin, the hunts, the jousting, and the spirited horses caparisoned with velvet blankets.

The passion for adventure had brought them together in the hour of war. Their rough camaraderie enabled them to rise above their defensive individualism and the greed that exudes from them because they have all been onlookers at the banquet of life, watching it through the window of a lighted palace, standing in the spot where the public generally attends such festivities.

This small, motley group constitutes one of the main components of Mexican society. Their characters had been shaped by extreme contrasts.

Vivid imagination, thirst for glory and adventure, and the Renaissance strength that impelled them to undertake insane exploits were mixed with superstitions, sharp-toothed selfishness, and the terrible contradictions of the Middle Ages. Their sensuality and greed kept them in continual conflict with their religious beliefs. They loved Christ, and yet for money they did not hesitate to commit the worst atrocities; they had a passion for freedom, but could not live without slaves; they exalted chastity as one of the essential religious virtues, and yet raped Indian women; they lived under the rule of law, and were unable to understand justice. At the bottom of their hearts, the medieval devil carried on eternal warfare against the powers of heaven. At times, the heroic dream of knight-errantry engaged their minds in a sweet, austere dialogue with Amadis of Gaul, and the music of his romance rang in their ears. Some of the pictures moving through the historian's inner world were of the Roman and the Arab, the Cid and Ximena, the feudal lord galloping through his walled village, the acolyte who says amor for amen when he looks at a pious beauty.

But when their days as warriors ended, these men would undergo a radical change. They were to cease being Spaniards and to become Spaniards in America, known as Indianos. The Conquistador conquered by his Conquest was already foreshadowed by the uprooting of his life and the collision between everyday living and old and new self-interest. Like a serpent shedding its skin, the adventurer leaves behind him a dangerous stage of his life and becomes a sedentary creature, a new-minted nobleman or a cruel and petty overlord.

The figure of Hernán Cortés dominates the mass of the Conquistadors. He is at once the luckiest and the unluckiest of all. In great measure, he embodies the virtues and defects of the comrades to whom he gave a vigorous historic significance just because they were *his* men. The greed, the contradictions, the rootlessness, the metamorphosis from Spanish soldier to New World entrepreneur, the drive of each to become an "aristocrat" by main force, the streams from feudalism and the Renaissance that vitalized them—all reached their maximum expression in Cortés. With Cuauhtémoc, he is our grandsire—the white one—and for his grandchildren to understand him, it is essential to fix him in the drift of the new society.

The Metamorphosis of the Conquistador

A love of ostentation, prodigality of character, and vainglory were almost always traits peculiar to the Spaniard who had settled in the Indies, and Hernán Cortés was no exception to the rule. Even in his days as a prosperous farmer and notary on the island of Cuba, he was spending more than he earned entertaining his friends or buying his wife costly dresses. But what adventurer ever lost sleep over his debts? They were, so to speak, one of the social facts of life that no one ever managed to avoid if he wanted to prosper in the Indies. When all is said and done, the Conquest of Mexico—and the conquests carried out in the Indies too—owe more to the moneylenders than to the Spanish Crown. Hernán Cortés mortgaged all his property before he left Cuba, and he owed such a considerable sum to various creditors that he could not have paid it off in a lifetime devoted to agriculture and petty official pilfering.

His comrades in adventure were in even worse straits. The moneylenders—they, too, trusted in the lucky star and the heroism of their debtors—would sell them a crossbow for forty pesos and a sword for fifty. A horse cost from eight hundred to a thousand pesos, and the surgeon-barbers who went along with the army treated the wounded on credit, but at very high prices.

If Hernán Cortés conducted himself like a "brave and daring captain" in Cuba before he actually was that, in Mexico he became a great señor (if we overlook the comical excesses of a *nouveau riche*) from the moment the city of Tenochtitlán fell. His city and country houses were the richest and most spacious in New Spain. From the first, crenellated towers, façades of cut stone and tezontle, patios surrounded by columns, beamed ceilings of cedar wood, and noble apartments set the style for a type of dwelling that was to prevail throughout the colonial period, without perceptiblie modification.

His staff of servants was made up of majors-domo, many pages, footmen, waiters, and tasters. Although he was neither a hearty eater nor a tippler—he ate simply and drank nothing but a glass of wine and water at midday—his table was princely. He owned table services of gold and silver and sumptuous table linen; musicians, dancers, and jesters entertained at his banquets. Games of chance meant little in his life, but on the other hand he loved horses—he had a seat like a riding master, as one of his biographers tells us—feats of arms, and hunting. He dressed with somber elegance, in the style of the Spanish nobles, and his jewels were a diamond ring, a gold chain from which hung images of the Virgin and Saint John the Baptist, and a medallion for his cap.

He heard Mass and read his Book of Hours every day. He was sincerely devoted to the Virgin, Saint Peter, Saint John the Baptist, and Saint James, the patron saint of the Spanish soldier; "he gave alms every year as a duty of conscience," and when he was taken seriously ill on his tragic expedition to Honduras, he ordered the shroud of Saint Francis to be kept ready for his burial. Of all the Conquistadors of America, he was the most tolerant and the least cruel, although he disgraced his name many times by such unjustifiable crimes as the slaughter at Cholula and Tenochtitlán and the torture and murder of the conquered Emperor Cuauhtémoc. Though he was a devout Catholic and considered himself a champion of Christianity, he belonged to that strange period when sin, injustice, and insensitivity to another's pain went hand in hand with penance, the hair shirt, the Crusade, and heroic piety. Furthermore, he never opposed the moral laws of his environment, even though he kept a harem in Coyoacán and was capable of strangling his disagreeable wife Catalina Suárez when he considered her an obstacle to his aspirations to a title of nobility.

Hernán Cortés always saw things in the large. A man of many facets, he was, *mutatis mutandis,* a hero of the stature of the Duke of Alba and Alexander Farnese, the military leaders who consolidated Spanish power in Europe on another stage. More than any other Conquistador in the Indies he was moved by the universal spirit, that feeling of being above himself, which was the essence of Spanishness, in Américo Castro's judgment. His ambitious dreams surpassed reality, however great reality might be. At the same time that he was building the city of Mexico, he was organizing expeditions to Tuxtepec, Michoacán, Oaxaca, Colima, Zacatula, Honduras, and Guatemala, and he personally undertook the conquest of Pánuco. He was dazzled by the gleam of gold mines, the pearls and precious stones waiting to be discovered in the East, not to mention "many other secret and astonishing things."

The Conquistadors possessed to the fullest the modern spirit of investigation that characterized the men of the Renaissance, with the difference that the world was the Conquistador's laboratory, his books the tantalizing pages of nature and the undiscovered countries of the unknown world. The secret of his strength lay in the insatiable desire to find the hidden nature of things, to penetrate the great, unrevealed mystery of the universe; and his desire was so exigent, so boundless that each new conquest and each new discovery, far from satisfying it, heightened it to the point where Asia was thought of as a magic fruit within hand's reach.

Unlike Christopher Columbus, a dreamer who left his conquered lands to disorder and ruin while he pursued the phantom of Cipango, Cortés was a combination of visionary and practical man. During the three years that he acted as governor without royal permission, from 1521 to 1524, when he set out on his trip to Honduras, he succeeded in outlining, in general, the solid and characteristic structure of the viceregency, and the lords of the various provinces that had been conquered by his captains hastened to render him their vassalage. "In this manner," says Lucas Alamán "a nation was formed from all these separate parts, and this precious element of national unity came to be the foundation of the greatness the republic may attain some day, if it can be preserved." There was Mexico, without any national unity, but there it was, with its diverse landscapes and climates, with its woodlands and its plains, its men and their various languages, their arbitrary dress and customs, and its sacred mystery, unique and impenetrable, dressed in skins and hiding behind the solemn mask of the Spanish empire.

Cortés established Spanish dominance over the entire native world with remarkable speed. Streets, fountains, aqueducts, monasteries, churches, and mansions modified the landscape; soldiers and prospectors built villas and discovered minerals; ships weighed anchor for distant ports; a city government was set up; gunpowder was manufactured; cannon were cast in foundries; and the encomienda, the cornerstone of the viceregal economy, was established.

Even Cortés trembled at sentencing millions of Indians to slavery. But he knew that this act of almost universal degradation was an inevitable part of the transformation he had begun. In line with the custom he followed throughout the Conquest, he did not present his decision officially sanctioning that institution of the encomienda as a voluntary one but rather as an extreme measure he felt he was forced to adopt under pressure of circumstances. He washed his hands before the emperor, and considered himself blameless; which was tantamount to declaring his innocence to history. He took into account the heavy and constant expenses of the king. He writes:

And above all, the constant importuning of Your Majesty's officials and all the Spaniards; and as that could in nowise be ignored, it was almost necessary to deliver the chiefs and natives of these parts into the hands of the Spaniards, in view of the persons involved and the services they have rendered Your Majesty in these parts. . . .

On the one hand, he had to harden himself "to compel the natives to serve the Spaniards, in the manner of the islanders," as he states in his Third Letter of Report; on the other hand, "without that, the Conquistadors and settlers . . . could not support themselves." The dilemma thus stated brings us to one of the most important attitudes of the Spaniard in America. Neither the Conquistadors nor the subsequent colonists were able to live in America without the labor of the native slave, on whose shoulders the new society was built, grew, and prospered. Slaves built the churches, the houses, the highways, and the aqueducts, and worked the mines. They made possible the encomienda, the institution that satisfied the Spaniard's twofold aspiration to a higher income and a life based on the rights and perquisites of a feudal lord.

Lucas Alamán finds it interesting that the conditions of the encomienda prevailed *sui generis* during all the centuries of the colony. Everything that was hastily improvised at the very beginning, the municipal government, the encomienda, the subjection of the native chieftains, the labor system—all those institutions, oppressive as well as benevolent, which issued from the hands of Cortés—were actually to last over the course of the years, in their original form, exactly like figures on the antique clocks that parade around the church towers, activated by ancient machinery, repeating themselves forever as a living contradiction to the fleeting hour they announce.

The Conquistador became the first victim of the colony he had created. The evil nature of colonialism, which was to mark his sons and deform their characters, had its origin necessarily in the nature of the victorious soldier. Like all other Conquistadors, in Europe or the Indies, Cortés was to be not the governor but the obedient vassal of the authorities whom the king saw fit to appoint in New Spain. It is easy enough to imagine what this meant to the proud feudal warlord. Before the laurels on his brow withered, he was to take second place to some functionary, neither hero nor scholar but a dreary lawyer who viewed the world myopically over the top of his inkwell.

When Cortés was banished from Mexico by the treasurer Estrada, who became governor of the colony in his turn, the Conquistador expressed his bitterness by telling Charles V "that he gave thanks to God that those who had come to exile him from the lands and cities he had won by so much of his own and his comrades' blood were unworthy of any esteem, or of holding the positions they occupy." The Estrada episode was by no means unique in the career of Cortés. From 1521 to 1528, the year the harrassed man fled from Mexico to present his case to the emperor, the Spanish authorities tried every means they could find to relieve him of power by appointing governors and commissioners of their own—Tapia, Garay, Estrada, Ponce, Aguilar, and the members of the first Audiencia, headed by the rapacious young Nuño de Guzmán—or issuing orders for his arrest. If the sight of a Columbus in chains was not duplicated in the case of Hernán Cortés, it was only because sheer accident thwarted the royal intention of removing him from New Spain.

The conflict that ensued between state policy and the feudal leanings of the Conquistador was resolved in favor of the Crown, thanks in great measure to the chivalrous spirit of that Spanish adventurer who placed loyalty to his monarch above every other consideration. Cortés had cause and means to spare for rousing the country to rebellion. He never did it. He smothered his resentment, renounced any thought of taking by force what had been denied him, and far from becoming a rebel, resigned himself to the role of an eternal supplicant and played it for the rest of his life.

The Pale Sun of Glory

Like Columbus, Hernán Cortés had his unparalleled hour of glory on his return to Spain—a glory that was eminently deserved. He had left like any other obscure immigrant, his chattels on his back; after an absence of twenty-four years he returned, one of the most famous men of his time. He was a kind of Marco Polo, who bewitched Spain for a moment with the magic of his marvelous reports. His letters were translated into Italian and Latin, and the story of his courage, his cold sagacity, his rare good luck in conquering vast kingdoms full of marvels with a handful of stouthearted men, was on every tongue everywhere. And here he was, this fabulous man who had escaped the flint knives of the Aztecs, who had fought hand to hand with thousands of fanatical warriors, the soldier who had been granted the privilege of conquering the Emperor Moctezuma. Here he was in Spain, no legend, but a man of flesh and blood.

The splendor of his entourage far surpassed the retinues of Christopher Columbus. Two sons of Moctezuma had come with him, three young men of the high nobility of Tlaxcala, Indian entertainers who could juggle logs with their feet at dazzling speed, and acrobats who could fly like birds from a tall pole to which they were tied with ropes that would unwind to incredible lengths.

Once more were enacted the scenes that Spain had witnessed in 1493. The balconies were hung with tapestries and banners; the bells swung wild and free; dwarfs, albinos, Indian freaks, scarred soldiers, servants carrying plaques and feather fans on poles, and the birds and animals Cortés described in his letters of report to Charles V paraded through the streets. Powerful mules, richly caparisoned, closed the procession, and this time they really carried the wealth of the Indies.

The women were especially interested in the person of Cortés. He was on horseback; his velvet cap concealed his hair, which was beginning to gray; and his black clothes emphasized the pallor of his face. His expression was a blend of dignity and the grave humility that distinguishes some Spaniards.

By that time he had become so obsessed with the desire to marry a woman of the Spanish nobility that the common woman who acclaimed him as he went past never caught his eye, nor did the strapping wenches there to see and be seen in the markets where he paused for a time in his travel to Madrid. But during his triumphal tour, he met a group of high-born ladies in the Guadalupe Convent; the captivation was mutual. To them, he was the victorious soldier, who had set all Europe talking about his exploits on the field of battle, and the uncommon lover, who kept a harem in Mexico stocked with native princesses and Spanish adventuresses. To him, those women who bore illustrious names were the richest prize to be won by the Conquest: the goal he must reach in order to become an aristocrat, a road on which he had set his feet the moment he had won his conquest. With his usual persuasiveness, he told the ladies about fantastic cities and sumptuous pagan courts, and finally he gave them gifts of pearls and golden jewelry, as Marco Polo had done in Venice.

When he knelt before Charles V, the emperor raised him to his feet and talked with him, visibly pleased. A year later, in 1529, he granted Cortés the title of Marquis del Valle, carrying with it twenty-two towns and twenty-three thousand vassals, "which he had chosen in preference to the entire kingdom of Michoacán that was offered him," a knighthood of Saint James, the two palaces of Moctezuma situated in the Plaza Mayor of Tenochtitlán, and two hunting preserves.

His status as a millionaire astonished Europe and aroused envy even in the empress. Among the jewels he gave his bride, the beautiful young Doña Juana de Zúñiga, daughter of the Count of Aguilar and niece of the Duke of Bejar, were five carved emeralds, one in the shape of a rose, another a trumpet, and a third a fish with gold eyes, "the work of the Indians, which contemporary authors call marvelous"; the fourth was a bell decorated in gold, with a large pearl for a clapper, and the fifth a cup, with an overlay of gold and silver that proclaimed this proud motto: *Inter natos mulierum non surrexit major* (of all men born of woman, none could surpass him). The five precious stones were valued at a hundred thousand ducats, and some Genovese jewelers from Seville offered forty thousand for only one of them.

Despite this second pinnacle of triumph, however, his star was declining rapidly. Bernal Díaz, his old and forgotten comrade, judges rightly as he surveys the life of his chief that luck was with him only during the Conquest of Mexico. The fact that his appointment as governor of New Spain was never ratified, and the greed that prompted him to interpret the grant of twenty-three thousand vassals as if each were the head of a family, which would have quadrupled at least the original grant, caused him countless disappointments.

The Grandeur and the Miseries of Victory

When Cortés returned to Mexico in 1530, open warfare with the authorities further embittered him. He became involved in struggles for pre-eminence, over lapses in etiquette, over trifles. The lawsuit about his vassals was to last longer than his life. In 1532 he complained, "I haven't a gold peso to spend on the things I need." Obviously, he was exaggerating. His enormous marquisate included parts of the valleys of Mexico, Toluca, and Michoacán, embraced Cuernavaca, Cuautla, and Oaxaca on the south, and extended to the coasts of the two oceans. This vast territory offered everything, from the eternal snows of the volcanoes, the forests of conifers, the cold lands of the high prairies, to the wonderful temperate climate of the high cordilleras, and the tropical coastlands. It was a kingdom, a boundless field for experiment where a stubborn, ambitious man could successfully establish every kind of crop and every kind of industry known to the world. This is precisely what Cortés did. He built sugar mills in Vera Cruz and Guerrero, began silk culture in Yautepec and later extended it to several other provinces, encouraged cattle breeding, planted wheat, hemp, flax, and cotton, and worked the mines of Zacatecas and Taxco and the gold-bearing placer streams of Tehuantepec.

In 1540, when the ill-success of his lawsuits forced him to go again to the royal court, he launched into jeremiads. All he asked, he said, was

a small part of that vast whole with which he served His Majesty without cost to his royal person in labor, danger, or planning, nor cost in money to pay the people who did it and who had served so freely and loyally not only by the land they had won, but by the great quantity of gold and silver and precious stones from the spoils they had found there.

Bernal attributes the misfortunes that befell Cortés "to the curses heaped upon him by the soldiers for not having remunerated them for their services as liberally they asked," for the historian could not otherwise explain how an obscure treasury official might prove harder for his captain to handle "than winning the land from his enemies."

From 1540 to 1547, the year of his death, Cortés dwindled to a shadow of himself. The man who began life as an adventurer and soldier of fortune ended his days sunk in melancholy thoughts. Even the long lawsuit that had absorbed him so fully could no longer hold his interest. On February 3, in a final letter to the emperor, he begged for a quick decision,

because if it is delayed, I must let it go and return to my house, for I am no longer of an age to travel from inn to inn; rather, I must conserve myself to straighten my account with God, for I have a long one and little life left to spend in discharging it, and it is better to let my estates be lost than my soul.

Life is brief, the catalogue of sins long. In the prime of his life he had been ruled by sensuality, thirst for leadership, the will to command; now that he had grown old and death was near he was tormented by the thought of adjusting that long and tangled account, and remorse gnawed at him incessantly.

He spent his hours in Spain between the affairs of the world and those of the soul—his practical sense never deserted him. He presided over a kind of academy where the audience would suggest lofty subjects for conversation. The men who met with him were a cardinal, a viceroy, and several men of letters, among whom Francisco Cervantes de Salazar must be mentioned. One of the themes chosen for May, 1547, was suggested by the serious illness of Francisco de los Cobos, Charles V's powerful prime minister, and was stated as follows: "The anguish of a rich and powerful man on quitting this earth." Although we cannot know what reflections that subject inspired in Cortés there in the academy, we can make a guess at them, thanks to the testament he filed at Seville on October 11 of that same year. Humboldt, who had it with him during his voyage to New Spain, declared that it was "a great historical document, worthy of being rescued from oblivion," and Mr. G. R. G. Conway, to whom we owe the best edition of it, wrote that Cortés "demonstrates in it a far from common talent for business, an excellent memory, and a cordial tolerance."

The Spaniard Who Made Good in America

"First of all," the will reads, "it is my wish that if I die in these kingdoms of Spain my body be laid to rest in the church . . . until it be time, and may seem so to my successor . . . to remove my bones to New Spain, which I hereby charge and order to be done within ten years, or earlier if possible."

Hernán Cortés heads his last will and testament with this stipulation. He issues a peremptory order that as soon as the last shred of flesh shall fall from his bones—those adventurous and argumentative bones which seem to play hide-and-seek through the centuries—they were to be taken to New Spain. In no other clause does he seem so categorical as in this one, for Hernán Cortés, "the Spaniard who made good in America," as they called him at court, was already an American, a man uprooted from his own country who had linked his destiny to a new land, that he had won by the strength of his arm.

He felt like a stranger in Spain. The ringing of the bells and the shouts of the multitude, which had acclaimed him on his first return visit to the peninsula, had faded from his memory. On the other hand, the injury done him by Charles V is not inviting him to the council where the fate of Tunis was being debated still pained him like a fresh burn. Of Spain, he bore in mind the uncomfortable inns, the bitter lawsuits, the hostile royal chancelleries where his urgent legal business slumbered undisturbed. Spain had haggled over his claims, impoverished him, gnawed at him, deceived him, considered him a foreigner. Everything had been quite different in Mexico. Here he had won fame and wealth. The Indians looked on him as a god, and in spite of the Audiencia, he could live like a prince on his own domains, expend his energy on creative pursuits, and renew himself in his palace in Cuernavaca, lying on the colonnade watching the green flood of the forest, the flight of the birds, and the gleam of virgin snow on the volcanoes as he breathed the warm, perfumed air of his paradise.

His will deals next with his funeral. All monks of every order in the city were to attend it, as well as fifty paupers dressed in hoods and long dark garments, who were to follow the coffin holding lighted torches. Unless he should die after twelve o'clock, Masses were to be said on the day of his death in all the churches and monasteries in the city, and in the ensuing days five thousand more Masses, to be apportioned as follows: one thousand for the souls in purgatory—he himself was a sure candidate for that dreary place of punishment, and he felt obliged to placate his future companions in distress—two thousand in memory of his soldiers who had perished in the Indies, "and the remaining two thousand Masses"—let us use his own words—"for the souls of such persons as I may have some accounts with that I may not know of." Then came a list of the religious establishments that were to pray his soul out of the horrors of purgatory and win him the name of benefactor. A convent for nuns and a hospital were to be built with his funds in Coayacán and a secondary school for the study of civil and canonical law in the city of Mexico.

The will goes into great detail about burying the dead and making life comfortable for the living. He was to be buried next to his mother Doña Catalina Pizarro and his two small legitimate children Luis and Catalina in Texcoco. His wife Juana de Zúñiga was to be paid back the ten thousand ducats which she had brought as a dowry and he had spent on launching the fleets for the conquest of the Spice Islands. At the time he made his will he was arranging the marriage of his daughter Maria to the heir of the Marqués de Astorga, and had paid him in advance twenty thousand ducats of the hundred thousand agreed upon for her dowry, and he ordered the payment of the remaining eighty thousand. His other two legitimate daughters, Catalina and Juana, were to receive fifty thousand ducats each, and his bastard sons Don Martin and Don Luis, whom the Pope had legitimized in 1529, were to receive a thousand ducats a year as long as they lived, but in a codicil added some days later he canceled Luis' legacy and bequeathed it to the powerful Duke of Medina Sidonia.

He felt a deep affection for his illegitimate daughter Catalina Pizarro, whose mother was Leonor Pizarro, and he remembered her in his will, bequeathing her the village of Chinantla and the tribute from it, the income, and several herds of cattle. He left ten thousand ducats each to Doña Maria and Doña Leonor, and did not forget his female cousins, his wife's ladies-in-waiting, and their servants. At that final hour he kept in mind the smallest details of his rather theatrical life. He had once forced his head groom and his butler to pay him some money which they swore had been stolen from them; now he ordered it returned to them, and he did not forget an unpaid bill from one of his tailors.

Naturally, his greatest concern centered on his first-born son, Martín Cortés. The line of primogeniture granted by Charles V would be founded on him, and he would carry the title of Marqués del Valle. His inheritance would come to him at the age of twenty-five, at which time the Duke of Medina Sidonia, the Marqués de Astorga, and the Count of Aguilar would relinquish their guardianship over him.

Bernal Díaz, retired from the world in Guatemala, did not forget to place a modest wreath on the tomb of his old captain. He bent his head over the paper and his wrinkled old hand grasped the pen in its strong fingers and wrote: "After he had won New Spain, he had no good fortune . . . perhaps for that reason he will have it in heaven, and I myself believe so, for he was a good gentlemen and very devoted to the Virgin and the Apostle Saint Peter and the other saints."

His hand paused, and he fell into a long silence. The broken helmet, the shattered lance, the emperor's scepter, the slain Indian were all lying on the dunghill of history, turned to dust, eaten by worms. Bernal closed his eyes, and his lips murmured again and again: "May God forgive him his sins, and me mine." Above the glory, tarnished by this world, the green branch of piety was blossoming. And piety in that age was a symbol of hope.

7

The Ávilas

A FAMILY OF DOOMED MEN

A dark and dreadful fate hovered over the members of the Ávila family. The first of them to appear in Mexico was Captain Alonso de Ávila, who came from the island of Cuba with Hernán Cortés. According to the detailed portrait of him drawn for us by Bernal Díaz de Castillo, he won fame as a valiant soldier even though he played no part in the expedition of the Conquest after the disaster of Noche Triste. He was thirty-three years old in 1519, well built and pleasant-faced. His speech was clear and expressive. He treated his comrades generously, but at the same time, like any Spaniard of the sixteenth century, he liked to command and not to be commanded; he was boisterous—fond of noise, Bernal explains in another mention he makes of the young captain—and inclined to be invidious. Hernán Cortés, unable to put up with a man so like him in this key aspect of his temperament, got rid of this dangerous officer by sending him to the island of Hispaniola as procurator, under the pretext that the Tribunal of the Indies would have to solve some of the problems posed by the Conquest recently begun.

Alonso de Ávila carried out his mission efficiently and returned with "good news" to Mexico City after Tenochtitlán had fallen into the hands of the Spaniards. Cortés then appointed him auditor for the colony—he was the first in New Spain—gave him the important encomienda of Cuauhtitlán, and, possibly because he still viewed him as a rival, entrusted to him and to Quiñones, the Zamoran, captain of his private guard, the mission of delivering a portion of the booty won in Mexico to the Emperor Charles V.

From the beginning, Alonso held a position far superior to that of most of the adventurers connected with the actual Conquest. He was a prosperous encomendero, an ambassador, the recipient of a fantastic amount of treasure—Bernal Díaz mentions among several jewels "the gold wardrobe that Moctezuma and Guatemuz once owned"—and as if that were not enough, Cortés, with his prodigal generosity, had given him several gold ingots.

The ambivalent destiny of the Ávilas was to occupy high positions, only to sink later and dramatically into suffering and poverty. Quinoñes, Alonso's partner, was stabbed in a fight over some women on Tercera Island, and Alonso had to continue his voyage alone, never dreaming that destiny was about to make him the victim of one of the most famous episodes in the history of piracy. When the profile of the Spanish coast was already visible on the horizon, the fleet of Juan Florín attacked his ship—Hollywood has exploited this kind of assault so often that we need not trouble to describe it—and carried him off to France with the stolen Mexican booty. Francis I, the monarch who had asked once too often to be shown Adam's last will and testament and who on that account had been denied a slice of the world by a meddlesome Pope who divided it between the Spaniards and the Portuguese, felt that providence was restoring to him some of the wealth of the Indies, even though it had come by the dark road of piracy; and he toasted the valor of his hungry corsairs who had handed him this great historical revenge on a platter of Mexican silver.

Alonso spent two years in a French prison, and upon his return to Spain, minus Moctezuma's treasure and Cortés' gold, Governor Francisco de Montejo appointed him auditor for Yucatán and marched with him to the far-off peninsula, a region without rivers or mountains where the Maya still lived by their ruined pyramids. These Indians were fond of bathing, of magical symbols, and of cutting off the heads of white men as the finishing stroke to their cruelty.

The second of the Ávilas appeared in Mexico in 1524. He was a brother of Alonso, named Gil González de Benavides. This obscure Caribbean adventurer, whose life is a long, unanswered question, joined

Cortés on his disastrous expedition to the Hibueras. After his return to Mexico, he managed to have Alonso send him a power of attorney from Yucatán, "so that he might have to himself and make use of the village of Cuauhtitlán," and soon became an outstanding figure among the first encomenderos in New Spain.

He was married to Doña Leonor de Alvarado, by whom he had five children: Gil González de Benavides, the eldest; Alonso de Ávila, named for his uncle; two daughters, María and Beatriz; and a young boy whose name is not known. He lived in a magnificent house adjoining his brother's, which occupied the corner of the royal streets of Ixtapalapa and Tacuba, and he enjoyed an annual income of more than twenty thousand pesos, for, apart from the village of Cuauhtitlán, whose tributes he took in his brother's absence, he had the encomiendas of Ixmiquilpan and Xaltocan in the state of Mexico, and those of Zirándaro and Guaymeo in the district of Pátzcuaro.

The titles held by Gil González to his numerous encomiendas are not very clear. He was a typical *manos blancas* who succeeded in getting hold of the richest pieces of land without having taken part in the Conquest, to the great chagrin of the real Conquistadors. Juan Suárez de Peralta, our sole guide through the genealogical labyrinth of the Spaniards in America, a man who, like any good Creole, rejoiced in a sharp tongue and loved poking into the origins of the colonial fortunes, accuses Gil González of keeping his brother's villages through fraud and the practice of black arts, to the end that Alonso died in Yucatán "almost desperate; and they say he cursed his brother and prayed to God to be pleased to render him justice and that neither his brother nor his children might enjoy the estate, and so it was."

Thanks to the research of the author of the *Tratado de las Indias,* we are able to note that the sudden wealth of Gil González, his concealment of it, his manner of living, and the position of his sons must have been somewhat obvious, for the dying man's curse was to be carried out, sooner or later, by the will of God and the help of the devil whose job it was to take care of such low, nasty, but unavoidable duties. At any rate, although the rascal Gil González was not lucky enough to be punished in one stroke for his sin, he soon began to pay something on his debt. The last of his children, while still very small, drowned in a water closet. This child's ignoble death was the first of the devil's acts in fulfilment of the Conquistador uncle's curse. The second presented greater difficulties, as Suárez de Peralta put it—naturally it had to do with a woman—and the devil had to work on it for many years. But it is only fair to acknowledge that he carried it out with a malevolence and a deployment of dramatic resources worthy of his most elaborate and ambitious undertakings.

This is the story: Gil González was very proud of one of his daughters, named María, and he intended that she make an advantageous marriage. This aristocratic Creole girl, like all the ladies of her time, lived in strict seclusion. Not only were a thick wall, heavy window grilles, and a spike-studded door interposed between María and the sensuality of the outside world; she had, in addition, her duennas, her ladies-in-waiting, and her mother watching over her. Yet the defenses of a colonial household and the surveillance of a mother, however wise we may suppose her to have been, were not enough to conjure away a prophecy that was to have a fatal ending regardless of preventive measures. The devil was not outside in the street, nor in the church, nor in the ballroom, but inside the house itself, incarnate in the person of a servant named Arrutia, who rode beside his master's horse and who, insult upon injury, was not even a white man, but a despicable mestizo. Let us leave to Suárez the responsibility for the inevitable comment: "They became entangled in a tender flirtation, and to further their love each pledged, with obvious damage to the honor of her parents, their betrothal in marriage."

Some hint of this forbidden love affair leaked out and "in order that their shame might not be published in the village" her brothers Alonso and Gil—at this time the father may already have died—got rid of the mestizo by shipping him off to Spain.

Days later, Alonso approached his weeping sister and said, "You must go to a nunnery, sister, for it is my wish, and it would be best for us that you become a nun (and you will do so) where you will have everything you need, and you will be treated well by me and by all your relatives, and you need not raise any objection to this, for it is proper."

And so María was immured in a convent, but she refused to take the veil, hoping that her lover would come back; but even this feeble hope was extinguished by the hard wind of misfortune. Her brothers deceived her and "forged letters saying [Arrutia] was dead, and they told her of it, and then she took her vows and led a most unhappy life." "Fifteen or twenty" years later, enough, in any case, for Captain Alonso de Ávila's curse to have worked upon all the members of the family, in a manner that we shall see later, the private drama of the nun reached its inevitable denouement. The exiled Arrutia—"he who loves truly forgets late or never"—arrived in Vera Cruz and wrote her a letter announcing "that he was alive and in this country." Fainting spells? Yes, the nun "fell to the ground in a swoon." Tears? Yes, and lamentations, too. "Then she began to weep and to lament that she could never enjoy the one she had loved so much." Madness? Sad to say, in the end María did lose her reason. Is that the last of it? Anyone who knows the sixteenth century, and knows a little about the devil as manipulated by Suárez de Peralta, also knows that this story must end with a flourish of hellfire; the survivor of this collective and indiscriminate curse must go into the convent garden and hang herself from a tree, so that her soul may perish along with her body amid the chanting and laughter of an unleashed throng of gay, triumphant demons.

After Suárez had Captain Alonso de Ávila die, cursing his brother, Gil González de Benavides, on his deathbed; after he had flung open the door to damnation for Sister María de Alvarado and had filled chapter XXXIV of his *Tratado* with all the horrors that we, careful to keep faith with his spirit, have attempted to reproduce here; he hastens to compose the following responsory as a footnote to the office for the dead, solemnly, and with emotion: "All the children of Gil González de Benavides came to a truly pitiable end, and it is meet for all who learn of it to pray to our Lord for their souls, and that He may take them to His bosom."

A Privileged Seat at the Table

Until the time of the arrival of Martín Cortés, the young Alonso de Ávila could consider himself the most privileged Creole in New Spain. His position as a younger son was no obstacle to his inheriting the encomiendas of Xaltocan, Cuauhititlán, Ziránrandaro, and Guaymeo on the death of his father, while Gil González de Benavides, contrary to the custom of the period, was left nothing but the dreary village of Ixmiquilpan. Alonso did not trouble himself unduly over his encomienda. A manager collected the tribute regularly, and a capixtle—a sort of a foreman—conscientiously performed his duty of exploiting the Indians. The rich encomendero—his annual income was twenty-five thousand pesos—never visited his estates, except for Cuauhtitlán, and that only for a short period. The city offered too many attractions for a young Creole to take much of an interest in the progress of agriculture and industry or the lives of his slaves. Every month the nice gold pieces arrived on his desk, in some mysterious fashion, in exchange for the corn, blankets, pottery, and animals that had been delivered as tribute, a tribute that Alonso was able to collect through the efforts, not entirely clear to him, of some unknown uncle with the same name as his.

From Alonso's house, situated a few steps from the university on aristocratic Calle del Reloj, he could see the Plaza Mayor, the scaffolding of the cathedral, and the high colonade of the city hall.

He had married before he was twenty, possibly to conform to the customs of the day. His wife was Doña María de Sosa, daughter of the treasurer Don Alonso de Sosa and Doña Ana Estrada, who in turn was the daughter of Don Alonso de Estrada, one of the famous treasurers of New Spain at one time. All the Estrada daughters had made advantageous marriages with distinguished men in the colony, and one of the sons, Fray Juan de la Magdalena, "had the glory" of translating the *Escala espiritual de San Juan Olimaco,* the first book published in the New World.

In addition, Alonso's wife was the niece of Doña Juana de Sosa, married to Admiral Don Luis de Castilla, perhaps the most powerful and influential citizen of Mexico City. A counselor of viceroys and a public official, this man who had come to Mexico as an ordinary settler was also a miner who had struck it rich. In his house, which was near Alonso's, he kept an armory, a host of servants, a superb stable, and a retinue like a feudal lord's. "Even the servants' cups used in the kitchen were of silver," Dorantes de Carranza declares, "and in his lifetime he gave away more to the poor and the hidalgos than a very liberal king might have given."

Thus Alonso de Ávila belonged to the society of encomenderos, mining men, and public officials because of his rise in life, his wealth, and his wife. He himself held the post of alderman in the city council, a body that not only fixed a man's place in society but also assured a preponderant place in the colony to the Creoles through their participation in the government.

The children of the Conquistadors or the first settlers who had had the good luck to inherit important Indian villages were strangers to boredom. Alonso frequently gave dinners, suppers, and balls. The days of the Viceroy Don Antonio de Mendoza, when ladies would faint at banquets as a result of overindulgence and when men would chase the native serving girls brandishing a half-eaten turkey leg in a greasy hand, had passed into history. Majors-domo no longer had to watch the dinner guests lest they carry off the silver vessels, because merrymaking was the Creole's natural milieu, as international adventure and warfare had been his father's. In the Ávila house musical instruments were played at all times, costly dinner services were set on the table every day, by the light of perfumed candles; and Alonso was adept at composing impromptu verses or at making love to the ladies and thereby giving an ingenious and daring twist to his dinner parties.

The realistic scenes from La Celestina, the most popular book of the sixteenth century, cast their shadows against the backdrop of that life, giving it a color and freedom which the other segment of society—the domain of the religious orders and the penitents—vainly strove to combat with disturbing pictures of rattling chains and the agonized cries of souls in purgatory to the living sinners who had forgotten them. The toothless mouth of the shrewd procuress, that stitcher-up of virgins deflowered too soon, was never far from Alonso's ear: "Enjoy your youth, every good day, every good night, the good food, and the good drink. Keep it while you have it. Be damned to him who wastes it." Her advice was followed to the letter. Alonso was not fond of history—that could be left to more unfortunate Creoles—he never fell into the sin of composing heroic cantos in his own honor nor did he bother in the least about saving his soul from the flames of hell, for after all, to a youth of his age, there was time enough and more before he would need to regret his past.

Nothing is more lost than the "mur" [mouse] that knows nothing but his hole. If that be closed to him, there will be nowhere he can hide from the cat. Look at all the dangers a one-eyed man must run! A soul alone neither sings nor weeps; a single act does not make a habit; you will seldom see a lone friar on the street; a partridge flying alone is a marvel seen only in summer; dining alone soon destroys appetite; one swallow does not make a summer; a single witness is not the entire faith; he who has only one set of clothes soon wears it out. What can you expect, son, from this number one? I can tell you, he has more troubles than I have years on my back. Take even two, which is pleasant company as far as it goes: For you have two ears, two feet, and two hands, two sheets on your bed, and two shirts to change about. But the more you wish for, the better things will go for you; the more you drink, the better you feel; honor unshared is only a ring on the finger. So then, just between us, take the cash and let the credit go.

In his fondness for women, and in other matters, Alonso was all docility, and the procuress could lead him by the hand.

On feast days Alonso took part in the horse races, the mock wars, the jousting, and the ring tournaments. In the mornings he exercised his horses in a nearby meadow; after dinner he played field sports, and in the afternoon and after supper he gambled at cards and dice, wagering large sums. Hunting, one of the favorite sports of the gentry; cavalcades and promenades; extended visits to the encomienda, where he reigned like a potentate, with the power of life and death; the demands of a punctilious etiquette; and an exquisite toilette—these filled his days to his complete satisfaction.

We do not know well the first-born son of Gil González de Benavides, but he is a mere shadow alongside his brother; a somewhat reserved man and a recently widower. Alonso made his presence felt in the life of the colony, in one way or another. He carried the royal standard in the Procession of the Flag; he was the animating spirit at parties and dances; his curly hair, the fine sweep of his mustache, his elegance caught every woman's eye. There was no spot he did not fill with grace and charm.

A Glimpse into Alonso's Household

In the middle of the sixteenth century the most important room in a hidalgo's house was the armory. Alonso owned a helmet, a coat of mail with brassart and cuisse, gloves, gauntlets, two mailed corselets, two cuirasses, and two pairs of greaves, so that he could take part in the tournaments armed cap-á-pié. The warrior's accoutrement was completed with three halberds, two pikes, six lances, and numerous shields. Compared with this supply of antique hardware, his firearms were not at all plentiful. Two arquebuses and a pair of pistols were "his entire stock."

His stable included a handsome white horse, his favorite, whose proud bearing is immortalized in the chronicle of Juan Suárez de Peralta; two blacks, a schooled bay, a hack, a dappled mare, and a tall, powerful black mule. Two stallions, one gray and the other black, were hitched to his wife's red satin litter whenever she went calling or to church, for carriages were still unknown in 1565.

The trappings and the velvet saddles, black, purple, or yellow and trimmed with gold nails, the Cordovan pillions (as the padding which covered the horse's haunches was called), the breast-strap strung with little bells, the various types of bridle bit—one for long stirrups, a curb bit for show riding, and the bit for short stirrups—the crimson and orange harness, the silver headpiece, also with bells, and the horsecloths—all represented a real fortune.

A survey of the Ávilas' wardrobe reveals both the love of costly fabrics and garments which characterized the late Middle Ages and the zeal to surpass which lent its tone to the days of chivalry. A list of Doña María de Sosa's garments exposes to the impious public gaze "a satin petticoat with velvet flounces," a "colombino" (dove-gray) dress trimmed with silver passementerie, and another of olive green; also some long pleated skirts, a sleeveless bodice of brocade and another of white satin; two pairs of sleeves, one of embroidered crimson with gold and baroque pearls, and another of purple satin trimmed with silver. The lady also owned three complete outfits, some skirts, two pairs of sleeves, and two loose gowns that could be made into new dresses with the aid of some imagination and a diligent needle. This finery, meager for so eminent a lady, was rounded out by a mantle of red damask embroidered in silver, a purple cloak, also worked with silver, and one lone, funereal velvet hat, with no trimming.

Unlike the male wardrobe of our day, men's clothes then were richer and more brilliant than women's. Aside from his severe warrior's garb, Alonso had six taffeta hats as against the poor little black one of Doña María's; to her one mantle and little cloak, three magnificent damask capes, a velvet cape embroidered in gold and lined with brown damask, a short collared cape of blue velvet, a long cloak, and three short cloaks, one of white cloth with white trimming, one of black satin trimmed with fox and gold passementerie, and one of black satin lined with plush. He had eight surcoats—short jackets worn over the doublet—of satin and velvet, and he owned many pairs of hose, which fitted the flesh like a glove, from the waist to the toes, and emphasized the manly contour of the leg. His hose were of black velvet, crimson and gold satin, and white satin with silver laces; his doublets, like his suits, cloaks, and underclothing, were trimmed with passementerie, braid, and embroidery of silk and precious metals.

Our feminine lingerie, with its soft fragile richness or its complicated and deceitful underpinnings, which is shamelessly exhibited in the windows of the most centrally located shops, was non-existent in the sixteenth century. The complete inventory we have of the Ávilas' clothing mentions only six man's shirts and two woman's chemises and no garments of a more intimate or sinful character. Our capacity as investigators of the past leads us not only to expatiate on this aspect of life but to speculate about the vexing problems that must have faced Alonso de Ávila's wife because she had only a couple of chemises to her name. To add to our perplexity, we do not know whether the said chemises were trimmed with lace or ribbons or adorned with the embroidery which so improves such garments in our eyes.

Jewels were worn to enhance the richness of clothing, to an extraordinary degree. One might wear at one time ten emerald and diamond rings, six earrings of gold, crystal, and pearl, religious miniatures, and a gold belt from which hung a dagger and no fewer than forty-eight cords and loops of gold and crystal, to decorate a costume. Outward display seems to have been the law governing household economy. Our inventory lists seven beds of velvet, fine scarlet cloth, and gilded wood, tapestries and chests, armchairs, writing cases lined with skins and Cordovan leather, and numerous items of silver. It also mentions four linen sheets, a counterpane trimmed with scarlet velvet, and a single bed with sheets, pillows, and mattresses. It speaks of spoons but is silent concerning knives and forks. The staff of domestics who served this elegant couple was made up of two Spanish manservants, two pages, and seven Negro slaves. A clergyman had charge of the education of their small children and doubtless he also functioned as the family's private chaplain.

To that first generation of Mexicans, life was an endless feast, smoothly borne to table upon the backs of thousands of anonymous slaves. Alonso de Ávila and the Creole youth of New Spain lacked the wit to learn their lesson before bloody experience would hammer it into their souls. The hardships of their fathers had no meaning whatsoever to those naïve, cruel children; they were sunk in their feudal dreams, and when tragedy surprised them, it destroyed them with ease and flung them, defenseless and dumbfounded, into dishonor and death.

8

Martín Cortés

SECOND MARQUÉS DEL VALLE DE OAXACA

Ours is essentially a tragic age, so we refuse to take it tragically.
D. H. Lawrence

The image that Spain presented at the middle of the sixteenth century was that of a medieval castle invaded by a troupe of people educated in the free and joyous atmosphere of the Renaissance. Old customs and sentiments, superstitions and beliefs from the past were bewilderingly and arbitrarily mingled with the new sensibility—the talent for living that radiated, like rays from a life-giving sun, from Italian Humanism. Actually, Prince Philip was not at all the "Demon of the South" reflected to us by the cloudy mirror of history. In 1554, he was twenty-seven years old and somewhat unstable mentally. He threw himself into tournaments and hunts with a frenzy, adored dancing, and loved to sing and play the guitar. His skin was white, his hair and beard golden—he was known as the Fair Prince—and his natural dignity was combined with a youthful grace that was not without strength.

That same year Charles V, on the point of relinquishing his world empire, conceived the plan of marrying his son to Queen Mary Tudor. By thus converting England to Spanish Catholicism, he thought to place himself in a position from which he might easily overthrow the numerous enemies, among them the Pope, who ringed him about. Philip obediently consented, and the costly preparations for the wedding were completed in April. On May 14 the young prince left Valladolid for Alcántara to meet his sister Juana, who was to be regent of Spain during his absence. He was accompanied by a glittering suite of a thousand knights, among them the Marqués del Valle de Oaxaca, firstborn son and heir of the Conquistador of Mexico.

On June 3 the company arrived at Benavente. The festivities were brilliant. Before the young prince's eyes passed floats with enormous cardboard elephants, a ship flying the English and Spanish flags, and a girl "lying on a coffin, mourning for Cupid, who followed her on horseback; on reaching the royal stand he flew into the air by means of a rope tied around his waist, and at the apex of his flight set off fireworks." Interludes by Lope de Rueda were performed—as in Shakespeare's staging, the scenery was nothing more than wigs and a curtain—and bullfights and mock tournaments were held. The crowd, waving torches, marched beneath the tapestry-hung balconies where Philip watched the public celebration with his deformed son, Prince Don Carlos.

In the "holy and fearful" town of Compostela, Philip knelt beside the sepulcher of Saint James Apostle, patron and help of Spanish soldiers, and received the queen of England's envoys, headed by the Protestant John Russel. A few days later he embarked at Coruña and crossed the channel on the *Espíritu Santo,* a huge merchant ship with a sculptured and gilded prow, which flew the royal standard of Spain "more than twenty meters long, with Philip's coat of arms embroidered on purple damask," escorted by hundreds of small vessels.

In London the prince, in black velvet and silver, spoke Latin to the queen's counselors—"he had not come seeking men or money but because God had ordained that he marry their virtuous sovereign"—and at the end of his speech he downed the gigantic basin of beer they had poured for him, without blinking an eye.

Mary, his betrothed—the Pope remarked later that he could not say whether Philip was her husband, her nephew, or her cousin—sent the Earl of Pembroke from Winchester to meet him with a retinue of two hundred knights dressed in black velvet and a company of bowmen carrying the red and yellow banner of the kingdom of Aragon. It was raining hard that morning, but Philip paraded on horseback, mounted on a beautiful horse with his red cloak of state spread proudly over its crupper; that same evening, attended by twelve noblemen, he held a private interview with the queen. The nocturnal walk, through gardens made mysterious by trees and fountains, brought to mind legends of Amadis of Gaul and King Arthur and held a flavor of romantic adventure that vanished the moment the company stepped over the threshold of the salon where, deeply moved, the middle-aged, ailing sovereign awaited them. With the same courage he had shown in tossing off the beer in front of her counselors, he kissed the hand of his betrothed, according to the custom of the British court.

The marriage ceremony was performed with a solemnity never before seen in England. At eleven in the morning Philip appeared, making his way through the crowd that thronged about the cathedral. He was dressed in white and covered with a golden cape embroidered in pearls. The queen arrived half an hour later, also dressed in white and gold, "dazzling for her diamonds, if not for her beauty."

At the close of the Mass and the medieval marriage ceremony, one of the knights at arms called in Latin: "Philip and Mary, by the grace of God, King and Queen of England, France, Naples, Jerusalem, Ireland, Defenders of the Faith, Prince and Princess of Spain and Sicily, Archduke and Archduchess of Austria, Duke and Duchess of Milan, Burgundy, and Brabant, Count and Countess of Habsburg, Flanders, and the Tyrol, in the first and second years of their reign."

Three years after those ostentatious ceremonies, when Philip had become poor Mary Tudor's widower and the dream of Charles V had vanished in smoke, Martín Cortés marched with Philip in his campaign against France. Martín, who had already played a part on two solemn occasions in the life of the prince, was also present during the monarch's first great battle—"his experience had been confined to the brief Perpignan campaign at Alba's side"; but we do not know whether Martín was there as a soldier or simply attached to his household. Be that as it may, the position he held in relation to Philip was quite different from his father's to the emperor, who had lived in seclusion in the monastery of Yuste since about 1557. Philip was no soldier. At thirty, in the prime of his life, he would have to take to his bed after jousting in a tournament, and the exercise of the chase, his favorite sport, made him ill. Contrary to the feudal tradition of the Spanish kings, who had always fought at the head of their armies, he stayed a long way from St.-Quentin on this occasion, as his 150,000 soldiers advanced under the Duke of Savoy, and he learned from messengers what was going on at the front. Thus, without intending to, he ushered in the era of modern warfare. In other ways too he departed from the customs of his day; when he was in Cambrai, he received a horoscope sent by Nostradamus, from Paris, but he burned it unread.

The battle of St.-Quentin was short and easy. The right flank, commanded by Alonso de Cáceres, was made up of Spaniards and Germans; the left flank was the infantry regiment of Navarrete plus some Walloons; and the center was entrusted to the celebrated Julián Romero, commanding his Spanish troops with English and Burgundian reinforcements. The cavalry kept guard over the rear and provisioned the lines.

On August 10, Saint Lawrence's Day, a part of the army routed the eighteen thousand French under Montmorency near the walls of the city, and with almost no casualties the Spaniards killed six thousand men and took two thousand prisoners. On August 11 Philip appeared, dressed in his burnished armor, to receive amid artillery salvos the homage of the captured enemy flags and to embrace Savoy, who knelt before him to kiss his hand. Then, instead of attacking Paris, which could not have withstood him in the absence of the Duke de Guise, he organized a solemn procession to a nearby church where he vowed to build a monastery dedicated to Saint Lawrence, the new and miraculous patron of Spanish victories.

This was the king whom Pope Paul, in a conversation with Navagero, castigated in the following terms: "Philip eats meat in public on fast days and during Lent, because he says the weakness of his stomach forces him to. Eat in your own room, you rascal, and do not set the world such a scandalous example, for you know that is one of the Lutheran dogmas!"

The battle of St.-Quentin was both the first and the last warlike act of Philip II. After 1558 he almost never left his kingdom, and already he was beginning to dive joyously into the ocean of paper that came across his desk from the most distant corners of the world.

Soon after his return to Spain with the monarch, Martín Cortés married his niece Doña Ana Ramírez de Arellano, by whom he had a son named Fernando, after his grandfather. It was then that he decided to end a court career that could not offer him any brilliant prospects and to settle down in Mexico. Philip proved generous to his faithful companion. On January 29, 1562, in Madrid, he signed an order purchasing Martín Cortés' main house in the city of Mexico, and in Toledo, on September 16, he issued a decree by way of farewell which granted Martín unrestricted use of all vassals living within the boundaries of the marquisate. In this simple, amicable manner, the lawsuit that Hernán Cortés had pursued in vain through many long and bitter years was settled in favor of his son, who had performed no notable services for the Spanish Crown.

A Little King in Spanish America

The second Marqués del Valle de Oaxaca, heir to the riches and the name of Hernán Cortés, returned to Mexico under auspicious conditions. The settlement of the suit that had sapped his father's strength made him a little king in Spanish America, in the flower of his youth—he was born in 1532 in Cuernavaca, or so it is believed. Within the imprecise boundaries of the eldest son's extensive estate, he was a law unto himself. He appointed the ecclesiastical and civil authorities and set the amount of tribute: a tithe plus first choice of harvests and herds; his vassals were obliged to render him the personal services "which they had been accustomed to giving to the Aztec emperors." His cultivated lands, his industries, his mines, his cattle, and his thousands of slaves brought him an annual income conservatively estimated at fifty thousand pesos and, in addition to the sacred prestige surrounding the figure of Cortés, he held a title of nobility that was unique in New Spain. Although by birth and descent he was the first gentleman of the Creoles, Mexico was strange to him. His father had taken him to Spain when he was eight years old, and he had lived since then as a courtier at Philip's side.

The great events he had chanced to take part in—the disaster at Argel, the campaigns in Flanders, the marriage of his monarch to Mary Tudor, the battle of St.-Quentin, and the fervid scheming of the Spanish court—do not appear to have marked his character appreciably.

The epitaph he composed for his father's tomb, which Gómara cites with evident bad faith, may give us some idea of the utter mediocrity of this wretched scion of the great Conquistador and the importance granted him because of his lineage:

> *Father, who by an awkward fate*
> *Held this lower half of the world*
> *And enriched our age by your valor,*
> *Rest now in peace eternally.*

Martín was accompanied on his voyage to Mexico by his wife Doña Ana Ramírez de Arellano and his half-brothers, Don Martín, son of the famous Doña Marina, and Don Luis, whom the Conquistador had fathered by the Spanish woman Antonia Hermosillo and whom he unexpectedly disinherited in a codicil shortly before his death.

In the household of the Marqués del Valle and the society of the period, Don Martín Cortés, the bastard, represented a curious human type. The concessions made to natural children in the Europe of the Middle Ages were denied him in Mexico, according to the genealogist Baltasar Dorantes de Carranza, in whose opinion bastards should be deprived of employment, social honors, and economic compensations by the mere fact of their illegitimate birth.

Don Martín Cortés added to this indiscretion mixed blood, although that serious drawback was somewhat offset by the fact that the Pope had legitimized him and his other bastard brothers. Although by blood and birth he stood between his father, the Conqueror of Mexico, and his mother, the most famous Indian woman on the continent, his education drew him entirely into the European orbit. He retained the innate qualities of the Indian, such as the silent heroism he was to manifest later during the difficult trials that awaited him, but he thought and acted in every way like a Spaniard.

While still a young child he had been snatched from Doña Marina's arms and sent to Spain. His status as an exceptional mestizo—he was an eloquent testimonial to the might of the empire—determined that he would enter the service of Prince Philip and later of the empress. While still very young, he fought at Argel and in Germany, "where he left the field wounded again and again." He was admitted to the Order of Saint James in Spain, married Doña Bernaldina de Porras, and lived on the two thousand ducats a year which Hernán Cortés had willed him, which actually meant living at the whim of his half-brother, the marquis. His long absence from Mexico, his title of knight, and his services to the Crown made him just as much a stranger in his own country as the legitimate Don Martín.

The two most famous sons of Hernán Cortés, the dark man and the white man, represented two prototypes. The bastard founded a long line of mestizos whose Indian blood, far from supplying a creative and stimulating force, imposed a fundamental insecurity. The legitimate son, in his turn, started an endless chain of lazy, absentee Creole landlords. Their ascendancy over others was based as much on their newly aristocratic lineage as on the wealth they had inherited, almost always at the cost of slaves conquered in a manner that failed to distinguish between brutality and the miraculous intervention of the divine will.

The Heyday of the Creole

Suárez de Peralta tells us that the news of Martín Cortés' voyage to New Spain "brought great happiness to the land, especially to the sons of the Conquistadors, who had truly longed for it." One of those delays so common to the navigation of the time demonstrated the anxiety people felt for him while they waited. They could learn nothing about him for many days, and they began to fear that the ship had suffered an accident. All the spiritual resources of the period were mobilized to combat whatever danger he might be in, and after public prayers, supplications, vows, and processions, a courier arrived with the word that Martín was safe and sound in Yucatán, where his wife had given birth to a son. Without a pause the city exchanged deep solemnity for wild festivity. People congratulated one another, greeted the good news with ceremonies, and gave balls and cavalcades; the Viceroy Don Luis de Velasco met with the city council and the social elite to plan a program for Martín's reception.

A great many Creoles went to Vera Cruz to meet him, or "at least to Cholula." "The flower of the country," knights, priests, and monks, swelled the procession as it moved along. As in the days of Hernán Cortés the roads were strewn with flowers, the Indians danced in the square to the music of flageolets and teponaxtles, and their leaders offered Martín the magisterial silver staves.

From the moment he stepped off the ship the Marqués revealed, contrary to all expectations, a character totally unlike his father's. Hernán Cortés was a born diplomat. He owed his greatest victories more to his wise and patient arguments—Bernal recalls that he could talk anyone out of anything—his persuasiveness, and his unaffected camaraderie than to his arms. He treated captains and the humblest soldiers with equal deference, and when he received the first Franciscans who came to Mexico under Fray Martín de Valencia, he knelt on the earth and reverently kissed their hands. His son, on the other hand, wore his arrogance like a cloak. He would not show his escorts the proper courtesy, nor would he bother to grant them their proper places in the hierarchy.

If Hernán Cortés and his firstborn son were unlike in their manner, their appearance differed equally. Although all the portraits of the Conquistador were painted toward the end of his life, and not by great artists, they succeed in capturing something of his ambivalent nature. The disappointments he had suffered had not extinguished the flame of daring resolution in his wide, deep-set eyes; his mouth expressed the energy and sensuality of a man used to dealing with women and to being obeyed; only his bent, graying head revealed the change that age had wrought in him as, in sadness and perplexity, he looked his last on a world that had lain at his feet and which he had never understood.

The Hospital de Jesús contains an oil painting of great interest: it is not only the one known portrait of Martín Cortés but also the only one of a Creole directly descended from the generation of the Conquistadors. We see in it first of all the portrait of a gentleman and not a man of the people. The fashionable full black beard and mustache cannot give authority to a face of such stereotyped mediocrity that fluted ruff and plumed hat only emphasize it. The sword hilt, running out of the oval of the painting, is plainly out of proportion to the small hands and courtly wrist ruffles. The artist seems to have felt that, in the absence of any significant features, he needed to emphasize the puffed sleeve of the doublet and to paint a large coat of arms of the marquisate across his chest. This expedient, while it shows the painter's limitations, also removes any doubt concerning his illustrious model's lineage.

The anonymous portrait befits both his figure and his life. Suárez de Peralta, a Creole who kept in close contact with Martín Cortés during his stay in New Spain and who is always partial to him and to his family, describes the impression his gross discourtesy had made on his fellow citizens:

And ever since the marquis set foot in New Spain, he made himself detested, more so each day, because he persisted in using the familiar address of *vos* to all the knights and monks and in denying them their proper place. They felt this very keenly, and his bad reputation later traveled as far as Mexico City; he was very much criticized, and many even vowed they could not bear him, and the love they had borne him and the wish to see him vanished as the result of that habit.

In Coyoacán, where the Conquistador had built his country seat, the neighbors received his son "as a most royal person" regardless of his insolence. Then came the great city festival. Three hundred horsemen dressed in livery held a contest in a field. The horses, adorned with costly trappings, coursed across the grass. The masters of ceremonies, the fanfares, the gleaming armor must have reminded him of the royal festivals he had taken part in.

At the end of the preliminaries, he made a triumphal entry into the city. The same three hundred knights, in the same garments, led the march, followed by two thousand citizens on horseback in black cloaks. Ladies, "and those who were not," glittered with jewels on the balconies hung with tapestries under velvet canopies. And so they came to the palace. The viceroy, ill with gout, received Martín in the doorway of the "grand ballroom," leaning on a cane, and there they clasped hands and embraced. There was much backing and filling over the delicate question of who was to take the right side, an honor that Martín finally yielded, to everyone's pleased surprise. In the evening Don Luis de Velasco gave a splendid supper "and then the marquis went to his house and the viceroy stayed in his."

A Creole Paradise, Ghosts, and Paper Wars

The social calendar changed with the arrival of Martín Cortés. Suárez de Peralta, who found himself swept along by the mad whirlwind of gaiety, whether he would or no, describes it thus: "No one could talk about anything but fiestas and galas, and so there were more of them than ever before." The palace of the marquis, left long ago in the hands of his manager, opened its doors to the knights and gentlemen of New Spain. Sumptuous dinners and suppers were prepared every day, and in the evenings huge sums were gambled away at cards. Martín, who must have found the strict etiquette of the Spanish court intolerable, was revealing an insatiable appetite for pleasure, and his imagination labored tirelessly to offer new excitements to his guests. He introduced the *brindis*—"this had never been the custom in the country, and no one knew what it was"—a pastime similar to that enjoyed by the rich and idle young men of the Tsarist aristocracy.

The brindis started with a challenge to see who could drink the most wine without falling down. The major-domo would bring up a large supply of bottles, the guests would place their bets, and the two contestants, loosing the cords of their doublets, would pour wine into themselves; there was to be no stopping until one of the pair rolled under the table almost apoplectic, dragging tablecloth and glasses with him. The game had its rules. Anyone who refused to accept the challenge had his cap cut to pieces publicly as a sign of deep scorn at his pusillanimity. Cruelty did not fail to show her ugly face: "During the dinners and suppers anyone's known failings might be discussed, even though he was present."

The Creoles were also very fond of masquerades. It was enough for someone to say at table, "We're having a masquerade tonight," for a hundred men to ride out in the streets in disguise. We can imagine the carnival scenes created by numbers of drunken men secure in their disguises. Some would woo the women, going from window to window on horseback; others, more daring, went into the houses of rich merchants with beautiful daughters and took the greatest liberties.

The devil—that active devil whose power Hernán Cortés had broken with sword and lance—delighted in using the young Cortés as an instrument for his infernal designs. "The matter reached such a pitch," Suárez remarks, "that many already in the power of the devil are still walking around." The monks hurled Catiline diatribes from the pulpit and advised fathers to safeguard the honor of their families. Since undoubtedly the women disregarded all admonitions and refused to retire from their windows, the families decided to keep watch over them; but the crafty Creoles, scorning reprisals, would blow passionate love notes through long blowguns decorated at the tip with flowers.

Hunts, tournaments, cavalcades, card games, drinking bouts, and balls followed one another uninterruptedly and made a happy Arcadia of the colony. One party led to another, and a big one was paid for by *echando la casa por la ventana,* by going all out. If Martín's hospitality and his ungovernable fondness for pleasure won him the good will of half the Creoles, his avarice and his choleric temperament alienated the other half. Soon after Martín's arrival a relative, a rich landowner named Hernán Gutiérrez Altamirano, gave an opulent supper for him. On "presents and gifts" alone, he spent the incredible sum of more than two thousand ducats, but this did not prevent Martín from entering a claim against some lands of his, "which seemed very wrong to everyone; and from then on, they were wary of the marquis and noticed how many similar things he did, which proved to be the cause of his downfall."

The honeymoon of the viceroy and the encomenderos that started with such bliss swiftly turned sour. An irresistible force had met an immovable body. On the one side was Don Luis de Velasco, the monarch's representative, supported by his active relatives and the administrative and economic resources of the colony; on the other, a group of land-owning Creoles threatened with the loss of their encomiendas, who saw in Martín Cortés, by virtue of his position, the defender of their rights. Unfortunately, the man lacked the vitality and shrewdness needed merely to maintain the privileged situation of his own people. Stiff pride of caste and his exalted idea of himself led him to provoke incurable resentments and breaches of etiquette, already all too frequent, in his punctilious and legalistic world.

One such breach served as a pretext for a battle which had been brewing a long time between him and Don Luis de Velasco. Shortly after he came to live in the city, Martín ordered a large silver seal that bore his coronet and coat of arms, above this unbecoming inscription: *Martinus Cortesus primus hujus nominis Dux Marchio Secundus.* The first time his agents used it on payment of the royal duty, Hortuño de Ibarra confiscated it, on the grounds that in his opinion the use of a seal so similar to the one used on royal writs constituted something like *lèse majesté.* The viceroy not only upheld Ibarra but ordered the initiation of a suit over the matter and sent it on to Spain.

Matters worsened with the arrival of the Visitador Jerónimo de Valderrama. The viceroy prepared to meet him, accompanied by the leading knights of the city, as was the custom; but Martín refused his invitation without even a reply. Instead of joining the official entourage, he went ahead by the Ixtapalpa Causeway on August 16, 1563, followed by his lance page, welcomed the visitador, and returned with him to where Velasco's retinue was waiting. Unable to reproach Cortés for preceding him, Don Velasco promptly found a way to chastise him publicly without injuring his own authority. He ordered his secretary, Turcio, to tell Cortés that his page must step out of the entourage because no one was allowed to show any insignia as long as the Audiencia was flying the royal standard.

War had been declared. Martín suffered the first blow, but he quickly returned it. "The page," he replied, "will remain in the retinue." The viceroy issued an ultimatum. "If the marquis will not obey, he must be forced to do so." Turcio was running from one side to the other, the soldiers were waiting for the order to throw themselves on the lackey, and the marquis, standing his ground, was raising his hand to the hilt of his sword when Valderrama stepped into the dispute and diplomatically persuaded Cortés to withdraw the page with his pennoned lance a suitable distance from the royal standard.

It looked as though the viceroy had won the day, but that was not the case. Valderrama, perhaps mindful of the story about the poisoned custards with which Hernán Cortés disposed of his predecessor, Luis Ponce de León, finally accepted Martín's invitation to stay in his house, thus suggesting that he took the Creole's side.

Jerónimo de Valderrama is a figure of blurred outlines. Some moldering bundle of papers may contain the traces of his life, but not even the contours of his face, his age, his family background, or his personal inclinations are known. The inquisitive student of the past is always powerless to dispel the fleeting shadows in his line of vision. One must resign oneself to accept sketchy outlines, incomplete likenesses, and backgrounds so clouded and puzzling that history becomes a ghost story. This is precisely the case with Valderrama, as—to be perfectly frank—it is with the majority of the actors who play a part in our book.

The visitador, a mere suit of clothes that moves through the air like a phantasm, signs a paper from time to time, dictates an agreement, turns in a report, and travels mysteriously from one place to another, never losing his spectral quality.

What were the consequences of Valderrama's ghostly act? They were many and varied. First of all, the epistolary combats that had broken out among the colonial inhabitants were exacerbated to a degree that seems hardly conceivable today. Archbishop Montúfar wrote venomous letters denouncing the monks; the monks filled their voluminous correspondence with horrors they attributed to the archbishop; the viceroy complained of the Creoles, the Creoles of the viceroy, and Valderrama complained in writing about all of them except his friend Martín Cortés. To the visitador, Velasco was an apathetic functionary who patronized only his own people; business was carried on largely through flunkies, and the oidores were all equally inept; the monks spent enormous sums on building monasteries and preached "that the pestilence that was wreaking such havoc was God's punishment for the king's sins, and that as long as the country had no monarch of its own it would not be governed well." As for the Indians, Valderrama was sure that no matter how they were harassed and maltreated, they would follow the advice of the monks and go into hiding to avoid paying their tribute.

Another, and not the least, of the consequences was that Valderrama doubled the tribute to be paid by the Indians; he rescinded even the exemptions from payment that had already been sanctioned and he issued an order fixing severe punishments for the tardy—all unreasonable and contradictory measures. Although these orders came from a royal representative, they were met by vigorous opposition from Velasco, who regarded himself not only as the king's deputy—administrative tangles are always devilish—but also as omnipotent and sacrosanct in his own person.

Valderrama was categorical. He petitioned Philip II for the removal of the viceroy and the members of the Audiencia, and without waiting for the Council of the Indies to rule on his radical requests, he dismissed the oidores Villanueva and Puga from office—the latter was Dr. Vasco de Puga, author of the famous abridgment of cedulas which bears his name—and sent back to Spain. Thus he opened the first chapter, as it were, of a long novel of appointments and removals from office, of embattled appearances and disappearances, that have provided abundant material for countless generations of Mexican chroniclers, historians, and dramatists.

Martín, for his part, opened fire on his enemies, counting on the support of the ghost who was living in his house. Was the Audiencia trying to block completion of the building he was putting up on the Volador? Sue the Audiencia. Did the Bishop of Michoacán claim he had some right to his lands in Santa Fe? Sue the Bishop. Had the municipal government refused to recognize that the boundaries of his villas in Coyoacán and Tacubaya were contiguous with the outskirts of Mexico City? Sue the municipal government.

The secretaries were busy night and day copying allegations and judgments; the lawyers were making their fortunes and exchanging terrible blows. Meanwhile the gentlemen, not satisfied with having started that avalanche of paper that threatened to engulf them all, sent letters in the greatest secrecy to influential friends in Spain, asking them to bolster their claims with the help of Philip II's counselors.

The viceroy was not resting behind the lines during these battles. Without undue harshness, he had written to the Council of the Indies, reporting the arrogant and bad-tempered behavior of Martín Cortés and the shocks and annoyances he provoked. But when Valderrama doubled the tribute the Indians had to pay he was prompted to greater severity, for he had always been their sincere protector. On June 22, 1564, he wrote to the king, telling him that "in the villages of the marquisate more than sixty thousand Indians are living, which ought to produce 84,387 pesos annually, a population which exceeds by 37,000 persons and an income which exceeds by 47,000 pesos, the first grant made to Hernán Cortés."

The viceroy never had the satisfaction of finding out what success he had had with his shot. A few days later, before his report could reach Philip II, he died in the house of the official Hortuño de Ibarra, on July 31, leaving in charge his oidores, Pedro de Villalobos, Jerónimo de Orozco, and Licentiate Ceinos, dean of the Royal Audiencia. The three men combined were not able to exercise any part of the authority the dead viceroy had wielded. Velasco had known how to rule with the velvet glove. He was an aristocrat but at the same time he loved the

Indians, and as the royal representative he did not allow insubordination. To this just man, the Creoles were a lot of unruly youths whom he could control merely by threatening them from afar. He had known how to suppress in time the insolent acts of Martín Cortés without any need for extreme measures, and he maintained order, even though the proud land barons, stronger than ever, were suffering a real attack of panic.

9

The Creole Paradise and the Serpent

The Gospel doth advise
Be on guard for wolves will prowl
'Neath fleecy skins disguised
Thus stealing by surprise
From herd and flock and fowl.   Juan de Timoneda

Into that gay, civilized Creole paradise, where the fountains flowed with wine, the turkeys and hams hung from trees, the inhabitants dressed in satins and brocades, and gold appeared mysteriously on the desks of the encomenderos, crept a cruel and active serpent. Paradise, a feudal miniature of hunts, cavalcades, and balls, rested on an illusion of ownership, and the serpent, like everything evil and everything good in the colony, was made of paper and appeared in the form of a royal decree which aimed at snatching the enjoyment of their beloved encomiendas from the Creoles.

The Spanish Crown had been trying to suppress the encomienda from the moment it was established, in order to avoid a fight to the death between the Spanish American barons and the centralized rule of the kings. The passing of time did nothing to soften the conflict; on the contrary, it made it more violent. But none of the Crown's efforts, not even the famous New Laws, decreed in 1540 at the inspiration of Fray Bartolomé de Las Casas, had met armed resistance from the Conquistadors. Loyalty to their monarch, possibly the outstanding characteristic of the Spanish soldier, had been put to severe tests, but had never broken. They limited their protest to shouting, blustering, and filing petitions with the courts. The extreme venture was a plot to dress in mourning for the reception of the Visitador Tello de Sandoval, whose duty it was to enforce the laws; but Viceroy Don Antonio de Mendoza managed to dissuade them from this rather ridiculous gesture.

The incessant wrangling had a serious effect upon the Indians and on the development of the colony. Don Joaquín García Icazbalceta, in his biography of Archbishop Zumárraga, writes:

No one was doing any building or undertaking any long-range work; everything was up in the air; the Indians were being cruelly plundered and the land was becoming impoverished and depopulated. So palpable were the consequences of that precarious foundation of the public wealth that the monks themselves, generally so opposed to apportionments of property, went to law more than once, because they were consistently the sole means of alleviating the lot of the Indians and of giving some stability to the land.

The arrival of Martín Cortés gave the Creoles a confidence and security hitherto unknown. By birth and by the devices on his coat of arms he was a Creole far superior to the Spanish functionaries who traditionally despised those born in the colony. Further, he was an encomendero of sufficient stature to challenge the power of the colonial authorities with his wealth and the number of vassals. The problems of his class were his problems, and whatever the others suffered, he must feel in even greater measure; hence he could not possibly remain on the sidelines during a dispute.

Velasco's death injected life into the Creoles' party. Valderrama was on their side, and the oidores were three old and skittish lawyers whose principal task was to follow court proceedings and sentence petty criminals. Without a vigorous authority to hold them in check, the Creoles now showed openly the scorn that gentlemen have felt from time immemorial for the magistrate's ruff.

Their spirits were buoyed up by the tacit agreement that was whispered through the city. Nothing was thought or talked about but the implacable necessity of perpetuating the threatened encomienda, at any price. Meetings and caucuses were held, and exclamations and loose talk charged the already tense atmosphere with electricity. There was much talk of "dying for their estates and their honor," "of their determination to make the Marqués del Valle king, for "he had more right to the land than the king of Castile," and "of the very grave injury His Majesty had done the country by letting it go to waste everywhere because most of the encomiendas were already in their third generation."

The fear of being dispossessed of land their fathers had conquered, and of being left in poverty, drove them mad and, says Suárez de Peralta, bringing his unshakable devil front and center,

As the devil found the door open for him to do his work, there was always someone to say, "Body of God!" We're nothing but hens; the king wants to take the food out of our mouths and the roof from over our heads, so let us take his kingdom away from him, make off with the country, and give it to the marquis, for it is his, and his father and ours won it to their cost; let us not see this grievous thing.

Martín Cortés, who had become a leader of colonial life, still could not count on the fellow-feeling of all the Creoles. His air of a big chieftain, his stupid pride, and his arrogance had aroused resentments and disaffections which created numerous enemies for him.

One of the many armed encounters that were to transform the capital of New Spain into a replica of bloody Florence and its battles between rival factions occurred in Calle del Martín Aberraza on April 5, 1565. Bernardino de Bocanegra and his brother, Hernando de Córdoba, were on one side, and Juan Suárez, Alonso de Peralta, Alonso de Cervantes, and a man named Nájera on the other. They all drew their swords and began to fight furiously. The Bocanegras must have been highly skilled swordsmen, for, despite the number of their adversaries, Cervantes was lying wounded on the ground when the guard intervened.

Martín apparently took the side of the Bocanegras. He visited their house frequently during the trial and heaped favors on them, while he tried to crush their opponents who, for the most part, were sons of men who had been loyal to his father, the Conquistador. Suárez attributes this partiality to the attraction Martín felt for Doña Marina Vázquez de Coronado, the wife of Nuño de Chávez de Bocanegra. At that time Mexico City was small enough that nothing could happen without being instantly reported. The citizens lined up on one side or the other; everybody knew all about everybody else's "weaknesses and faults"; they turned the most trivial events into questions of life and death, "and as the period was, in addition, one of pride and bravura, and this was fostered by the fashion of wearing swords at all times, arguments commonly ended with blades drawn . . . in the streets and the public squares."

The rumor that Martín was "carrying on with a lady," whose name lent itself to off-color witticisms, provoked a great battle of slanders, anonymous letters, and poison-pen verses. One day as Martín was drawing a kerchief from his nose, he came upon this quatrain:

> As God's my witness a good man
> Won this land for Marina.
> And now, upon my word, this one
> Will lose it through her namesake.

Whether or not this second Doña Marina was amorously involved with Cortés, as Suárez de Peralta hints with his usual malice (he rejects the nickname of "the Saint," which her contemporaries gave her in recognition of her virtue), the verses reveal the atmosphere of intrigue, petty quarreling, and subtle insult that surrounded the society of the sixteenth century.

In this period of confusion it was Martín Cortés who directly or indirectly provoked the skirmishes and dissensions that occurred constantly. From the moment of his arrival in Mexico, he had followed the practice of adding to his retinue any person of rank whom he might chance to meet in the street. The marquis would no sooner make his appearance, followed by his squire, than men would change course and go to greet him and join his entourage. This homage was far from voluntary. His friends performed the courtesy gladly, but disgruntled Creoles and Spaniards, exaggeratedly jealous of form, rendered it with clenched teeth, and only waited for some pretext to excuse them from paying the required homage.

A chance came almost unsought to the high constable, Juan de Sámano. At one casual encounter he had the audacity to proceed on his way, once he had greeted Cortés and removed his cap. Unless it was promptly corrected, such a serious lapse might mark the beginning of the end for Martín's feudal world. Don Luis Cortés was charged with reprimanding the haughty Sámano. The constable excused himself, claiming urgent business; Don Luis then suggested that if he was in such a hurry when he met his brother, he might very well slip around a corner or duck into a house "so that people would not be aware of his disrespect," but Sámano managed to avoid a showdown and before long, as Cortés had feared, other dissidents were following his example.

Although the marquis' whole party took a hand in the matter and threatened with a merciless drubbing anyone who would be so insolent as not to abandon his duties and follow Martín, Sámano's example was followed by Juan de Valdivieso. He was a twenty-three–year–old Creole, the owner of four villages in the Mixteca and houses and orchards valued at forty thousand castellanos, and distantly related to Martín into the bargain, through the marriage of his sister Doña Guiomar de Escobar to Luis, the bastard.

One morning Valdivieso was in the Santo Domingo gateway as Martín chanced to pass by, and the arrogant youth made no move to join the retinue. At this unforgivable offense, Don Luis halted his horse and said, "Señor Valdivieso, see here."

To which his brother-in-law replied, "Wherever Your Mercy commands."

The conduct of Luis Cortés in these encounters may justify the codicil disinheriting him which his father had added shortly before his death. As an officious lickspittle to his brother he was the one to convince the would-be strayer that he must follow the pennon of the marquis whenever he appeared in the streets. On this occasion he was also the man charged with tweaking the rebel's ears, but as they never met on the field of honor, he had to be content with challenging him to come to his house, situated on the spot where Monte de Piedad now stands.

On May 7, Valdivieso met the appointment, accompanied by Hernando de Bazán. Luis was on the upper colonnade that ran around the patio, and they became involved in a bitter argument. Cortés argued that Valdivieso's relationship obliged him to respect the custom, and Valdivieso took refuge behind the shield of his dignity as a gentleman. Finally, seeing that his brother-in-law would not give in, Luis loudly forbade him to call him brother from then on or to set foot in his house again. Swords were drawn, and Bazán was trying to make peace when three servants, ranging themselves beside Valdivieso, forced him to run pell-mell downstairs under a rain of sword-thrusts.

In the small square before the marquis' palace, the fight grew hotter. A number of the gentlemen in the city—Comendador Leonel de Cervantes; Juan Suárez de Peralta, the man who reported the incident; Mayor Juan de Sámano; and Juan Gutiérrez de Bocanegra, among others—foregathered immediately and positioned themselves beside either Luis Cortés or Valdivieso.

The townspeople, loath to miss an opportunity to watch the señores destroying one another, rushed up en masse and encouraged the fighters with shouts and whistles. The oidores had been informed of what was going on by the clerk of the court, Pedro Morán, and by common consent they met and ordered the town crier to announce a fine of two thousand pesos to be imposed on anyone who did not withdraw to his house immediately.

Luis Cortés and Hernando Pacheco were held in the town hall, and Valdivieso, being of lesser rank, was thrown into the public prison; but they were all released very soon because the Audiencia did not have the courage to impose much of a penalty. By the end of that same month, Agustín de Villanueva and Baltasar de Aguilar, "two of those who had lost face in the Bocanegra affair," were traveling through the streets in armed bands, looking for a quarrel with Martín. But Martín, forewarned, was going about escorted by his brothers, his friends, and his servants armed with garrotes hidden beneath their capes. No blood was drawn. Thanks to a host of mediators, Cortés gave up the thought of revenge, and the pitched struggle was resolved in a peaceful meeting where Villanueva's faction agreed they would merely gnash their teeth and lift their hands to their caps as the marquis' entourage filed proudly past his adversaries.

On June 17, another incident occurred. At ten-thirty one night, during one of his rounds of the city, Julián de Salazar disarmed one of the marquis' servants of his sword. Martín was at dinner at home when the servant told him what had happened. He sent out another servant and a page in livery to recover the weapon. The two men, armed with long swords and bucklers, behaved with such insolence that the mayor decided to disarm them, and they returned home shortly with a list of false grievances. Martín rose from his table in a rage and went into the street with his bodyguard and, meeting Salazar on the wooden bridge near the city hall, he heaped insults on him and took the confiscated weapons from him by force.

The Dark Line

Who was the first man to conceive the idea of a "country-wide uprising"? The trial that followed the so-called conspiracy of the Marqués del Valle reveals it in full course, and the angry judicial inquiries held in the sixteenth century to expose the guilty were as fruitless as the deductions of the historians of the nineteenth and twentieth centuries in their attempts to decide which bold brow was deserving of that crown. All that we can be sure of is that the private outbursts, the secrecy, and the constant irritation that the threat of imminent seizure provoked, and that faced them always, like a scarecrow, at length induced a widespread discontent and an atmosphere infected with rebellion, which was heightened by the incredible feebleness of the oidores.

All the obscure, ambitious, and somewhat eccentric characters who emerge in the hour of revolution now make their entrance on our limited stage, without previous notice, asserting their right to a place in history. Licentiate Espinosa de Ayala, a clergyman and prebendary of the cathedral; one of his friends, half rascal and half churchman, named Pedro de Aguilar; the two brothers Baltasar and Pedro de Quesada, a pair of youths without office or benefice; and Cristóbal de Oñate, an adventurer from the Peruvian wars, known as "the Boy" to distinguish him from his Conquistador uncle of the same name—all of them, scenting conspiracy, flocked to the house of Alonso de Ávila with a daring proposal.

The Licentiate Espinosa, who seems to have been on good terms with Alonso, took over the introductions: "These gentlemen have been most eager to see Your Mercy to kiss his hands and offer their services."

"I kiss Your Mercies' hands," Alonso replied, "and you may consider this house and all that it can offer you your own."

"My Lord Don Alonso, Your Mercy well knows," the prebendary explained, "the great discontent existing all over this country because of His Majesty's new decree that the encomenderos' grandsons may not inherit their encomiendas. . . ."

"I do not believe there is such a decree," Alonso interrupted.

"I swear to God by this cross," the priest exclaimed, "that a friar swore to me he had seen it and read it."

"Your Mercy seems to believe firmly that there is no such thing," added one of the group, "but we have heard what the Señor Licenciate says, and to make assurance doubly sure, the oidores do not pretend otherwise."

Shorn of circumlocution and courtesy phrases, to put it briefly, the men were talking of "arousing the country to rebellion." Alonso protested, then threatened to denounce them, and finally agreed to join with the daring Licentiate Espinosa de Ayala.

In this shadowy and unconvincing manner, Alonso de Ávila crossed the line separating respectable citizens from those flirting with crime and entered a dark and forbidden zone. The wealthy hidalgo was not moved by any compelling desire to exchange the splendor and security of his life for a conspirator's hazardous career, but matters had come to an intolerable pass. What would become of them if they were deprived of their slaves and lands? They would have to find work, beg alms, even dishonor themselves by working with their hands.

The Creoles were exasperated by an event that in other circumstances would have provoked only an innocent outpouring of ink and sealed paper. Two royal decrees had come with the fleet, under General Pedro de Roeles, that touched the port of Vera Cruz in September, 1565. One, based on Viceroy Velasco's reports, reinstated the suit over the number of vassals in the Del Valle marquisate; the other was the result of the suit filed immediately after Martín's first use of the silly seal which arrogated to him the title of duke, more than two years earlier, and restrained him from using it. These two decrees gave rise to a rumor, which spread mysteriously with the speed of a plague, concerning a third royal order decreeing the abolition of the encomienda.

Thus ended the long war of nerves, and the heavy machinery began to move slowly. From October to December, 1565, several meetings were held where untidy plans were discussed, weapons were readied, and the usual sin of amateur conspirators was committed. Compromising letters were exchanged. One of these, composed by Luis Cortés and Licentiate Ayala de Espinosa, announced that Alonso was in Mexico City for the purpose of advancing the conspiracy. This was sent with some others to three priests from Toluca in care of Pedro de Aguilar.

Aguilar met Alonso in one of his Indian villages, "situated between Cuauhtitlán and the estate of Gabriel Logroño." Alonso read the letter, then took the messenger into a closed room and said to him: "Señor Aguilar, these things are very secret and very intimate, for there are rascals whom a man cannot trust, and as Your Mercy is such a good man whom I hold as a friend, I shall tell you all that takes place concerning this affair."

Aguilar, better known by the disrespectful nickname of Aguilarejo (meaning, roughly, Eagle Beak), was moved. Never in the obscure life of this small-time rascal had an authentic gentleman revealed to him secrets of such importance. Through the window of the room he could see a cultivated field and hear the mournful songs of the Indian slaves. All that wealth was the property of the hidalgo who called him friend and confidant, without being asked, and he sat by his side, as equal to equal.

According to Alonso's statement, the Marqués del Valle had summoned him to his palace and told him in the utmost secrecy "that it seemed to him the king wanted to take the food out of all our mouths." They had discussed the matter carefully, and after looking at it from every angle they had concluded that they ought to arouse the country to rebellion, kill the oidores, the officials of the colony, and the son and brother of the dead viceroy, "may he rest in peace," Don Luis and Don Francisco de Velasco, both unsubornable partisans of the monarch. Yes, the king must be made to understand that he was not dealing with submissive vassals but with men who were ready to defend their estates with their lives.

The plan for the conspiracy was outlined. The means of carrying it out had not yet been determined, but already there was an unmistakable finality in its general outlines. But what was even more important, it brought about an agreement between the powerful Martín and Alonso de Ávila, who could enlist all the Creoles whose encomiendas were in jeopardy. Alonso then went on to reveal that he had spent four or five days in Mexico City engaged in "putting it into operation," and concluded the interview by giving Pedro de Aguilar a letter in which he promised to return to the city as soon as he possibly could.

A Masquerade: The Beginning of the Conspiracy

Alonso de Ávila made his appearance in the city on a Sunday, not by night as might be expected of a conspirator, nor with his face hidden in the folds of his cloak, but leading one of the noisiest masquerades recorded in the history of the colony. Those Creoles! The sound of barbaric music could be heard from afar, drowning out the ringing of the Sunday bells. Little by little the tumult drew near the Plaza Mayor, where the burghers and their pious ladies were coming and going at that hour.

The masquerade burst into the plaza to the muffled beat of the teponaxtle and the wailing of the flageolets. Alonso de Ávila, on horseback and followed by twenty-four horsemen, was dressed as the Emperor Moctezuma Xocoyotzin. A mask hid his face, but he was wearing the crown, the sumptuous mantle, and the sandals in which the unfortunate monarch had appeared before the astonished eyes of the Conquistadors more than forty years before. Behind him came musicians and dancers, and at the end of the procession, many slaves from the Cuauhtitlán encomienda, dressed in white and carrying stalks of flowers and enormous earthenware pots from which arose the piquant smell of Mexican cooking.

The masquerade crossed the plaza and came to a halt with a loud gabble of voices in front of the palace of the second Marqués del Valle de Oaxaca. Martín came through the gate, surrounded by pages bearing halberds, and Alonso got off his horse, half concealed by the smoke that arose from the censers, saluted him in the Aztec manner, then crowned his wife with a garland of feathers. A "buffoon" in the crowd that was watching the spectacle shouted appropriately, "Seize that crown, Marchioness!"

The instruments struck up once more. The gentlemen in the retinue passed out beautiful bouquets—called *suchiles* in Náhuatl—which held love poems and appropriate slogans. The one Martín chanced to be given contained a sentence not at all difficult to interpret: "Fear not the fall, for it is only to rise higher."

The mummery ended with the distribution of the bouquets. The whole thing was an attempt to represent the entry of Cortés in Tenochtitlán. Then, while the Spanish musicians tuned their instruments and the majors-domo were busy with the preparations for a ball in Alonso de Ávila's house, the masquerade moved on through the streets of the city.

At nearly midnight, the supper that Alonso had ordered to be made ready in his encomienda got under way. All the dinner service, made by the potters of Cuauhtitlán had been painted with this device:

and the marchioness' wine jug was larger than the others and also painted with that disturbing monogram. Even before the supper had ended, the oidores had one of those pitchers in their hands. The set of dishes, recently come from the wheel of the native potter, was new evidence of guilt. The proud crown and the capital R could be translated as an imperative "Thou must reign," addressed to the heir of Hernán Cortés by the Creoles.

When the tablecloths were removed, the mummers again rode through the city streets. By the light of torches, the Creoles held mock battles with balls of clay filled with flowers or ashes thrown at the leather shields, and daylight found them still engaged in this horseplay. Reeking of wine, white with ashes, they turned their horses homeward, taking care not to stumble over the sleepy merchants on their way to first Mass.

A Mirage of Words

The conspiracy, which had officially begun with the masquerade, the ball, and the youthful high spirits of that Sunday, was far more serious than the oidores suspected. With his mind made up to carry the rebellion forward, Alonso gathered together the interested principals in the armory of his house on the following Tuesday. Cristóbal de Oñate, the Quesada brothers, Aguilarejo, a wealthy Creole named Baltasar de Aguilar, Gil González, Licentiate Espinosa de Ayala, and Captain Baltasar de Sotelo were all there. Three of Alonso's servants—Gonzálo de Núñez, Juan de Victoria, and Méndez his major-domo—stood guard at the doors. The metallic sheen of the armor, the pistols, and the swords reflected the candlelight and filled the plotters with confidence. Alonso, seated at the head of the table, was stroking his golden mustache. A noticeable change had come over him. His fragility, his slender white hands, and the still delicate contours of his face seemed to be stamped with a manly resolution.

One of the Quesada brothers spoke. "I understand that Alonso has a plan. We should like to hear it."

"It's very simple," Alonso answered. "First of all, we must organize platoons of ten armed men under the command of a captain. On Friday, the day that the oidores meet in council, one platoon must meet surreptitiously in the main doorway of the royal apartments; a second will seize the armory. Meanwhile a third will enter the council room and put to death the oidores and the visitador."

"Is it necessary to kill them?" Baltasar de Aguilar asked.

Alonso, quickly: "And what else can we do with our enemies? If we do not kill them, they will kill us."

Oñate interrupted. "Let him go on with his explanation of his plan, or we shall never be done."

"When the oidores are dead, a prearranged signal will be given by one of our men who is to be posted near the fountain in the patio; this man will pass it on to another conspirator posted in the gateway to the street, who will be required to wave a red cape."

Several of the men exclaimed, "What is the point of that complicated system of signals? And waving a cape in the air?"

Alonso again: "Friends, that red cape will tell Licentiate Espinosa that the moment has come to ring the big cathedral bell twice."

"Would you please tell me," Espinosa interjected, "what is your object in having the bell rung twice?"

"That will be the signal for other platoons who will be already in their places; they will enter the houses of the royal officials and the Velascos and kill them," Alonso replied.

Espinosa was insistent. "But do I have to be in the bell tower?"

"Well, does Your Mercy suppose I can be killing the oidores and ringing bells at the same time?"

Espinosa, sighing: *"Allea jacta est."*

Quesada, quickly: "And then what? Ten stabbings won't settle everything."

"Then what? We'll throw the bodies into the square and make a bonfire of the papers in the archives, so it will be quite clear that royal justice has ceased to exist. The marquis, for his part, will be in charge of the square and he will speak to the people."

"Not all the encomenderos are on the side of the rebellion," Cristóbal de Oñate argued.

"We've taken that into account. We shall buy the defectors and the lukewarm ones with the money we seize from the royal coffers. Once we are masters of the city, Don Luis Cortés will march out with a squadron and take the fortress of San Juan de Ulúa and the ships in the fleet. The bastard, Don Martín Cortés, will march on Zacatecas and the other cities in the interior, and Francisco de Reinoso will be trusted to capture Puebla de los Angeles."

Everyone was hanging on Alonso's words. Lord, how easy, how feasible it all was! One man gives a shout in a corridor, another answers from the patio, still another waves a red cape as though inciting a bull, a bell rings twice, and the servitors of the tyrant vanish through a hatch stabbed in the chest. In the second act, a handful of brave little soldiers sallies forth, and behold, the king's fleet gives up without a struggle, Puebla de los Angeles, Zacatecas with its silver mines, Jalisco with its wheat fields—all New Spain surrenders by some verbal magic and falls into the hands of the Creoles.

And what then? Then comes the apotheosis, the grand celebration where fireworks shoot Bengal flares into the sky, cannon thunders, and a royal crown held by angels descends upon the head of the Marqués del Valle. "Philip the tyrant is dead! Long live Martín I, King of Mexico!"

The lovely delirium would not end there. Dukes, marquises, and counts would be created, a Creole nobility linked with the old Aztec nobility; the land would be reapportioned—"there was plenty for everyone"—the doors to world trade would be flung wide open, and the prelates, knights, and governors would be summoned by the sovereign and would swear the customary oath of allegiance to the king.

The conspirators had not neglected a chapter on international relations, and they thought first of all of the Pope. Dean Alonso Chico de Molina would present the pontiff with a load of rich treasure and implore him to grant the investiture of the kingdom. He would also negotiate an export treaty with the king of France, in exchange for a right of way through his territory on the way to the Holy Land. Licentiate Espinosa de Ayala was trusted not only to announce the capitulation by ringing the bell twice but also to execute the delicate task of rescuing Martín Cortés' eldest son from Seville and bringing back the heir to the throne on a ship carrying a cargo of Spanish wine.

Qualms of conscience? The man who thought of the wine with which to celebrate the victory had a convincing justification. The theologians who had lined up with the encomenderos, chief among whom were Don Chico de Molina and the Franciscan monk Luis Cal, argued that New Spain belonged more rightly to its conqueror, Hernán Cortés, than to the king who was trying to ruin it by unjust laws. Everything that had been said in secret was restated emphatically at the meeting of the conspirators. The tyrant Philip II must be made to understand that his subjects were men who knew how to defend themselves and their interests.

This plan for a rebellion, destined to be the first of a series stretching from that day to our own, was nothing more than a mirage of words. In the time of the Conquistadors, action was suited to words; they prayed to God, laid about them with their maces, and that was the way they made war. But the Creoles, brought up in another atmosphere, had lost the ability to face harsh reality. They had inherited nothing from their fathers but the fondness for narrative, the pleasure of the anecdote—the fascination with the word, both for its musical sorcery and its savor on the tongue, the word that did not transcend life but merely floated in the air held up by its own magic, as a heavy cloud will hang motionless above the yellow soil of the high meseta in winter.

New recruits were won every day. Alonso de Ávila, in one of the many meetings, showed a list with the names of a hundred and twenty conspirators and Martín Cortés, for his part, had written to his friends in Guatemala inviting them to join the revolt. They had replied that as soon as the countryside of New Spain had risen up in arms, "the same thing will be done here, and they will answer obediently and take the oath of vassalage."

A Flash in the Pan

The Friday set for the uprising went by, and the Creoles did not launch the revolution. What had happened? An accident as unnecessary and childish as the one that had set in motion the machinery of the conspiracy now put a spoke between its wheels and halted it. Alonso de Ávila, showing a legalistic turn alien to his character, had taken it into his head to have the plan for the rebellion set down in writing and signed by every man. As might have been expected, Cortés refused to put his name to the incriminating document, and the other conspirators argued that they would play their parts in the affair without having to attest it by their signatures.

A few days later, the Marqués del Valle was a changed man. When the conspirators went to him to offer him the crown of Mexico, he received them standing up and told them: "I would gladly help you, but I fear nothing would come of it and that in the end we should lose our lives and our property." It so happened that before his time a distant relative of his, Gonzalo Pizarro, had had a similar attack of delirium and had lost his head on the block. Thus the marquis was able to give them a grim example on the head of his ambitious kinsman; his uncertainty, apparent from the beginning, had grown. On the very day of the masquerade he had informed the visitador of the existence of a conspiracy, and had gone through the farce of arming his men. Not long afterward he told Valderrama himself, in the greatest secrecy, of a new plot. His version of it was that the Creoles would rise in Texcoco during a mock tournament that was planned in celebration of the wedding of Alonso de Cervantes. But when the conspirators themselves pressed him, he maintained that the uprising should be postponed until the arrival of the new viceroy, and that it would be best to wait until the decree seizing the encomiendas had been issued. In effect, then, he had coolly bowed out and was saying far and wide that these men were not to be trusted in the slightest.

The full weight of the conspiracy then fell on Alonso. In his house mysterious conversations went on in the armory between one hand of cards and the next deal. His parties became so lavish that they attracted new partisans, but without the decisive support of Martín Cortés the rebellion sustained itself only by inertia. In his fashion, Alonso was making every effort to keep the fire burning. One day he passed around a list containing the names of a hundred and twenty members of the conspiracy; another day he vowed that if the marquis persisted in being so evasive, he himself would force him at dagger's point to head the enterprise. Then again, he would decide to go ahead on his own account, as the only responsible leader, "for he was ready to die and he knew he had been informed upon."

On January 1, 1566, Alonso fell ill, and a period of calm ensued. Martín Cortés, vacillating between ambition and fear, presented himself to the Creoles as a willing if remote partisan, while to the visitador and the oidores he appeared to be a loyal vassal who could be trusted to inform them of the slightest attempt at rebellion among his own people. Martín, badly frightened by his own clumsy and characteristically secretive double game, preferred in the end to ignore the whole dangerous thing and wanted to accompany his wife to Toluca in February, but the visitador and his oidores dissuaded him from that plan on the pretext that they needed his help.

The departure of Valderrama, at the end of February or early in March, would rob the Creoles of a steadfast and powerful ally. In vain Cortés pleaded with him to postpone his voyage until the arrival of the new viceroy, and even wrote to him at Puebla, describing the conditions of unrest that prevailed all over the colony. (That would be one way to improve his health.) His attempts were useless. Without Valderrama there making a nuisance of himself, the Audiencia took effective command for the first time and began to assemble evidence of the conspiracy. Then the situation changed radically.

As the revolutionary efforts of the Creoles began to slacken and finally came to naught, the authority of the oidores rose proportionately to unprecedented heights. Curiously enough, neither of the opposing forces was at all successful in concealing its machinations from the other. Fray Miguel de Alvarado, the Augustinian prior and a relative of Alonso de Ávila, had full knowledge of what the Audiencia was engaged in; he interviewed Villalobos in an attempt to substantiate the secret information, and succeeded in dragging from him a promise not to go ahead with the judicial investigation. The marquis lent his support to the friar's persuasions. Indeed the country remained at peace, and the foment subsided into the whispers and nonsense of excitable people.

10

Ashes on the Forehead

I feel a great desire to lay aside, once and for all, those wars, barbarities, hecatombs, martyrdoms, actions of state, high-sounding names and disguises; a great desire to approach some very simple subject, narrowly chan-neled; the ordinary matters of ordinary people; of some human being, in short, I mean an actual figure; I don't know of what stamp or how he would be . . . but I should want him to be absolutely authentic and totally mine—do you understand?—totally mine.

Franz Werfel

On April 5, 1566, the conspiracy collapsed from within. Baltasar de Aguilar revealed the facts concerning it to Don Luis de Velasco, and, "almost by force," Velasco prevailed upon him to sign a detailed statement informing on the plot, which the brothers Alonso and Agustín de Villanueva also signed as witnesses. They represented the group of those loyal to the king and inimical to the marquis and his cohorts. Don Luis de Velasco, the future viceroy, was a discreet and intelligent man, waiting only for a chance to avenge himself on Martín for the grievances suffered by his father; the confusion and cowardice of his enemy made it easy for him to seize his chance.

Martín Cortés was reaping what he had sowed. The rebellion plotted by Creoles had failed because of the opposition of a group of counterrev-olutionary Creoles, as was to happen later in 1810.

On April 7 and 8, the dates of Palm Sunday and Holy Monday, Pedro de Aguilar made confession, took communion, and then informed two Dominican monks of the plot; though he did not confirm his accusation officially until May 28, the Audiencia had knowledge of it on that same Monday. Other denunciations came with a rush. Ayala de Espinosa followed in the steps of his accomplice, and the brothers Quesada, seeing the entire structure of the conspiracy threatening to topple over on them, brought their accusations to the court. Pedro de Aguilar went still further. He promised to remain in the conspiracy "the better to learn the truth," in his own words, "and, of course, to continue always to report on it, for my intention is now and has always been to serve His Majesty to whom I owe fealty as my king and lord."

What else could be expected of such people? Not one of the principal conspirators could be trusted, unless it was the reckless Alonso de Ávila. The Quesada brothers were "a pair of restless, debauched, and poverty-stricken youths." In addition, Pedro was beside himself because some relative stood in the way of his marrying one of the girls with whom he fancied he was hopelessly in love. Espinosa de Ayala, the prebendary of the cathedral and one of the most active instigators of the rebellion, justified the bad name that most of the clergy of the sixteenth century had earned for themselves. Alonso himself had dismissed him from his village of Zumpango where Espinosa had been vicar for selling a herd of pigs he had no right to. Unemployed and ill, he took refuge in the natives' hospital, which he left at night, dressed as an Indian, to carouse in the disreputable sections of the city where he kept some women—one Cristina de Arriata, a mestiza, and another named Leonor Ortíz—on the money he had got by pawning chalices and holy images from the hospital chapel.

The facts in our possession concerning Pedro de Aguilar, "Aguila-rejo," defined his character in a few broad strokes. This sly rascal, ostensibly engaged in selling cacao, had fled from Campeche in 1554 one jump ahead of the law; four years later he was wearing a cloak and bonnet; in 1565 he donned cape and sword; he loved gaming, drinking, and wenching, and he generously shared his village strumpets with his host, friend, and carousing companion Espinosa de Ayala.

Cristóbal de Oñate, in 1565, was a youth of twenty-three who had already seen something of the world. As a young boy he had entered the service of the Conde de Niebla, and he traveled with him to Peru when the count was appointed viceroy. He did not make his career in the Indies, however; at Niebla's death he sailed for New Spain, seeking the patronage of his uncle, Cristóbal de Oñate, the Conquistador. Here, by his own confession, he had been the *cavaliere servente* of Catalina de Salazar, Oñate's wife, and importuned his uncle for the money to go back to Spain.

On Wednesday of Holy Week, Baltasar de Aguilar went to the monastery of Santiago where Martín was lodging and told him of the betrayals. Martín asked for the keys, locked the doors of the monastery, and rode out with Bernardino de Bocanegra and his servants to comb the city. Aguilar returned on Holy Saturday with Agustín de Villa-nueva to try to make him see the danger he was running. On Easter Monday the marquis tried to exculpate himself to Villalobos the oidor. Was it his fault if some rash fellows had used his name in their loose talk? Had he himself not informed on the alleged plot? Villalobos calmed him. There was no evidence pointing to him, and the whole scandal dwindled into puerile braggadocio.

Creole Splendor

No sooner had the oidores returned to their favorite occupation of instituting lawsuits than the Creoles suffered a new bilious attack. Diego Ferrer, their court solicitor, informed them at great length by letter that the Council of the Indies was opposed to granting enco-miendas in perpetuity, and wished they would not insist on it. Meetings began again. Alonso de Ávila made his boast. "With his own hand and in the open street, he would kill the oidores himself with his pistols." The marquis spun his web of dreams of royalty, and the plan of the new conspiracy sported unexpected Renaissance trimmings. According to Torquemada's version of it, the uprising was to take place on June 21, San Hipólito's Day, during the solemn Procession of the Flag. At the corner of Calle del Tacuba and the marquis' little square, around the clock tower that flanked the square, the conspirators were going to build a large man-of-war, a kind of Trojan horse with cannon and soldiers concealed inside it. Once the parade arrived at the palace, the bastard Martín Cortés would descend from the clock tower to the ship at the head of armed men, start a mock battle, snatch the royal standard from the ensign—Alonso de Ávila was the standard bearer that year—and proclaim the marquis king; a volley of shots would give the signal to begin slaughtering the authorities.

All during June, Martín Cortés and his friends were so busy preparing the festivities to celebrate the christening of his newborn twins that this new conspiracy must be attributed to the overwrought imagination of the Franciscan historian.

The knowledge that they had been informed upon did not seem to worry the Creoles. The christening was to take place on Saint Peter's Day—the saint to whom Hernán Cortés had been most devoted—and the city wore a look of unusual activity. The merchants in their dark shops were selling lace from Flanders, rustling brocades, satins bright with metallic thread, and heavy velvets; the tailors, as at the time of Charles V's funeral, kept their needles constantly threaded. The knights had their armor polished, and the ring of hammers and the shouts of servants who were running a thousand errands throughout the city could be heard on all sides.

On June 30, rockets and bells brought the citizens out of their houses early in the morning. From time to time the wind billowed the tapestries and pennons hanging from the balconies, and their gold and silver embroidery glittered in the morning sunlight. Despite the threat of a second flood that had seemed imminent for several days—high water lapped and groaned against the pilings of the bridges—that morning was a respite between showers, such as poets love:

> *Everything is scented with summer, everything showers*
> *earth with soft sighs, and its essence is the fresh*
> *amber which nestles in the flowers.*

The Arabian *souk* on the Plaza Mayor had been transformed. A covered wooden walk—four yards high and six yards long—trimmed with flowers, escutcheons, and flags, extended from one of the balconies of Martín's house to the pardoners' door of the cathedral. The Indians, according to their custom, had transplanted a grove of trees, complete with rocks and streams, and set it in the heart of the city. Hunters armed with arrows, macanas, and blowguns chased the birds, tigrillos, and foxes that ran loose among the trees. The European music of violins, sackbuts, and lutes blended with the Mexican flageolets and teponaxtles, just as the world of medieval Spain met the world of the natives, united in honor of the grandchildren of the founder of their country.

Toward the middle of the morning, the procession began to cross the stage. At its head were the godparents, Don Luis de Castilla and his wife Doña Juana de Sosa, in plumed hats and glittering with jewels and rich fabrics. Twelve knights dressed in white point lace escorted Don Carlos de Zúñiga and Don Pedro de Luna, who were carrying the children, but when they came to the entrance to the covered walk, two knights in armor cut them off, and a mock battle ensued. One by one the guardians of the newborn children fell, until the godfather, drawing his sword, overcame the challengers with ease, and the procession resumed. The populace loved these medieval mock battles, and the gentlemen usually made no effort to shorten them.

When the dean, Chico de Molina, had poured holy water on the tiny heads of Pedro and Juana—Pedro was to be the last male descendant of the Conquistador—the procession resumed at the doors of the cathedral and was received with a booming artillery salute, bells, and the shouts of the people.

That night there were fireworks, a mock tournament, and a masquerade. Oxen, turkeys, and chickens crackled on the spits, and the marquis' cooks fed the citizens. Two great hogsheads of Spanish wine supplied the drink. Through the open windows of the palace the sounds of guitars and lutes and the merry voices of the diners reached the crowd.

The Creoles, in the grip of the devil, moved from a banquet to a dance, all unaware that during the festivities, mysterious groups of horsemen were roaming the city, keeping them under surveillance. Orozco, muffled in his cape, the Velascos, and a number of soldiers were putting the finishing touches to a busy day. Never had they felt closer to rebellion than on the day consecrated to the Apostle Saint Peter, amid festivities more appropriate to a king than to a marquis, as contemporary writers put it.

What Were the Princes of Aragon Doing?

The early days of July were filled with echoes of the baptism. The game of plotting had ended, and all anyone could recall of it was relief that it had not brought any unpleasant consequences. The city dropped back into the lazy rhythms of other years. The three oidores, ostensibly devoting themselves to settling the numerous lawsuits that poured into the courts every day, had actually been spending their whole time collecting evidence against the Creoles. By July 14 a pile of accusations, testimony, and detailed reports had accumulated on the desks of the council. All the angry exclamations of the Creoles, their committees, their plans, their speeches, their comings and goings, were set down there on paper, with terrible legal power, and all that was left for the oidores to do was to set the date and the manner of arresting the conspirators. This was no simple problem. One false step, one poorly timed arrest, one breath of scandal would give the Creoles cause to resist and the much-feared rebellion would be begun.

The arrival of a ship carrying royal decrees and letters from Spain in Vera Cruz gave the oidores their chance to arrest Martín Cortés outside his house without causing a scandal. On the afternoon of July 16 they sent a messenger inviting him to be present in the council hall to hear the results of the royal lawsuit. Martín crossed the square on "a jet black horse with a most beautiful bearing," followed by his lance page. The plaza was packed with people eager for news. The marquis, wearing a wide doublet of light-colored damask suitable for summer, his sword at his side, greeted his friends, smiling and confident.

"Ah, what good news we are about to hear!"

Two guards opened the doors of the great hall, and the oidores offered him a bench, then took their raised seats.

Orozco addressed the court in a voice that trembled somewhat: "Command what must be done."

Ceinos rose, saying: "Marquis, you are a prisoner of the king."

"Why am I taken prisoner?" Martín asked, unable to hide his astonishment.

"For treason to His Majesty."

"It's a lie!" shouted Cortés, raising his hand to his sword. "I am no traitor to the king, nor has anyone of my lineage ever been."

That was the first and the last manly impulse that history records of Martín Cortés. He had fallen into the hands of his adversaries, and neither his oaths of loyalty nor his hypocritical accusations availed. Three obscure lawyers, timid and not overly respectable, had caught the proud marquis, owner of thousands of slaves, by a childish trick, and the future king was held prisoner in his own imagined throne-room, accused of treason to Philip II. Nothing could be done. He delivered his useless sword to Ceinos, and was taken, half fainting and surrounded by guards, to one of the apartments of the Casas Reales, which had been designated as his jail. Suárez de Peralta writes: "He did not understand that he was in prison for being what he was, nor that the case could not have been set up without the king's consent to his seizure."

The high constable, Juan de Sámano, was ordered to arrest the brothers of the marquis. He found the bastard Martín Cortés at home, completely unaware of what had happened. Sámano approached him without preamble: "Those gentlemen," he said, pointing to his companions, "have come for Your Mercy."

Martín ordered his cape and sword but, as he made a move to gird it on, the constable stopped him. "Your Mercy may not wear this, because he is going as a prisoner."

"Why am I taken?" asked Martín, in almost the words his brother had used.

"I knew nothing," Sámano answered, "except that I have been sent to take Your Mercy prisoner, and as such I shall take you."

Out in the street, they had him mount the marquis' black horse; a lackey took the reins, two more held the horse's head, and Sámano escorted the former soldier to the Casas Reales, where a room had been prepared for him next to his half-brother's. Luis, the most belligerent of the family, was arrested without offering the slightest resistance.

While Sámano was taking the bastard Martín by surprise, the mayor, Manuel de Villegas, an intimate friend of Alonso, appeared at the Ávila house. No thought of the "pistol shots" by which he had intended to do away with the oidores entered Alonso's mind, and he handed over his sword with indifference. Gil González was seized on his way home from his encomienda, and he and Alonso were thrown into the dark cells of the courthouse dungeon in the rear of the city hall.

That same day the dean of the cathedral Alonso Chico de Molina and the priest Maldonado were jailed in the tower of the archbishop's palace, which served as a prison for the laity. One of the most distinguished Bible scholars, the guardian of the convent at Tlatelolco, was detained in a cell in his own monastery under serious charges.

On the following day, Comendador Don Luis de Castilla and his son, Pedro Lorenzo de Castilla; the brothers Bernardino Pacheco de Bocanegra, Nuño de Chávez, Luis Ponce de León, Hernando de Córdoba, and Francisco Pacheco—all five of them sons of the prosperous encomendero Hernán de Bocanegra; Lope de Sosa, Alonso de Estrada, and Alonso de Cabrera, blood brothers of Alonso de Ávila's wife; Hernán Gutiérrez de Altamirano, one of Ávila's closest friends; Don Juan de Guzmán; and many other Creoles of the highest ranking families in New Spain were all put under house arrest and threatened with death if they went outdoors.

Tyranny's Little Spree

The justices were in the saddle. In the beginning, they had been obscure satellites of the brilliant Don Luis de Velasco, and after the death of the viceroy—the one chance they might have had to rule—the despotic Valderrama dismissed his colleagues Villanueva and Puga from office and made them feel his contempt by labeling them useless. After Valderrama's departure, while the threat of conspiracy hung over their heads for months, they had had to pay their respects to Martín's wife, smile at the marquis, and suffer the scathing remarks, the secret meetings, and the slights of the Creoles. Then in a few days, these timorous, useless old men became absolute masters of the colony, by a trick that was to become familiar to the inhabitants of independent Mexico at a later date. The conspirators had delivered themselves over, bound hand and foot, and they were besieged with oaths of loyalty and promises offered them daily by the few feudal lords who had escaped justice.

The everyday aspect of Mexico City had changed too. The gates were already guarded by the time the bastard Martín entered the Casas Reales as a prisoner. For the first time, cannon loaded with grapeshot were placed in various strategic spots around the Plaza Mayor, and several platoons combed the city, rounding up citizens. Everyone was chal-

lenged with the customary *"¿Quién vive?"* ("Who lives?"), to which
the obligatory countersign was a saint's name and the stammered "King
Don Philip, our lord."

The soldiers patrolled the city night and day, never unbridling their
mounts. The records mention that volunteer guards under the command of Francisco de Velasco, who had been appointed Captain
General of New Spain, even committed the sacrilege of entering the
churches during divine services with the fuses of their arquebuses
lighted, searching for rebels.

Other absurd precautions were taken. Four hidalgos guarded the
apartment serving as Martín Cortés' prison, and even members of his
family were not permitted to see him. "As cowardly and remiss as the
oidores had been in the beginning," says Orozco y Berra, "so puffed up
and vindictive did they become in their hour of triumph." The petti-
fogging lawyer who had spent his life scribbling legal writs on foolscap
and envying the gentlemen could now boast of his power to harass the
Creoles, and, as usually happens during such little power sprees, so
frequent in the history of America, they merely made themselves
ridiculous.

One night a peaceable merchant named Villaberche was walking
through the Plaza Mayor on his way home when he was halted by the
night patrol with the requisite *"¿Quién vive?"* Hard of hearing, the
man understood he had been asked "Who goes there?" and he hastened
to reply, "Villaberche." The guards leaped on him, lifted him off his
feet, and carried him to the ditch that ran in front of the Casas Reales,
shouting, "Body of God! So Villaberche lives, does he?" Nearly overcome by the rain of blows the partisans dealt him, the burgher, cured of
his deafness, shouted, "No one lives but our lord the king!" He would
have been killed on the spot if one of the guards had not recognized him
and gone to his aid: "Stop, stop! For the love of God leave off! Don't
kill him!" he exclaimed, and in the end they helped the trusting
Villaberche out of the ditch. Battered, streaming with water, he went
home and next day he shut up shop and swore to stay behind locked
doors until not a soldier could be seen on the streets.

The city was in great turmoil, and the people made a thousand
conjectures. Those who hated Cortés and his friends "were saying
things they had been suppressing, on the pretext of serving the king,

and making plain what they had not dared to before." No one felt safe. Everyone feared he might be flung into prison at any moment, on orders from the Audiencia, and that he might forfeit his property. The friends of Cortés did not ask about him because they did not dare to, and once the case against the Ávilas had been filed, not a single lawyer would voluntarily undertake their defense.

Creole Literature and Other Excesses

The trial of the prisoners opened on the very day of their arrest. Alonso and Gil, as might be expected, denied all charges brought against them by the Audiencia that were based on the statements of the traitors. The three oidores laid aside their ordinary business and almost lived in the courtroom, taking testimony from witnesses and assembling the counts against the Ávilas; they set peremptory limits on adjudication. They dispensed with the usual expedient of dragging the truth from the accused by means of torture, and they conducted the trial so speedily that the brothers were sentenced by the end of July. They were condemned to be beheaded. Their heads were to be exhibited on pikes, their property to be confiscated, their houses razed, and a mark of infamy was to be posted on the spot they had occupied, as a warning to restless Creoles.

After hearing his sentence read to him, Alonso struck himself on the forehead and said, "Can this be possible?"

The clerk of the court replied: "Yes, sir, and it would be best for you to make your peace with God and entreat his pardon for your sins."

The condemned man persisted. "Can nothing else be done?" When he heard a second negative, he began to weep and lament. Suárez de Peralta, who has left us a detailed report of all that happened, for he was a witness close to events, seizes the occasion to compose one of those tender, tearful scenes which decorate his chronicle in such profusion.

Alonso is in his cell, surrounded by monks, clerks, and guards. The tears overflow his eyes and spill over his white face, "which was very handsome," and he was "a man of high breeding, and so well-cared-for and polished that they called him the queen."

After a while, the chronicler fetches a great sigh from his hero and has him speak with his face and beard wet with tears, this moving piece of rhetoric:

My children and my beloved wife! Can it be possible that this is happening to a man who meant to give you ease and great honor, after God, and to whom fortune has given such a contrary twist that you will be forced to see the head and countenance you loved on a pike, exposed to the weather and the night watchman, like the heads of the basest and most infamous of men whom justice punishes for atrocious and ugly deeds? Is this how you hoped to see me honored, my sons? Deprived of the privileges of a gentleman [here the disgraced aristocrat raises his voice] it would have been better for you to have been the sons of a lowborn father who never knew the meaning of honor!

In spite of the negative answer given by the clerk of the court, there still remained the recourse of appeal. The oidores accepted it when it had been drawn up by a wretched lawyer (of their selection), and after reviewing it they reaffirmed the sentence on August 2. Alonso was so stunned by the blow that he refused to sleep or eat while the last futile maneuver by the defense was being made.

Torn Carnations and Pitiful Embers

Preparations were under way for an unusual event in the Plaza Mayor. The August clouds floated like great heavy angels in a dusky orange sky. All the gentlemen of the city, on foot or on horseback, stood guard at the mouths of the streets, and artillery was emplaced. "In this way," says Suárez de Peralta, "the oidores protected themselves against the great fear that gripped them."

Ladies in bonnets, knights, merchants, Indians, mestizos, mulattoes, and Negros crowded together so closely that they seemed fused into a single compact mass. Everyone was weeping silently. The rich dried their tears on fine handkerchiefs, the poor with the backs of dark hands.

A play of light and shadow ushered in the night, and as dusk crept into the doorways surrounding the plaza with a belt of darkness, the battlements were still sharply defined against the summer sky. One window in the palace was lighted. The flame of a torch appeared amid the darkening throng, and then, as if that had been a signal, torches, lanterns, candles, and street lamps sprang to life; the faces of the weeping women emerged from beneath their veils, washed by a flickering yellow glow, and the beards of the men looked black against their white ruffs.

The palace clock began to strike eight over the noise of the rattle of chains and pulleys, as the condemned men were brought from the city prison. Across the drawbridge came Gil González de Benavides, with an escort of men on horseback. He wore a green wool riding suit and high leather boots. Behind him, mounted on a mule and surrounded by Dominican monks who were there to help him die well, came Alonso de Ávila. He wore velvet hose, a satin doublet, and a cloak of damask lined with fox fur. His hair was covered by a cap trimmed with gold and plumes, and if his nervous hands had not been telling the beads of an orangewood rosary—his sister, Sor María de Alvarado, had sent it to him in prison—anyone might have thought he was going out for one of his usual airings. Both men were wearing the clothes in which they had been arrested, and the feet of both were chained. When the people saw them, they cried and shouted. "The storm of weeping was such," Suárez de Peralta records, "that it was awful to listen to."

The prisoners knelt on the scaffold, recited the phrases of reconciliation, and ratified their declarations before the clerk of the court. Then an unprofessional headsman laid Gil out on the block "like a sheep," and "caused him to suffer some time, which was a very great pity," but finally managed to behead him. The outcry and the sobs of the people made his brother turn his head. Only when he saw the decapitated body of Gil did he understand that he too must die. Sobbing, he fell on his knees and began once more to recite the penitential psalms.

His white hand was twisting the tips of his mustache mechanically, and as the Miserere began he slowly raised it to untie the strings of his doublet. He was probably trying to gain time. Life had been one long festival for him, an uninterrupted game in which he had been lucky, and he could not believe that it was all about to end in such an unexpected, ugly fashion. He still cherished some hope. At the last moment the oidores would repent and grant him his life; his Creole friends would try to save him; angels would awaken him from a nightmare, and life would flow on, gay and leisurely, as in the past. But time was passing, and the longed-for miracle was not forthcoming. Alonso tried a pitiful appeal. With his eyes fixed on his house, visible from the scaffold, he cried, "Ah, my sons, and my beloved wife, and all whom I am leaving !" Fray Domingo de Salazar, later appointed bishop of the Philippines, hastily interrupted him.

"This is not the time, señor, for Your Mercy to do that; instead you should look to your soul. I hope in our Lord that your soul will fly straight to Him, and I promise you that I will say a Mass for your soul on the day of my patron, Saint Dominic."

Alonso again began the Miserere, and the priest, fearing an uprising, addressed the people: "Gentlemen, commend these gentlemen to God, for they say they are dying justly. Does Your Mercy not say so?" he asked, turning to the condemned man.

Alonso assented weakly. His eyes were bandaged—"It was easy to see how much he feared death," observes Suárez, whose horse's head was touching the planks of the scaffold—"and the moment he was laid down he raised his hand, uncovered his eyes, which seemed to revive him a little. He then spoke some words to the priest in secret. Then he bowed his head, the headsman gave him three blows, and his decapitated body fell noiselessly to the ground. Antonio Ruiz de Castañeda, one of the encomenderos, raised his eyes to heaven and, tearing his beard, swore to avenge these deaths.

The execution ended very late for the hours the colony kept. It was eleven o'clock at night when the crowd dispersed to their homes, bewildered and deeply moved. A smell of stables and of dust, smoky torches and spilled wax, filled the brightly lighted plaza.

Creole Honors to Their Dead

An anonymous ballad, written at the beginning of the seventeenth century, describes the episode as follows:

> *The bodies are headless now,*
> *stiff, ashen, and dead,*
> *carnations stripped of their petals*
> *as night finds their pitiful embers.*

Two men, followed by a monk carrying a taper, buried the Ávilas that same night in the church of Saint Augustine where the family maintained a private chapel.

The Creoles were fully aware that they had lost a decisive battle. The day after the beheadings a feeling of guilt and frustration was evident. "It was like a judgment," Suárez writes, "to see everyone saying openly that they had died as martyrs and that they did not deserve death." The conduct of the trial, the dramatic setting of the execution, the contrast between Alonso and the mean-spirited oidores—all defined in one bold stroke the line dividing the Spaniards and the Creoles. For all their apparent irresponsibility, their poor aptitude for action, their serious limitations, the Creoles formed a world apart, a united world of new people whose interests and attitudes were not only different from, but irreconcilably opposed to, those of the Spaniards.

In the icy moment of repression, some Creoles reacted like Antonio Ruiz de Castañeda. They expressed their indignation at the thought that they had been made victims of boundless injustice in words, without reckoning that words had been to blame for the failure of the conspiracy and the death of the Ávilas. The Creole's lack of imagination led him to view his timid defenders as martyrs; after all, they were defending his rights, and for that he exalted them and rendered them homage, thereby marking another difference between Conquistadors and Creoles. To the Conquistador, heroism was a goal, consciously achieved by his own efforts in Europe and the Indies. The Creole, born in a colonial setting, is misled by the distance between the word and the deed and he fails in his first try for independence before he has actually fought for it. He surrenders because he considers himself beaten in advance; when he comes face to face with tragedy he is as frightened as a child, and considers himself a martyr. He weeps over his martyrdom and plans his own funeral.

Suárez writes:

> Never had a day been seen of such confusion and great sadness, shared by everyone, men and women alike, as when they saw those two gentlemen brought out to their execution; for they were much loved, and rich and distinguished besides, men who had never done harm to anyone, but rather had always contributed to their fatherland and honored it.

A few days after the executions, as Juan Suárez de Peralta was making one of his usual rounds of the city, he halted his horse near the gallows on which the heads of the Ávilas were exhibited. They seemed to him sunk in a deep sleep, and he imagined Alonso as he had looked in the street on his last day, riding a beautiful white horse with trappings of embroidered velvet and followed by his lackeys and pages. "To see him in this state now!" A huge spike had been driven into his delicate flesh and his brain through his "fragile skull." The mustache that he used to stroke and twist and keep so neat, the "silky hair" that was "curled and dressed with such care to make it beautiful," now fell lankly down the sides of his face, exposed to rain and wind.

"And all because of the greatest of misfortunes! That rich gentleman, associated with everything that was best in the town, lost his life, his honor, his estates all in one moment and suffered the death of the lowest of ruffians." The Creole let his tears flow as he sat there on his horse. "In all my life," he concludes, "I do not know when I have wept so, at the thought of what the world has revealed in what I saw before me."

11

Tragedy, Expiation, and a Moral

The dead whom you kill enjoy good health.
Don Juan Tenorio

Throughout the trial, Martín had defended himself weakly. In all the pleas for acquittal entered in the course of his legal maneuvering, not a trace can be found of the sagacity and raw courage that had made the name of Hernán Cortés famous. Suárez de Peralta formulates this accurate judgment in summing up his attitude toward the oidores. "The confession which the marquis made was far different from what his intelligence and vivacity might have promised."

Undoubtedly there is a great discrepancy between the Creole's intelligence and vivacity and his manner of confronting life. As long as he is letting his fancy roam, playing, or conversing, the three things he liked best, the Creole reveals a refined mind, a soaring spirit, and a sympathetic understanding, but when the moment of action strikes, he suffers an obvious and painful truncation. We must take into account here that the Creole was his father's heir, but he departed from that legacy at times. He inherited greed, exile, an obsession with aristocracy, and, as we have seen, a fascination for words; but to all that was added an elegance and a feeling for rhetoric far beyond what the Conquistador, a man of the people, could appreciate. The periods in which they lived gave rise to their differences. The father had lived at the dawn of the Renaissance, when the newly opened world was offering itself, full of promises for heroes. Their hunger for glory and for earthly joys was satisfied by grasping the sword, crossing oceans, or conquering empires rich and strange. The son, on the other hand, was born in a colonial atmosphere peopled with echoes of the past, a smooth, debilitating atmosphere rotten with wasted creativity.

Nothing that was integral to New Spain belonged to him. Even the underpinning of his life—the encomienda—did not come to him as a solid inheritance, but on deposit, as it were, and subject to unforeseeable contingencies. He had its usufruct, but not its permanent possession. We must recognize in the Creole's desire to insure the perpetuity of the encomienda a strong urge for affirmation rather than greed. In spite of his wealth and his place at the top of the hierarchy, the Creole felt that he had been left hanging in midair. Alonso de Ávila and the Marqués del Valle, the two types of eminent Creole of the sixteenth century, held their property subject to the vicissitudes of a lawsuit; at any moment they might lose their slaves and the lands which were their reason for being.

A Sheep among Wolves

The oidores had had very little rest from July 16, when the rebels were arrested, to the middle of September. The trial of Martín Cortés was moving slowly. In spite of the weakness of his defense and his fall from grace, he was too powerful a man for the oidores to dare sentence him to the death suffered by the Ávilas. Luis, on the other hand, a second son and a bastard, could be sentenced straightaway—he was condemned to be beheaded and to lose his property—and they were confident that once the routine appeal had been denied, his empty, finicking, talkative head would be cut off.

That is how matters stood when the news reached Mexico City that the new viceroy, Don Gastón de Peralta, Marqués de Falces, and his wife Doña Leonor de Vico, had landed in Vera Cruz without previous notice. The viceroy was ignorant of the recent occurrences in New Spain. Three leagues out of Vera Cruz the master of a trading vessel had informed him casually of the deaths, imprisonments, and complications resulting from the conspiracy of the Creole encomenderos. This aroused the viceroy's suspicions, and he stayed on board ship for the rest of the day. On July 18 he disembarked, already concentrated on the problem. For five days he heard reports from various people and read a volume of contradictory letters, for whereas the partisans of the king described to him a state of dangerous insecurity, those on Martín's side spoke of peace undisturbed except for the weakness and cowardice of the authorities. As soon as he was able to form a judgment, he ordered the Audiencia to suspend all trials, and on July 22 he started on his way to the capital, with an escort of twenty-four halberdiers and twelve of his own servants armed with lances; he entered it on October 19, amid the customary festivities.

The viceroy's arrival was greeted with widely diverse reactions. The friends of Cortés viewed it as a miracle from God which would free many innocent men from the hands of the "judicial butchers." But the realists, in their pessimistic fashion, held the opinion that the Marqués del Valle "was in greater danger, because the viceroy would take care not to oppose the king." Suárez writes:

And it was wondrous to hear what was being said on one side and the other; and it is certain that if the oidores had understood the intentions of the viceroy, they would not have waited but would have beheaded the marques and his brother before the viceroy's arrival in Mexico City. This is quite beyond doubt, and I know it from someone who knows.

The Marqués de Falces, third viceroy of New Spain, was a worthy successor to Don Antonio de Mendoza and Don Luis de Velasco. His just and benevolent mind and his innate nobility were not suited to the spite and the machinations of the oidores. Once again, aristocrat and lawyer—swordsman and penman—had met face to face, and that confrontation was to revive an old conflict in which only the participants were different.

Don Gastón de Peralta immediately took steps to dissipate the atmosphere of terror that was hanging over the city. The artillery and guards posted in the streets were withdrawn. The prisoners' condition was eased. The viceroy examined the trial papers carefully, with the aid of the prosecutor Céspedes de Cárdenas, and he himself questioned several of the imprisoned men. Little by little, normality was restored. A ring tournament was held "with more than enough galas and inventions" in which Suárez de Peralta and Agustín de Agurto played leading roles "for, although [Agustín] was a man of letters, he was very much a horseman." Suárez explains, always mindful of the money spent on festivals: "The festival cost us a good many ducats, and we held it in front of the palace windows. The marquis was there with the viceroy, which was in itself no small insult to the oidores . . . They were most indignant."

The power they had acquired thanks to the favors of the Visitador Jerónimo de Valderrama had fled them overnight, in the brusque manner in which such things always happen to officials of the Crown. Don Gastón de Peralta destroyed the entire judicial edifice which they had patiently built. The realists, so active a short time before and ever alert to political change, prudently kept their mouths shut and tried to conciliate the Marqués del Valle, at any cost. Baltasar de Aguilar, one of the first of the accusers, was seen often in the palace or going out to hunt with the viceroy, and he even retracted his accusations and made friends again with Martín Cortés.

The oidores, elated by their easy victory over the Creoles, had become accustomed to exercising their power without fear of contradiction; they were far from being the meek officials of Valderrama's time. In secret, they began gathering incriminating data against their enemy, the new viceroy, in the same way as they had built the trap for the conspirators. "The things longest forgotten," says Suárez, "usually come out at the most damaging time." The oidores recalled that in his days as a courtier Martín Cortés had been singled out by the king of France in preference to other Spaniards in Philip II's suite; and this recollection, seemingly innocent, led to the equally forgotten fact that the fief of the Marqués de Falces, situated in Navarre, had been French originally, and that the marquis was related to the Gallic monarch. It was only natural and logical, then, that the two marquises with similar backgrounds had formed a partnership "to rise up against the country" with the aid of the king of France, "to whom they would grant the right to trade and a certain amount in tribute." The oidores bolstered this theory with certain convincing arguments. Falces had commuted Luis Cortés' sentence, which had already been confirmed on appeal, to the much gentler punishment of forfeiting his property and serving ten years in Oran at his own expense. Falces had had the temerity to attend a public festival in the rebel's company; he had used his influence to persuade the informers to retract their accusations; and he had consistently followed a policy of extreme benevolence that was bound to endanger the security of the colony.

According to Torquemada's statement in his report to Philip II, the resentment of the oidores reached outlandish proportions. They did not stop with a vague hint of rebellion, but spoke of exactly thirty thousand armed men whom the viceroy and the Marqués del Valle had raised for that purpose. How did they arrive at this exact number? Torquemada hastens to tell us. Don Gastón de Peralta, in the course of repairing and redecorating the palace, had commissioned a broad mural commemorating an early battle "and that was their grounds for saying that he was holding men against the kingdom, for they took what was being painted for live men," a conclusion which, while it reveals something about the way the history of the sixteenth century was written, also reveals something that is not to be scorned about Mexican mural painting.

The Marqués de Falces promptly dispatched his voluminous reports to Spain. He had added to the routine notification of his arrival and the summary of current business a report on the order and peace reigning in the colony, which was based on the statement of a great many witnesses. Both his correspondence and that of the oidores traveled by the road to Vera Cruz, signed and sealed, where a dispatch ship was waiting. But lo, the ghostly and rapacious hand of His Majesty's Prosecutor Ortuño de Ibarra, who had been won over by the oidores, performed a simple piece of legerdemain and made the viceroy's entire mail disappear, but took great care to insure that the bulky packet of charges and accusations drawn up by the oidores should reach its destination.

Don Gastón de Peralta, unaware of what had happened in Vera Cruz, continued to review the decisions of the court. It was evident that as long as the Marqués del Valle remained in the colony, the incidents fomented by the so-called partisans of the king and the Audiencia would continue. On the other hand, Martín's trial ground to a halt. The marquis had challenged Ceynos and Orozco, and this challenge, writes

Orozco y Berra, "was an indication that the other ministers would meet a similar fate, and then there would be no judges left to sentence him." Finally, after a great deal of legal maneuvering, it was agreed that Martín, Dean Chico de Molina, and Espinosa de Ayala, and their respective files, should be taken to Spain on one of Juan Velazco de Barrio's vessels.

Endless arguments ensued over the question of adequate surveillance over the prisoners during the dangerous journey to the port, and the oidores excused themselves one after another, for fear of a hypothetical assault by Martín's partisans. The sons of the high constable were related to Luis Cortés; and gradually all the other candidates for the job turned out to be incompetent or full of convincing excuses. In the end, the Audiencia put it to the viceroy to fulfill his agreement and was "content to apply pressure to their enemy and to throw the responsibility on him if some scandalous act should occur."

The viceroy used a gentleman's expedient. On February 22, 1567, he had Martín Cortés appear before the secretary Gordian Casasano and Don Pedro Bui, Knight of Calatrava, to pledge his allegiance as a *hijodalgo* to the rule of Spain that he and his wife would embark on the *Esterlina* and that he would present himself within a period of fifty days before the Council of the Indies "all under pain of what may befall a gentleman hidalgo or whatever he may incur if he should break or fail to fulfill his pledge of fealty."

The oidores cackled with vexation and alarm, unable to grasp the significance of the ceremony. The Marqués de Falces answered them disrespectfully. "Princes, galleys, fortresses, offices, and other things of great worth are entrusted to gentlemen hidalgos under their pledge of fealty; the marquis is leaving under the best safeguard of all, so great is its binding force."

The Stage Is Set

The oidores' exaggerated reports of the conspiracy and their venomous indictments of the Marqués de Falces arrived on Philip II's desk, while the viceroy's juggled correspondence remained in New Spain. Philip followed his usual practice of appointing deputy judges and placed the fate of the colony in the hands of the licentiates Jaraba, Alonso Muñoz, and Luis Carrillo, in a decree issued on June 26, 1567. These men were granted the power of passing judgment on the highest official and the humblest citizen alike. The sentences they passed could be reviewed on appeal only by themselves, and when once they had reviewed a case no further legal step could be taken, even if the monarch himself should intervene.

In order to grant these judges still greater powers, it was ordered that as soon as they arrived in New Spain the Marqués de Falces was to take ship for the metropolis and leave Licentiate Muñoz in his place, though without the title of viceroy.

The appointment of the judges and the dismissal of the viceroy soon became known in Vera Cruz, swiftly followed by news of the death of Jaraba at sea. The two deputy judges lost no time in demonstrating their good will. Informed of the departure of the Marqués del Valle, Muñoz struck himself on the forehead—all Suárez de Peralta's characters have this ugly mannerism—and exclaimed, "Can it be possible that he is not in the country, and that he is alive?" Carrillo commented, referring to the oidores: "How can it possibly be that those gentlemen have not bloodied their hands with the marquis' head? His Majesty would have been well served, and very thankful to them."

The deputy judges' disappointment was understandable. After spending their lives sequestered in the Council of the Indies, scribbling official papers and torturing insignificant criminals, they had been given the undreamed-of chance to occupy a position of power for the first time and to pass judgment on a genuine marquis, only to be greeted with the bad news that the prisoner had placed himself beyond their jurisdiction. What good were the other conspirators, all second- or third-generation Creoles, compared with the son of Hernán Cortés? A single case like that, skilfully handled, would have assured their preferment, and they might even have attained high position on the Council of the Indies or in the colonies. To offset their disappointment, they ordered the construction of a new prison before they even began their journey to the city. They could foresee that the cramped prisons then in use in Mexico City, the king's and the municipality's, would be inadequate to confine the prisoners whom even one hard-working judge would feel obliged to supply in a continuous stream. The deputy judges' orders were carried out with such dispatch that the prison was finished by the time they entered Mexico City. In his *Tratado* Suárez de Peralta likens it to the prisons of the Holy Office, with their tiny dark cells barred with heavy grillework and window openings "a palm and a half" in size, through which the prisoners' food was passed. They soon became famous, and many years later people were still calling them "Muñoz's dungeons" in memory of their benevolent builder.

The Impious Reign of the Penny-Dreadful

On the whole, the work of the busy judges can be compressed into one gigantic adjudication, one enormous trial almost unexampled in the history of America. Beheadings, imprisonments, and tortures went on every day, creating a chamber of penny-dreadful horrors. Let us take the case of Baltasar de Aguilar, one of the first informers. It did him no good to accuse the Marqués de Falces of coercing him or to claim that his first denunciation had been the true one. Muñoz ordered him put to the torture, "the fiercest torture ever seen," and kept him in prison "broken to pieces," irremediably condemned and watching death approach with a terror that rises from the pages of the *Tratado* and wets them with his tears.

Carrillo and Muñoz had hit upon a way of notifying the prisoners of their sentences that was not without theatrical imagination. After midnight the clerk of the court would appear in a cell, accompanied by a confessor and the warden of the prison. He would read the judges' decision to the victim and go away, leaving the representative of religion with the condemned man. At dawn, the mule that was to carry him to the scaffold, a crucifix, the headsman, and the town crier with his trumpet would all be waiting for him at the door.

Fortunately for him, Baltasar de Aguilar was not alone in his cell. He had as companions his old accomplices the Quesada brothers, who had been imprisoned for some inexplicable reason. The Quesadas had barely heard the news of the deputy judges' arrival at the distant mine where they were living before they rushed to Mexico City with the twofold object of "kissing their hands" and reminding them of the outstanding services they had rendered the king by informing on the existence of the conspiracy. But to their vast surprise, instead of being given a reward or at the very least some token of gratitude, they had been thrown into prison. They had no cause for alarm. "They bore their imprisonment very happily" in the security of their innocence, and devoted their time, when they were not being questioned, to the merciful task of consoling the stricken Aguilar. They promised to care for his children and look after his wife, who was a relative of theirs, in the sad but imminent event that he should have his head chopped off.

One night, after midnight, the warden Juan de Céspedes shot back the bolts and went into the cell with a monk and a clerk of the court. Aguilar, nearly out of his wits, picked up his crucifix and knelt, weeping and beating his breast, then began to bewail his fate and shout out his sins. Baltasar was completely undone; he crawled across the floor, embraced the monk's knees, and begged him to hear his sins. The monk talked about divine mercy, and the Quesada brothers, from their beds, attempted to calm their comrade and promised to have a great many Masses said for his soul. Then the clerk of the court began to read the sentence by torchlight: "Señores Don Pedro and Don Baltasar de Quesada, now hear this: the illustrious señores Don Alonso Muñoz and Don Luis Carrillo hereby sentence you to be beheaded and to forfeit all your property. . . ."

A romantic bolt of lightning, a totally melodramatic bolt, struck the cell and turned the actors in this drama to stone. The brothers rose from their beds, stunned. "Is that true, Señor Secretary?" The reply was admirable (if we may so qualify it, in keeping with the pathos of the scene). "Yes," said the clerk, "and you need entertain no doubt. So Your Mercies must avail yourselves of the little life that is left you by begging God's forgiveness and behaving like gentlemen, for this is the crucible in which men's courage is refined. Take comfort, Your Mercies, and make your peace as Christians."

Baltasar could not believe in his good luck until he saw the clerk of the court leave. He dried his tears, dropped the crucifix, and, stepping into the earlier role of the Quesadas, he consoled them and doubled the number of indulgences and Masses they had promised him.

The little bells of the escorts were heard very early in the prison gateway and people began to gather, certain that Aguilar was the next to be executed. Two mules and two crucifixes surprised the curious. When the Quesadas appeared, "it was wondrous to see the people beat their breasts and weep; their cries rose to heaven, for these gentlemen were well beloved and much honored, and in all the city there was no one who had thought otherwise than that they were the freest of any who served the king."

On January 8, young Cristóbal de Oñate left the prison, tied hand and foot, and was lifted onto a mule wearing a pack saddle. He was paraded slowly through the streets of the city, with his head bowed, while the crier Juan de Simancas, as at Quesadas' execution, shouted: "This is the justice which His Majesty has ordered done to this man for being a traitor and for having committed the crime of rebellion. He orders him hanged and quartered; he who does such must pay for it so."

No witnesses or weeping relatives were present at the execution of the stunned and helpless youth. By the middle of the morning his body hung from the gibbet in the center of the busy plaza, and the final warning of the crier seemed to hang over it with a thread: "Let no person dare to take this body from the gibbet without the consent of the gentlemen of His Majesty's council under pain of death."

At the same hour that Cristóbal de Oñate was hanged, Martín Cortés, the bastard, was being tortured in the dungeon. At that time he was more than forty years old, and his body bore the scars of wounds received in the service of the Crown. He was stretched on the rack and suffered all the agony of the cords. To every question he replied, "I have already told the truth, and I have no more to say than what I have said." Muñoz then ordered six pints of water administered to him, to break his resistance. At the fourth, Martín exclaimed, "By the most sacred name of God, have pity on me, for I shall say no more from now until I die." At the final pitcher—the tortured man was practically drowned—Muñoz stopped the torture for fear that the long-suffering mestizo would die.

There Was Gnashing of Teeth

The days that followed the execution of young Oñate were days of terror for the inhabitants of the city. No one could feel sure he would not fall into the hands of the examining judges. A man might be condemned to death for a word or for a silence, for taking part in the rebellion or for knowing nothing about it. The case of Baltasar de Sotelo illustrates well enough the manner in which Muñoz and Carrillo conducted the trials. Baltasar, a rebel captain in the bloody Peruvian wars, was arrested and imprisoned on the grounds that his brother, a wealthy alderman named Diego Arias Sotelo, had been among those suspected of taking part in the conspiracy. Questioned about his past in Peru, he showed a safe-conduct, and for the sole reason that his rank of captain was mentioned in it, the judges sentenced him to be beheaded. "He died," says Suárez de Peralta, author of the account, "like a good gentleman and a good Christian. Everyone pitied him."

Such sinister spectacles had become daily bread. People whose names had never figured in the conspiracy or in any previous court proceedings were suddenly marched off to the scaffold. Alvarado, an unknown soldier, and Alonso de Ávila's servants—Gonzalo de Núñez, Juan de Victoria, and Méndez, the major-domo—were quartered with little ceremony. Of the whole group, the major-domo "aroused the greatest pity," because he had reached the "honorable age" of eighty, and his hair and beard were white—"he had not a single hair that was not white"; he was gouty in both feet so that he had to climb up the gibbet on crutches.

The brothers Bernardino, Fernando, and Francisco Pacheco Bocanegra, of one of the leading families of New Spain, suffered unspeakable torments. All three had been subjected to the rack and the water torture and, although none of them ever confessed, Bernardino was condemned to death for his intimacy with the Marqués del Valle. He had made his last confession; the crucifix, the mule with its pack saddle, the monk, the hangman, and the crier were waiting in the gateway of the prison; then the city watched a scene that interrupted the monotonous parade of hangings and beheadings. Bernardino's mother and his wife and her relatives, escorted by prelates from the religious orders, came through the streets toward the Casas Reales. The women allowed their black mantles to drag on the ground; they were barefoot, their hair was disheveled, and they were weeping so "that it was the greatest pity to see them." When they were brought before Carrillo and Muñoz, they prostrated themselves on the floor of the audience chamber and begged in the name of Christ's passion to be granted an appeal. The judges—this was their one act of clemency—ordered Bernardino returned to his cell and later, on review, they sentenced him to forfeit his properties, perpetual exile, and to serve twenty years on the king's schooner.

Baltasar de Aguilar Cervantes was rescued from death by his aunt, Doña Beatriz de Andrada, the wife of Francisco de Velasco who was a brother of the lact viceroy. Doña Beatriz managed to have his sentence of decapitation commuted after judicial review to a punishment like Bocanegra's. Juan de Valdivieso, Antonio Ruiz de Castañeda, the imprudent encomendero who had torn his beard at the Ávilas' execution and sworn to avenge their deaths, and Garcia de Albornoz, another who perhaps had spoken rash words, were exiled from the city of Mexico for a period of five to ten years.

History Repeats Itself

Stacks of anguished letters meanwhile had been piling up on Philip II's desk—that intricate little world, that mirror, that fine sieve, that be-all and end-all of life in the Indies. The happenings of those three years could not be contemplated without bitterness. The unbroken parade of petty tyrannies, hangings, decapitations, dungeons, exiles, tortures, and unjustified confiscations, all the bloody garbage of the colony, had originated in the self-seeking crimes of a few scoundrels. The Ávilas had refused to confess, until a bishop dragged from them a stammered "yes" in order to calm the indignation of the people. The bastard Martín Cortés had denied his participation in the plot, like the other conspirators, and words spoken under torture cannot be given the weight of convincing proof. The papers that covered Philip's desk were the final fruits of that obscure colonial plot. Mothers, wives, and children called to him from across the ocean, begging for mercy. Alonso de Múñoz had gone completely mad. The charm and the influence of the Indies, that strange influence under which lawyers become bloody butchers, finally turned Muñoz's head, and he had to be speedily removed from New Spain. Philip signed a decree appointing Licentiates Villanueva and Puga to replace the deputy judges, the very oidores whom Valderrama had dismissed as useless. As the end of a complicated episode drew near, colonial history brought back onstage the characters who had long since made their exits.

Puga and Villanueva, restored and in the role of saviors, sailed immediately on a dispatch ship and arrived in Mexico on Tuesday of Holy Week. Over the city, from time to time, was heard the sleepy chirring of the wooden rattles. Almost nobody was in the streets. The gentlemen were making retreats at the monasteries and the commoners sought sanctuary in the churches, praying and chanting in front of the altars draped in purple.

Muñoz was in the monastery of Santo Domingo, participating in the Holy Week services from a canopied platform which he had ordered set up in the presbytery. He was surrounded by halberdiers and would withdraw later to the luxurious cell which the Dominicans had prepared for him.

As soon as Puga and Villanueva reached the city, they hurried to the audience room. Orozco, Ceynos, and Villalobos were sitting there motionless, dressed in black, reviewing cases and handing down decisions. When the royal decree was read to the oidores, and they learned that they were being reinvested with a power that had been in dispute for so long, their great rejoicing ill became their years, their beards, and their serious position. They leaped with joy and flung the court papers into the air—and then a difficult problem arose. Who was going to notify Muñoz of his dismissal? Ceynos, Villalobos, Orozco, and Puga, all cowed, refused the chance to take revenge on their irascible colleague; after a long argument, they agreed that Villanueva, the boldest of them, should notify him on the following day.

On Wednesday, a dark day, Villanueva went to Santo Domingo followed by Puga and the secretary Sancho López de Agurto. They were told that Muñoz was asleep in his cell and had issued peremptory orders not to be disturbed. Villanueva grew tired of waiting and had himself announced by a page, but another long half hour went by before Muñoz would let him enter the room.

"The deputy judge," Orozco y Berra writes, "had something distressing and repugnant about him." To judge by descriptions, his face was not exactly ugly but repellent, and his whole physical makeup exuded a horrible vulgarity, inspiring a feeling of nausea that has come down to us intact. His overweening pride was in the worst possible taste. An old man, stiffly pedantic, he always kept his cap on; he spoke without looking at his interlocutor, and to persons of high rank granted a slight inclination of his head. He kept around him at all times a guard of twenty-four halberdiers.

He received Villanueva seated in an armchair, contenting himself as usual by lifting a hand to his hat. Villanueva asked him, as a mere formality, how he had passed the night, and he answered drily that "he had spent it somewhat poorly and, were it not for his coming, he would not have got up." "With all due respect," Torquemada comments, "he seemed more like an arrogant god than a man." This surly reception exhausted Villanueva's patience and, taking the papers from his bosom, he handed them to the secretary Agurto, saying: "That he should read this decree from His Majesty and notify the Señor Licenciado Muñoz of it immediately."

The decree ordained that, within three hours of its being served on Muñoz, he was to drop all his business and leave for Spain without any delay "under pain of losing his property and his head at the hands of the Audiencia." The farther Agurto read, the longer grew Muñoz's face. At the end he was completely dumbfounded.

Torquemada, who saw the hand of providence at work in the removal of the tyrant from the stage, embroiders the final scene with a few dramatic touches. Muñoz, stripped of his platoon of halberdiers, left the monastery and, at the end of the three hours allotted him, fled the city in haste, accompanied by Carrillo, terrified of the people's vengeance. The two criminals were on foot and unattended, carrying their goods on their backs, and if some compassionate soul had not lent them horses they would have had to walk all the long, rocky way to Vera Cruz.

The Serpent Bites Its Tail

Since the conspiracy had been broken, New Spain had breathed a charnel-house air. Some victims moldered forgotten in their tombs, and others groaned in the dungeons or pulled oars on His Majesty's galleys while they waited for death. The field where the knights used to joust in mock tournaments had been abandoned; the widows were beginning to be resigned, and dangerous topics of conversation were avoided everywhere. The priest Espinosa, his accomplice Aguilarejo, the bastard Martín Cortés, his brother Luis, the Bocanegras, and so many others who had played a part in the revolt had made their exits, and we have no way of tracing their footsteps on the trampled highway of life. The Creoles, cured of their libertarian intentions, considered themselves lucky to receive a crumb from the viceroy, and the second Marqués del Valle de Oaxaca made up his mind to pursue his litigation, in the hope of recouping his losses and wiping out as well as he could the stigma of traitor that had besmirched his new escutcheon.

So fared the victims, guilty or innocent, of Mexico's first attempt at libertarian revolution. But what had happened to the executioners? Would they live in peace to the end of their days, trying to conjure away the punishment awaiting them in the next world by good deeds and a timely remorse? Fate, doubtless bearing in mind the literary implications of our story, did not will it thus, and wrote an epilogue that would bring together the judges and the condemned, the executioners and the victims in a spot where all would be held equally culpable. We alone can survey them, in their benevolence.

"The mysteries of chance!" Don Luis González Obregón says sententiously, taking his cue from events. The current attraction in the port of Vera Cruz might well justify the exclamation of this tedious reporter. The Marqués de Falces, accompanied by his wife and the members of his household, numerous convicts sentenced to exile from the paradise of the Indies, and the magnificent gentlemen Alonso Muñoz and Luis Carrillo were all met there, waiting for the arrival of the fleet that was to take them to Spain. There was no longer any appreciable difference between the viceroy, the oidores, and the conspirators. They had all been proud of their paper offices, and now, thanks to more recent papers, they had all lost their positions and their significance and were all subject to Philip II's justice.

While they were still in Vera Cruz, Licentiate Carrillo received the habit of Knight of Saint James, the last honor in his long career as magistrate, for after a few days at sea an attack of apoplexy struck him down. The malicious imagination of Suárez de Peralta plays upon that accident in one of those ruthless novelettes he was so given to writing. Although in the common opinion Muñoz was "most cruel" and Carrillo was considered mild, the truth was otherwise in the secrecy of the audience hall. The former was gentle while the latter often handed down "highly criminal" sentences, yet "all those who trembled before Muñoz and cursed him persisted in this mistake."

Now here was the hypocritical judge, lying helpless in his bed with his eyes rolled back and his mouth covered with foam in payment for his crimes. His jaws could be opened only by force, with sticks, to make him swallow certain medicines—"he was put to the torture in the same way he had had others tortured"—and he finally died. Then, "rather than cast him into the sea, they gave orders to open him, and take out his entrails, soak them in brine, and carry him to the nearest land, which was at Havana, where the ship would touch."

Suárez de Peralta's story does not end with Carrillo's death, however. The seamen superstitiously believed that his cadaver was bringing violent storms on the vessel, so they decided to wrap it in mats and lower it into the sea, suspended from a line; not even this extreme measure could divert the storms, however, so they cut the line unwillingly, over the pleas of Muñoz, and Carrillo's maltreated corpse sank forever into the Caribbean. Can you imagine the draperies with which our Creole author clothed his account? Yes; Suárez de Peralta said the expected things.

To think that the man in such a responsible office, who had killed men or granted them life at will, should be dealt such great torture; that he should be opened, naked and raw, and all his entrails exposed to view (a procedure unsuited to his dignity and his position and his habit as Knight of Saint James, as well as to the estates he owned and his noble blood), that he should be wrapped in some filthy mats covered with tar, tied up and placed where there was no reason for him to be, and to have the loathsome pages and cabin boys on the ship look upon him with loathing and hold their noses and turn their heads and flee from his evil smell and the sight of him. And that the body that had been used to turning over on very fine sheets in a very white bed, and which everyone had invited to take the best and most honorable place, had no place at all on the ship, not even with the ballast, but instead they cast him into the sea as they would a dog that had died. Truly, every time I come to this passage, I feel a great wonder and a great hatred of the world, and I should not have wished to be in his shoes; this will not be the first nor the last thing of that sort that will happen to him, and which our Lord will allot him in order for us to undeceive ourselves about what matters so much to us.

The great hatred of the world that this tyrant's lamentable end aroused in Suárez de Peralta might have been mitigated had he known that Carrillo's corpse was not cast into the sea but was brought to Havana where it was buried, probably with all the pomp due to his high office. Beyond question, "alongside his colleague, he was nullified, and if he played his part it was humbly and in a supporting role, in the shadow of the other man whose tool he was."

Suárez de Peralta, the gentleman, concludes his story with this moral lesson. Fray Juan de Torquemada, a Franciscan friar, author of a hodgepodge folio volume entitled *Monarquía indiana,* in which he plundered several historians who were his contemporaries, enlightens us on the last consequences of the conspiracy. The good Marqués de Falces arrived in Spain, was received by Philip II and given his discharge, and went home, where he lived out his days in the enjoyment of a clear conscience. On the other hand, Alonso Muñoz was granted an audience in which he had to listen to the "royal voice" saying, "I did not send you to the Indies to destroy the kingdom." "That was the terrible voice of Philip," Don Luis González Obregón explains in an aside, "the voice of the big tyrant reprimanding the little tyrant." Muñoz, the man who had never taken off his hat in greeting, the despot who was always guarded by twenty-four halberdiers, the judge who hanged hundreds of Creoles, tried to justify himself, but the "stern king"—the adjective belongs to González Obregón—coldly turned his back, and Muñoz died that same night. He was found sitting in a chair in his room "with his hand on one cheek."

This style of writing history is by no means confined to the Creoles. One professional historian, a Spanish Franciscan, did his work by opening the window of his cell and filling his papers with the scattered rumors that blew in. Neither man considered himself guilty of spreading wholesale falsehood. The Creole gentleman, Don Juan Suárez de Peralta, in his Madrid home, and Fray Juan de Torquemada, in his Mexican monastery, were merely writing the kind of rounded, moral history that people liked to read. The sixteenth century, packed with violent events and dramas, like our own century, refused to be bound by reality and was avid for such tales, but they had to be embellished with the moral lesson which our stories of violence and tragedy lack. What we regard today as a tiresome literary mannerism was a part of their life. To be sure, the eyes that looked at the world then were not our eyes.

12

The Creoles Mirrored in Their Prose

Why do I have to play the poor man in this comedy?
Must it be tragedy for me and not for the others?

Calderón

In 1878 the Spanish historian Don Justo Zaragoza exhumed and published Juan Suárez de Peralta's *Tratado* which helped to clarify, with all its exhaustive, gossipy, fascinating reports, the rebellion of the Creole encomenderos. Zaragoza's failure to establish the identity of the chronicler did much, however, to temper the joy of his discovery. With only a single proved fact to go on—one that Suárez himself had provided by identifying himself with the twofold title of "citizen and native of Mexico"—Don Justo followed his scholar's instinct and turned to the *Biblioteca hispanoamericana septentrional.* In that exhaustive index Beristáin verified that the Mexican Suárez de Peralta had written a *Tratado de la caballería de la jineta y la brida (Treatise on Horsemanship, the Mount, and the Bridle).* This gave him a second clue for his research. Don Justo, hot on the trail of this Creole phantom, discovered not only this extremely rare volume but also a *Libro de albeitería (Book of Veterinary Medicine*) in manuscript, which is still sleeping the sleep of the centuries on the shelves of the Biblioteca Nacional in Madrid. Yet even these new discoveries failed to dispel the mists shrouding Suárez's true personality. With all his clues exhausted and all avenues blocked, Don Justo armed himself with patience, studied confused references, established connections, and after gathering all the proofs he could muster, began to suspect that Suárez de Peralta might have been the son of Juan Suárez, brother to Catalina Marcaida, the first wife of Hernán Cortés. Suárez himself destroyed this ingenious and plausible theory by bitterly condemning in his book those who imputed to the Conqueror the crime of murdering his wife. And as "the first and most important of the accusers" had been the chronicler's presumptive father, Don Justo's deduction was abandoned for lack of documentary proof and left to join the growing number of historical enigmas. Then in the nineteenth century, another patient delver in the archives, Don Francisco Fernández del Castillo, at last succeeded in unmasking our Creole. As his discoverer had suspected, Don Juan Suárez de Peralta was indeed the legitimate son of Juan Suárez and the nephew of Catalina Suárez, the Conquistador's first wife, who died in her palace at Coyoacán one night in October, 1552.

Suárez's profound secretiveness throws light upon so many facets of his character that it is worthwhile to go into the subject more thoroughly. In his *Tratado,* Juan Suárez, a character apparently unrelated to the author, is described as a Conquistador who "owned Indians in encomiendas and was rich, and who, recognizing the vigor and boldness of Cortés, married him to his sister and did much for him as will be shown later." What did the rich encomendero do for the bold but insignificant court clerk from Cuba? While Cortés was a fugitive in the Antillean jungles, his brother-in-law swam turbulent rivers to bring him food; he advised the stubborn man to reconcile himself with Diego Velázquez; and when a courier from the government brought an order divesting Hernán Cortés of his command, he beat the luckless messenger and tossed him into a ravine.

Suárez de Peralta's desire to make a hero with a many-quartered escutcheon out of the modest Juan Suárez was based on the latter's one proved stroke of wisdom in negotiating for his three sisters. The first was almost certainly Diego Velázquez's mistress. But Suárez was also very complacent over establishing the lineage of Doña Catalina, to whom he always gave the title of marchioness even though she never actually held it, and that, added to the similarity of names, might be taken as proof of a deep-seated family affection, if Suárez had not labeled the accusation that Cortés had killed his wife "a great abomination" and a self-interested intrigue. In his eagerness to clear the Conquistador of all blame, he attributes the death of his aunt to a "childbed sickness," common to the women of his family, and with his penchant for apportioning both temporal and eternal blame, he goes so far as to say that the calumniators of Cortés had "paid or were paying for their crime in the next world." Yet Suárez, so ready with tears and with moral observations, knew for a fact that his own father and his grandmother had been the first to charge Cortés legally with murder, and he knew with equal certainty that his elder brother had acquired fifteen thousand pesos—a considerable sum at that time—as his share of the money awarded in settlement of the lawsuit entered by Juan Suárez de Ávila and his sisters as Catalina's heirs.

It was Suárez's unequivocal attitude that had seemed to invalidate Zaragoza's masterly historical reconstruction, and it moved him to exclaim:

A slight irregularity . . . an honorable conscience resists believing it, yet it is better to proceed in uncertainty about whether Juan Suárez was Doña Catalina's brother, in spite of the many circumstances that come together to affirm it, until such time as irrefutable proof may demonstrate it with perfect clarity.

Catalina's death affected Juan Suárez's position in New Spain. He shifted his attitude toward Cortés from that of brother-in-law and friend to that of opponent, and unquestionably the charge of wife murder that he and his mother brought was the most serious of the many accusations accumulated against Don Hernán in his famous impeachment trial. Whether or not it was true, Juan Suárez, noble descendant of the Marqués de Villena and former encomendero on the island of Cuba, acquired nothing but the poor repartimiento of Tamazulapa. He settled in Mexico City and married Doña Magdalena de Peralta, who bore him three children: Luis, the eldest son, who inherited the encomienda at his death; Juan, the chronicler; and a girl named

Catalina, after Cortés' dead wife. In due course his three children married the three children of Licentiate Alonso de Villanueva, a former ensign of Panfilo de Narváez.

Juan's position was far from easy. The second son of a colonial family had no very hopeful prospects in the sixteenth century. He was forced to keep up appearances as an hidalgo, yet the colony offered him no choice but to live at the expense of his first-born brother or to seek a miserable office in public administration or, as a last resort, to resign himself to holding one of the modest positions that were all the Church at that time offered to Creoles. Juan was too fond of life to don a habit or to spend his life in the viceroy's antechambers soliciting some ill-paid town magistracy; and he decided to help his brother with the family business.

Neither of the Suárez brothers ever hesitated to undertake any kind of enterprise. There were grist-mills operating on the family property in the outskirts of Tacubaya; they bred blooded horses; they dealt in several commodities, and were among the first to buy and sell houses—the favorite occupation of respectable Mexicans for centuries. In 1572, a shrewd trick on Juan's part backfired. He happened to owe two thousand pesos to the brothers Salvador, Juan, and Antonio Gómez Corona—some fraternal trio always seemed to preside over his destiny. These three sons of Gonzalo Gómez, encomendero and Conquistador, had grown tired of dunning him and decided to take the matter to court. Perhaps Suárez de Peralta had been expecting it to come to that; in exchange for a white horse and twenty pesos, he and his brother acquired from Hernando de Alvarado, the son of Fray Juan de Zumárraga's secretary, certain court records of lawsuits filed by the first bishop of Mexico in his capacity as Apostolic Inquisitor. Among these acquisitions were a charge of blasphemy against Suárez's father and another charge, filed in 1557, accusing Gonzalo Gómez of Judaism. The latter document was the basis of negotiation.

Using as an intermediary his cousin Leonardo de Cervantes, grandson of the famous Knight Commander of Saint James Don Leonel de Cervantes, Juan proposed to pay the debt by turning over the defamatory papers to the Gómez brothers. Instead of accepting the proposition, however, the Gómez brothers turned over all the facts to the Inquisition on May 1, 1572, and accused the Peraltas of being recently converted

Moslems, "a charge which had already been brought against them and which many people believed."

The case ended happily. The Gómez brothers, fearing that Juan might go off to Spain while he was out on bail, petitioned for an early settlement; the Inquisition merely seized the papers that were the cause of the dispute and issued a severe reprimand, and did not confiscate the two brothers' property.

Suárez de Peralta was an aristocrat whose coat of arms bore the proud motto: *Solo su virtud le ofende, fuerza ajena no letoca ni le preude* ("Only his excellence can harm him, outside forces can neither touch nor disarm him") was fond of horses and falconry, and he himself recorded that his brother spent two thousand ducats a year on the upkeep of gerfalcons and peregrines; throughout his *Tratado,* Suárez stands proudly on his position as a hidalgo; yet he did not hesitate to consign his father to hellfire in order to ingratiate himself with the descendants of Cortés or to resort for financial reasons to what, without mincing words, we must call blackmail.

Thus two seemingly incompatible types of man—the feudal lord and the scoundrel—blended curiously in Suárez de Peralta. He himself said that he wrote his *Tratado de la caballería de la jineta y la brida,* composed in 1580 and dedicated to the Duke of Medinasidonia, "because the exercise of horsemanship is the most useful and necessary one for gentlemen and for maintaining His Majesty's great service and strongholds in his kingdoms, especially in the Indies." This implies that when the Renaissance had flickered out in Spain and the fires of the Reformation burned with a dry crackling of vine shoots, Suárez fancied he was still living in the archaic, enchanted world of West Indian chivalry. His arms and his horse were always ready to answer instantly to the king's summons; he did not realize that regular armies had long ago relegated the gentleman warrior to a corner, like some archeological curiosity of the Middle Ages. His anachronistic feelings kept alive some of the lingering traces of the picaresque that he had picked up in the university of the Indies. A man of two periods and two worlds, Suárez reveals in the dream world of his chronicle and in real life the opposite beings that contended for his soul. The two live so close together that it is hard to judge when he is being an hidalgo and champion of feudal games, and when he is a *pícaro* who ought to be in jail.

A Landscape, an Herbalist, a Wet Nurse

In 1579 Suárez carried out his long-time plan of settling in Spain. The Creoles had lost a great historic battle and the paradise of the Indies became a miserably uncomfortable spot. The encomiendas—their *raison d'être*—were being liquidated, and the relics of the chivalric idyll, in which the Creole had figured as a principal, were collapsing helplessly before the triumph of the Inquisition, the arrivistes, the bureaucrats, and the money-changers. A cowardly man had no choice but to flee, and Suárez fled, seeking and even expecting to receive the protection of his lofty relatives.

The *Tratado de la caballería de la jineta y la brida* was published in Seville in 1580, and that same year, inspired by nostalgia, he began work on his *Tratado de las Indias,* which he completed in 1589. The chime of harness bells rang in his ears from across the Atlantic, and as the years brought their tinge of melancholy he kept seeing a lively picture of the gay or tragic events of his youth with the eyes of imagination. He had gone into voluntary exile from Mexico, but that did not mean he had ceased to love it. His *Tratado* opens with these words: "The Indies are the most fertile land ever discovered in the world, and the one most filled with all those things that are needed in the world for the service of man and his enjoyment."

Near the end of his manuscript, as he is telling us how Vázquez Coronado's expedition pursued the mirage of Cíbola only to find an out-of-the-way village in the northern desert, he is moved by his love for Mexico to exclaim:

New Spain happened once and only once in all history, for before another Mexico and its land may be discovered, we shall see the past and the present come together in body and soul, before the Lord of Heaven and Earth on that universal day of the Last Judgment.

He was a long way from being a writer. By his own confession, "he had only a little grammar, although much fondness for reading stories and dealing with learned people." Everything in his book that is not a historical report, an eyewitness account, or a quotation from a contemporary, boils down to a hasty, muddled string of commonplaces concerning the Indies. Writing history in the grand style of González de Oviedo was clearly beyond the reach of his hand, which was more accustomed to the bridle. His reading, which began and ended with the Bible, the indispensable Aristotle, and some second-hand classics and more or less official chronicles, must have caused him more than one headache. In the intricate and unfamiliar field of history, Suárez lost out because of his boundless ambition and his lack of order, like the Creole Baltasar Dorantes de Carranza, who shares with him the responsibility for the chronicles of the sixteenth century. The lively reporter of the execution of the Ávilas, who was there, whose horse's forehead pressed against the planks of the scaffold; the miniaturist who painted Viceroy Velasco's chivalrous manner; the poet who sang the rare virtues of his brother's falcons—he is helpless and out of control when he tries to imitate the ritualistic, conventional style of Oviedo.

No, "the sixteenth century was not fortunate in its literary prose." Suárez de Peralta, that "obscure Mexican Saint-Simon," wrote stumblingly, shedding tears and moral judgments, unclearly but simply, and entirely without literary affectation. If we grant that Cervantes de Salazar's Latin prose stopped with a topographical map, we must also deny to Suárez's far less ambitious prose an honorable place in the textbooks of literary history. His fate was to reflect, like a mirror and with a mirror's distortions, the image he was trying to dispel.

Suárez's opinions about the Conquest were those of his time. He was convinced that God had not given the Indies to the Spaniards gratuitously, but rather in due recompense for the expulsion of the Jews and the establishment of the Inquisition. This view was obviously sincere, for the chronicler himself and his father had had some unpleasant experiences with the Holy Office. The divine will was ever manifest. Had not Saint James turned the tide of many a battle, mounted on his white horse? Had not he himself seen the Virgin Mary blind the Indians by throwing handfuls of earth at them, with her own divine hands? But, even if the Spaniards could count on such powerful allies, the Indians were not bereft of aid. God acted through some of the natives, and the devil through others. Divine power and demonic power fought their eternal battle with swords and lances, or with arrows and macanas, and both used the Indies as an enormous prize ring where they fought their cosmic bouts.

But as the Homeric clash of battle faded, a kind of divination of dire events began. One of the antagonists, Satan, inexplicably undertook to spread demoralizing prophecies of imminent disaster. His hand was everywhere. He brought the dead to life, for a woman rose from her grave four days after being buried, lived on for twenty-one years, and even gave birth to a son. It was Satan who caused a bridge to sing his extraordinary song: "My haunches dance well when I am thrown in the water," and he filled the night air with warning lamentations—the idol Zihuacóatl cried, "Alas, my children, I must leave you now!" and a woman's voice spoke between sobs: "We are lost now, O my children! Where can I take you?"

Once, when Moctezuma sent some sorcerers to bewitch the Spaniards, they climbed to the crest of Tlalmanalco where they met the devil, looking for all the world like a drunken man. He was furious. "What do you want?" he asked. "What is Moctezuma thinking of? Is he awake now and does he remember terror? He has made one mistake already and it cannot be corrected, for he has caused many deaths, and destroyed many, and he has not done his duty by his god."

The sorcerers, quaking with fear, quickly built an altar and offered it to him on their knees. The devil—surely a devil not lacking in moral sense—took his place on it and continued, in a tone of frank pessimism, "You need not have come. I shall take no more notice of Mexico and I'm leaving you forever. I shall have nothing more to do with you or with your king Moctezuma. Go away, for I do not want to do what you ask me nor what he asks me. Turn around and look at Mexico."

The sorcerers saw Tenochtitlán going up in flames, and they fell to the ground in a swoon. That was the end of the Conquest. Suárez was able to read into the destruction of the conquered city the fulfilment of the prophecy of Saint John: "The prince of this world—the Prince of Darkness—will depart." And so he went away, vanquished not by Saint James alone, nor by miracles nor cold steel, but by the epidemic of smallpox that God had sent to the Indians—"it was a great help to the Spaniards, because [the Indians] could not fight owing to their illness and death"—surely a base and anti-Christian concept with which Suárez stains and prostitutes the divine victory.

He rounds out his view of the Conquest with a reflection on Alvarado's slaughter of the defenseless Indians. God had ordained that the

Spaniards be punished for their crimes, but as he did not want them all to perish, he sent them reinforcements: Narváez's soldiers. Suárez mourns for the lost souls of the murdered Indians, surely damned, and he ends piously and ineptly by quoting the blessed Saint John Chrysostom: "If the soul is lost, what is the body and what is it worth? Have ye another then to put in its place?"

His absurd pretensions to scholarship and his ignorance of ancient history led him to believe that Saint Paul's Epistle to the Romans might be applied to the Indians, because they were noted for their hatreds, dissensions, deceitfulness, disobedience to their parents—the Indian has always been praised for his deeply felt filial virtues—sins against nature, and above all their fondness for human flesh.

Sahagún, a student of humanity with much insight, was alarmed at the demoralizing effect of the colonial administration and recommended carrying over the customs and ancient laws of the Indians as the only possible means of saving them; Suárez firmly believed that the Conquest had been of great benefit to the Indians. He argues that in their pagan days, they had to walk more than eighty leagues, eating tortillas and roots along the way, in order to pay their tribute; whereas in the colony they could pay it in their own villages, "and consequently they felt quite rested and at ease, and they did not have to worry about anything but their own belongings, for now they all use pack horses and most of them go about dressed in the Spanish style and wear hats, breeches, and smallclothes." Yet this idyllic picture does not deter Suárez from describing Indians in the colony as the most drunken men he ever met. He claims that they would make themselves vomit so they could go on drinking, and that they generally entered taverns in groups of ten or twelve, leaving two friends at the door who would later lead them home. When the drinking bout was over, the Indians would take one another by the hand and the strange parade would stagger along, limp and babbling behind the guides, until one of them lost his balance. Then they would collapse on one another like ninepins and fall down, as in Brueghel's painting of the blind beggars.

Suárez shared the attitude of his class toward slavery. "If everyone has Negroes to serve him," he argues, "why should they forbear to make use of the Indians?" Both races were idolators and diners on their neighbors, and both practiced slavery themselves. In another paragraph he continues: "It is not fair to take the slave from his master if the master has a just title to him, any more than to make the free man a slave, and even less fair to give them all their freedom without any distinction only because some evil deeds have been committed."

Suárez occasionally sets down a sage observation to balance these convictions, which were a far cry from the Humanistic sentiments of his early years. In referring to the aboriginal Indian, he writes, "His only legal duty was to pay his tributes and services, to his overlords and gods alike," a summing-up of the human condition that is as apt today, after more than three centuries, as it was then.

In spite of his attitude toward the Indians as an encomendero, in one of his digressions Suárez helps us to understand the methods by which spiritual mestizaje, mingling of Indian and white, was gaining control of the body and soul of the proud Creole, without his realizing it. Speaking of the Indian herbalists, he says in his *Tratado:* "Those of us who were born there consider ourselves children of the earth and of the natives; they tell us many things, and all the more because we know the language, for to them that is a very seemly and friendly thing." In another aside he comes back to the theme in almost the same words, and lets this most important confession escape him: "The Indians hold those born in this land as their children, and their wives those whom they have nourished with their milk."

Pure symbiosis: the imponderables of the land, its silent labor to make a Spanish American of the Spaniard born in the Indies. New wine in old bottles. The Indian has broken out of his shell of suspicion, and the figure of a magical storyteller, often perceived in the childlike depths of the Mexican, comes forth in him. The Creole is a rootless entity, of little value in spite of his wealth and his comfortable family environment; whereas the Indian is a man out of antiquity, filled with natural wisdom, the secrets of nature, and marvelous stories. This slender man, dressed in rags, who eats snakes and flies, sees the Creole dressed in brocade as a son, and he communicates to him his solemn, powerful tenderness. And at his side is the native woman, the wet nurse who deserts her own children to give her breast to her master's white babies. The Indian servant and the Indian "nana" move through the Creole houses with their soft steps, and their task is to infuse a new feeling into that new man who made his first appearance in the New World.

A native landscape, a native herbalist, and a native wet nurse all poured their essences into the Spanish mold. It does not much matter that Suárez would deny the Indians, nor that he exiled himself voluntarily from the air of freedom, nor that, in the end, his class prejudices and his encomendero's pettiness should dominate him. Uprooting is never a way to free oneself from sadness and futile regrets. His Mexican heritage, which he touches upon only lightly, still led him to sign his books proudly as "citizen and native of Mexico," a title that was scorned in those days. And he wrote out of homesickness and love for his far-off land. For some reason he was ignored in Spain—he appears for the last time in 1590 as a witness to some statements made by Jerónimo Cortés, Martín's son, in applying for election as Knight of Alcántara; then, thanks to his *Tratado,* he was given back to Mexico. Now we are able to evaluate him and make him a part of our life, as the type of the poor aristocrat in the first generation of Mexicans. Certainly he could have done no more than he did.

Portrait of the Creole Courtier

Baltasar Dorantes de Carranza, author of the *Sumaria relación de las cosas de Nueva España,* unlike his colleague Suárez de Peralta, frequently referred specifically to his father, Captain Andrés Dorantes. "If the services of the Conquistadors were great," he writes proudly, "those of my father were miraculous." He did not exaggerate. Andrés Dorantes, a survivor of Panfilo de Narváez's expedition to Florida, crossed the enormous expanse of land from the Mississippi westward—Texas, Arizona, Sonora, and Sinaloa—with Alvar Núñez Cabeza de Vaca, Captain Castillo, and Estebanico, a Negro. They were ten years returning to Mexico City.

All the incidents of his adventure are recorded in that strange, stern, dramatic book that bears the brief title *Naufragios* (*Shipwrecked*). Alvar Nuñez's book opens with the roar of angry seas. The bodies of drowned men are lying on the beach; there are corpses on the rocks and corpses in the waters of the Mississippi. Rafts crowded with dazed madmen are sinking in the whirlpools and the heavy surf. But the two hundred fifty men marooned by the first wreck did not lose heart. They used poles and deerskins to improvise a bellows for a forge and melted down spurs, stirrups, and crossbows to make axes, saws, and nails. The palm trees supplied them with tow; the manes of the slaughtered horses gave them threads and lines and the horsehides became oars; and the men's own ragged shirts were made into sails. They set sail again with a little raw corn and no water, and again their boats, packed with sick and thirsty men, were wrecked in a hurricane. Alvar Núñez tells about it in a language totally alien to the boasting and selfish wailing of his sons, the later historians. He says: "I am telling this so briefly, because I think there is no need to set down in detail the miseries and labors we became involved in, for in view of the place where we were and the little hope of rescue we cherished, anyone may imagine everything that could happen."

None of those sixteenth-century men ever did set foot on the Island of Inevitable Doom, as they had expected to, but all of them actually took a ten-thousand-year leap across the short distance that separated their ships from that strip of American soil, a gigantic leap that took them back into the remotest prehistory, hungry, defenseless, and naked, to the realm of the woolly bison and the horror of complete helplessness. The marooned men built a fire and huddled around it "entreating mercy of our Lord God and forgiveness for our sins, amid many tears, each pitying not only himself but the others who were in the same state."

In the Indies, as a rule, Spaniards without weapons were enslaved by the Indians. Slavery, hard labor, and illness were destroying them. They kept themselves alive by pulling up, with bleeding fingers, the bitter roots that were their food. Their number dwindled from a band of eighty men to five, and then to four. The four survivors of the shipwreck, who, like their successor Robinson Crusoe, had a Negro slave with them—poor Estebanico who later died still under the spell of Cíbola—escaped one night during the wild dancing which celebrated the gathering of the prickly pears, and fled toward New Spain. They were not entirely helpless. During the years of their captivity they had learned that the Indians venerated sorcerers and medicine men, and they decided that it would be expedient to practice witchcraft. "They wanted to make physicians of us," Alvar Núñez says, "without examining us or asking for credentials. Their way of healing the sick was to blow on them, and with their breath and the laying on of hands, they drove the illness away."

Their magical reputation as healers preceded them across the deserts and the mountains and dictated their line of march. A mysterious voice would announce their coming and when they arrived at the villages men, women and children in war paint would come out to receive them, uttering blood-curdling cries as they shook gourds filled with pebbles and slapped themselves loudly on the thighs. "They were in great haste," Alvar Núñez writes, "to come up and touch us."

Their prestige grew enormously after they extracted an arrow tip that had been lodged for some time near the heart of a young warrior, and this and other cures—they drove away illness merely by blowing and saying an Our Father—enabled them to go safely from village to village, where they were surrounded by trembling and kneeling men; until after ten years they reached Mexico City. Their entrance was in keeping with their exploits. Baltasar writes that they arrived nothing but "skin and bones" in deerskin breech clouts, long-haired and shaggy-bearded, burned by sun and wind and covered with scars and huge calluses on their backs and shoulders from carrying heavy loads. People gathered to look at them "like something marvelous" and bullfights and mock tournaments were held in their honor.

After that remarkable trip to Florida, Andrés Dorantes never left New Spain. But he took part in the pacification and conquest of Jalisco, his only experience as a soldier in the New World, and when that was over, Viceroy Don Antonio de Mendoza officiated at his wedding to the encomendera Doña María de la Torre, widow of Conquistador Alonso de Benavides. Several children were born to them.

Baltasar, the eldest son, was born about 1543. His much-traveled father died before 1560, and Doña María married again and "neglected the children of her previous marriages." Ernesto de la Torre writes: "Baltasar grows up on Doña María's encomienda, and when he comes to Mexico City he spends the greater part of his time in economic dependence upon his mother's encomienda. She feeds and clothes him . . . giving him what he needs for the care of his person."

When he was fifteen years old, he fell "madly in love" with Marina Bravo, a little woman of fourteen, and married her "by an exchange of vows," a nuptial service that was hardly orthodox. Three months later, the Creole boy had forgotten his first love and had fallen madly in love again with another child of fourteen, named Isabel de Rivera, and contracted another marriage, again by an exchange of vows.

It would be impossible to guess how many marriages this precocious bigamist might have consummated if the Church had not intervened "when he asked for permission to marry by bell, book, and candle" and flung him into prison. Even so, Baltasar refused to formalize his pledge to Marina; an uncle of hers took a hand in the matter; the lawyers claimed that the prisoner was "a boy of tender years and little wit" and in the end Baltasar repented of his frivolity and the authorities pronounced "the first marriage valid and the second null and void."

At an age when other Creole youngsters were composing Latin epigrams, this future historian was launched on a career of dangerous adventure. On July 24, 1563, he escaped from the dungeon with the help of smuggled keys and an accomplice; when he was arrested again, he was sentenced to live outside the archdiocese and was fined 170 pesos which was paid by a rich uncle of Marina's, whom he finally married, against his will. He had several children by her. In 1604, the eldest son was at the Spanish court, seeking patronage.

In 1572, when he was living in Atzalán—an encomienda which he considered his, though it belonged legally to a daughter of his mother's from her first marriage—he was brought before the Inquisition, accused of having married for the third time and of forbidding religious instruction to "his" Indians.

We do not know how or when he began his career as a bureaucrat. In 1580 Viceroy Martín Enríquez de Almanza tried to have him brought to Peru—later Baltasar must have regretted refusing the invitation—Villamanrique gave him several jobs. After his mother's death, he had to resign himself to living otherwise than by the labor of the native slaves, for the coveted encomienda went to his half-sister, Doña Antonia de Benavides. He held successively the positions of lord mayor and royal officer in Vera Cruz (1588) and later became chancellor of the Royal Exchequer, and was given other posts of "great quality and prestige."

He never lost his fondness for women. When his first wife died, he married Mariana Ladrón de Guevara, by whom he had, he says, "a male child with his name" in 1604 "and several daughters."

We have no information about his death. In the *Sumaria relación*, Dorantes complains of a serious illness contracted by handling papers and reports, but inasmuch as in that same book he confesses to the viceroy with the greatest candor and no hint of shame that he was a victim of the malady of his century, it can be fairly supposed that his death, which occurred before 1613, may have been due to syphilitic lesions and not to literary activities, however lethal these may be at times, in more ways than one.

The Palace: Observation Post and Laboratory

The few facts of Dorantes' life that have come down to us balance out to his disfavor. The evaluations of the *Sumaria relación,* which constitutes his entire work, are equally unflattering. Pedro Henríquez Ureña calls him an excellent historian, but Ramón Iglesia asks whether he deserves that title, and Ernesto de la Torre, to whom we owe the best study of his collected papers, asserts that he wrote it under economic pressure.

This son of the man who raised the dead in the Texas deserts is a braggart who "boasts of being a documented historian" but "all his information boils down to" a bad compilation of extracts from three or four known authors—not Gómara alone, as Iglesia states. Undoubtedly he lacked the ability to elaborate an account, and he has no firm criterion, "for in his work, aimed at throwing light on the merits of the Conquistadors, the diatribes against their cruelties which appear to have been taken from the writings of Father Durán prove in the end not to be germane."

That is not all. Iglesia classifies Dorantes as:

a servile sycophant who can never praise the viceroy highly enough, all his praise being directed toward asking favors for the descendants of the Conquistadors who, he tells us tearfully, were living in the greatest poverty, some of them forced to beg alms at the doors of houses

and it is no less true that Dorantes was guilty of "drawing a rigid line of demarcation between the Conquistadors and the settlers who arrived later, whom he treats with insuperable rage and scorn."

It is curious to think that perhaps it is because of these very limitations, plus some not very remarkable insights, that Dorantes' testimony is of particular value, for without it we should have no very accurate understanding of the Creole and the society of his day. Dorantes belonged to a class that had been overthrown. Suárez de Peralta chose to seek the protection of his relatives in Spain when the gates of the Creole paradise closed at his heels. The author of the *Relación,* however, clung to the viceroy's coattails (to keep from sinking any lower), when he lost an encomienda that never actually belonged to him legally—"the village I managed to inherit was worth five thousand pesos in yearly income when it was taken from me, and I was left as naked as my father when he came out of Florida."

As a bureaucrat he was beyond reproach. He knew the palace secrets by heart and was a genealogist by temperament, one of those men, common to our country, who enjoy tracing their family trees for other people, never thinking that an examination of their own tree might reveal some more or less disgraceful twigs.

By 1604, when he was past fifty, Dorantes had become a model courtier. Like Gogol he was endowed with a very sensitive nose, and he sniffed cautiously at the universe of the viceregal antechambers, his nose like a reading glass. A newcomer might have been misled by appearances. How could he distinguish legitimate sons from bastards, gentlemen from scoundrels, arrivistes from those who had taken root in the colony long ago? How could he find out the dissimulators, the commoners, and the rascals when they were all falsifying their proofs of the purity of their blood and deceiving the viceroy with their trumped-up histories and genealogies? All that could be left to Baltasar Dorantes de Carranza. He was there for that express purpose, a genealogist by profession; that was why he decided to write a *Relación,* in which he could exploit his gifts as an observer and his long experience as a bureaucrat. We must not suppose that his literary leanings might lead him to follow the palace manners and customs disinterestedly. It piqued and upset him that rascals could obtain honors and favor through their campaigns, their intrigues, and flattery, at the expense of those who deserved these honors and had a right to them. The projected work would include a detailed report on the good and the bad petitioners, the unworthy scoundrels and the legitimate descendants of the Conquistadors, and thus help the viceroy to know whom to reward with grants and employment and to whom the coffers of the royal treasury should be closed.

Once our Creole had convinced himself that he was to be the guiding force of a new distribution of justice, he went to work. It was not easy to levy a careful census. In nearly three-quarters of a century the original tree trunks had sent forth many branches; some families had emigrated to distant provinces; some refused to give any information; others turned over false data, all of which complicated the genealogist's task. Sick and suffering from lack of sleep, he went from door to door, rummaged through archives, and "deciphered on" papers, until finally he finished the thick manuscript. One is "thunderstruck" at the conclusions to be drawn from his census. Of the 1,326 Spaniards who had taken part in the Conquest of Mexico, there remained only 109 children, 479 grandchildren, 85 great-grandchildren, and 65 in-laws, for a total of 738 persons, grouped in 196 households. These were the people eligible for the "offices and the provisions of His Majesty." The dead were not on his list, of course, for they already occupied the plot of ground assigned to them, nor were the sons of the Conquistadors who had become monks and priests. There were many of these and, legally at least, they were unable to carry on the houses, "as he calls the genealogies."

Dorantes cleverly manipulates his statistics to make a case for his own caste. To be sure, he reasons, some died in the war, but the greater number had emigrated because of grievances suffered under the past governors. "A roiled stream enriches the fisherman." Men who rendered great services had their property seized, and favors were granted to those who "came with their hands washed to eat the fruits that others had got by the sweat of their brows"; when the king finally dealt out justice and stopped "those upheavals which almost resembled tyrannical acts," it was already late in the day. Even though the Audiencia restored encomiendas and estates when it finally faced up to the impossible task of "reversing a world" it left matters in much the same state "with those who won this land and their sons feeling nothing but sorrow today. Those who came afterward got the best of the bargain, when all is said and done."

Dorantes knew there was a mystery hidden somewhere in this situation, but he refused to bother with it. He was aware that he would be accused of malice, and would make enemies and be repaid with curses for all his work, his loss of sleep, and his care, even though "the truth I follow is to serve this Republic in all things and I pray to God I may be thanked for it."

Mexico, Mother of Oddities

Dorantes offers an insoluble puzzle. On the one hand, he remarks that "preaching the Gospel with sword in hand and by bloodshed is a fearful thing," and on the other, that the saints helped the Conquistadors to an extent that left no room for doubt. "No one can understand this theology," he exclaims, slipping onto forbidden ground, but he catches himself in time and adds contritely, "The secrets of God and his judgments are inscrutable." One thing emerges clearly. The sins of the fathers are visited on the sons. There were few men of his stock who did not beg their bread at the stranger's door. The Bible helps him to express his indignation: "The unhappy men," he says in conclusion, "were left to crawl like serpents."

The idea that guilt was implicit in the warlike deeds of the Spaniards often emerges through his vision of a Spanish-American world ruled by mysterious and omnipotent heavenly forces. The misfortunes that befell the most illustrious figures in the Indies—Columbus, Hernán Cortés, Núñez de Balboa—arose from "wishing to preach the Gospel by shedding blood. That is not in the very least what God commanded his disciples when he sent them to preach to all the world." The end they sought—the conversion of the Indians—seemed good to the chronicler, but the means employed reprehensible. Their punishment was not long coming, "because the property they had acquired thus was all dissipated like smoke or like salt in water."

Despite this summary condemnation of violence, Dorantes' glaring inconsistency leads him to accept with pride the position of pleader before the king on behalf of the encomenderos, "so that the blood spilled may be present, may speak, may cry out, may be their symbol." The chronicler who had spontaneously condemned the shedding of Indian blood now undertakes to defend officially the blood spilled by the Conquistadors themselves, and this contradiction between what he writes and what he does demonstrates the inconsistency of his beliefs, and also to a large degree, the dramatic inner struggle between warring influences within the Creole. He vacillates between the Spaniards—he feels he is a Spaniard, as he says expressly in his *Relación*—and the Indians, whose plight he felt as a spiritual dilemma, owing to the redemptive doctrine of the best of the Castilians. There is already a trace of the American consciousness in this vacillation, this wavering that brings with it ignoble reservations. In general terms, we might say that in the sixteenth century a cultivated Creole was closer to the Indians than an educated Indian. For example, Muñoz Camargo, the odious historian of his province, puffs up Tlaxcala's part in the Conquest and his adherence to the Spaniards out of all proportion, and only because the noble Indian and the Creole hidalgo understood each other, and their common ambition for slaves and profits coincided.

One cannot read far in the *Relación* before finding some inconsistency. At times Dorantes conceives of the Conquest as an altar furnished with riches from heaven: "They were sending down permanent roots breadth of land and vassals, and fruits of fervent joy and gladness from heaven, and with them thrones for so many angels." The genealogist begins by rejoicing at the idea of provinces overflowing with colonists who are growing rich and "founding their bloodlines and lines of succession," but then he feels the prick of greed and goes on to prove painstakingly that some perpetuate themselves in Castile with what they bring back, and others are getting rich "when they never thought they would ever have enough, nor even emerge from beggary."

It was the same old story. The descendants of the Conquistadors had to crawl like snakes—only 55 owned encomiendas in 1604, a number reduced from 934 by his reckoning—and to suffer displacement by a cloud of lower-class *manos blancas*. Their bitterness and disillusion knew no bounds. The Creole's inability to scale himself to the reality of his condition produces rhetorical fireworks, and the style in which he expresses the tragic spiritual crippling of the dispossessed becomes more baroque than ever and foreshadows the literary madness whose dull, dark, heavy face will hover over the following centuries.

Here are three typical pages from his manuscript. Taking a deep breath, he begins his tirade:

O, Indies! O, Conquistadors, full of works, in the simplicity of those fortunate times, from which you took nothing but a fair name and eternal fame, while in days of greater services and greater exploits, you were despoiled of your own estates and the fruits of your services and great deeds, whereas those who ruled in the early years gave away your hard-won fruits to newcomers who merited nothing from the Conquest, now the season has come when more can be gained through deceit and lying and idleness and injury to his neighbor, when by selling wine or spices, cloth or old iron, a man can establish a great entailed estate, and blow up this world with feigned miracles without gratitude to God nor to those who raised him from the dust in all his nakedness to become so powerful.

O, Indies [he goes on amid more insults] the pimp for idlers, the seat of the bankrupt, the storehouse of lies and deceit, the inflation of fools, the destruction of virtue, the home of madmen and the French sickness, the picture of hell, the mother of oddities, the common fatherland of the un-natural, [you are] the sweet kiss of peace to the newcomer, and to your own sons an alien land, a knife in the back, a scourge to your own people.

He interrupts the parade of epithets—he has been calling the Indies wolf, fox, idol of Satan, and brothel of the good—to ask:

Do ye not know that your goods, your gold, your silver, and your precious stones cannot be passed on in this world? Do ye not see that they are movable goods and not roots? Everything is ending, everything is halting, and those who possess these things cannot entail their estates to their grandchildren.

This "digression and exclamation by the author," as Dorantes labels his diatribe in a marginal note, is in fact the center of and key to the *Relación*. It is directed to the heads of that house of madmen, the *manos blancas,* who favor the recent arrivals, in other words to the Spaniards who are responsible for carrying out the royal policy so inimical to the Creole interests. In view of Dorantes' frequent outbursts, González Obregón is surprised "at the firmness and gallantry in his style of expression." Indeed Dorantes was the Creole who voluntarily assumed the role of defender of his people. He champions them with the only weapon he has, his intransigent pen, and he does not spare his scathing arguments; yet at the same time he is a courtier who is likely to sink to the most servile adulation in order to ingratiate himself in his patron's eyes. The rotten world he has sketched, "Satan's school" in the Indies, could be transformed "into a paradise of angels" if the viceroy would use his magical powers and merely lift a finger. As Dorantes' pen traces the governor's name, it ceases spitting poison and pours out the finest and most moving of honeyed words in his repertoire. "We are living most contentedly," he exclaims, prostrating himself on the ground, "and we can never have enough of seeing Your Excellency or worshiping his shadow, because we love him"!

Bureaucratic Hell

When it came to the descendants of the first settlers—Dorantes was one of them—he maintains that they merited the same treatment as the sons of the Conquistadors. But only the first immigrants who had married into the families of the warriors must be included, although some of them "would rather be rewarded with the jingle of the cash box, since they did not awaken to the sound of the trumpet," and to show the viceroy precisely with whom he had to deal, he closes his book with a long appendix of distinguished colonists, listing seventy-five families.

Dorantes hated illegitimate offspring as much as he did the arrivistes. He is reconciled to descendants of the Conquistadors and mentions them all, not as hidalgos, but as nobles whose titles were given them for services to the king. But he cannot tolerate illegitimate children, much less if they had Indian mothers. He wrote to the viceroy: "My pen does not speak nor will it write about the bastards. Indeed it is better to leave them unmentioned, for neither ecclesiastical law, divine law, nor civil law will help them." Some pages later he reconsiders his proposal to "leave the bastards in the bottom of his inkwell" and decides to mention them, not in order to help them pick up some crumbs fallen from the table of government, but only to expose them to the viceroy as the most inopportune and numerous petitioners, so that he can slam the door in their faces as soon as he recognizes them. Those unworthy pariahs, "the get of dark women, not the light-skinned ones," are guilty of destroying the legitimate successions.

And, Most Christian Prince: in my opinion, though I say it as a man of cloak and sword, neither the King nor Your Excellency owes them anything, nor is it right that they should be given preference over the legitimate, for according to reasons of nature and law, of God and of justice, the properly born sons are the ones dealt with in the new laws, and the bread should be apportioned among them, not taken from them and given to this breed.

The Cavalier and the Nouveau Riche

Among the many claimants who were polishing the benches of the
viceregal antechambers with their wrinkled hose, the only ones deserving of help are the nobles. They are always the first to come and the last
to leave, with their pockets stuffed full of parchments and memoranda.
They spend many mortal hours in the audience hall, pale with hunger,
their delicate hands resting on the hilt of their swords, trying as best
they can to hide the holes in their boots. No one pays any attention to
these descendants of heroes who have set a value, not excessive we must
recognize, on every scratch their fathers got during the war; yet they
demonstrate a healthy optimism.

Whenever the genealogist thinks of this outcast breed, his eyes fill
with tears. He knows how far the palm of martyrdom can reach, for
"there is nothing more base and groveling than to resort to pretension."
What "wasted steps," what "doffing of caps," what shame these unhappy men have endured. And yet in spite of their thwarted hopes,
"what favors they imagine, though unable to perform them; what
enchantment and beauty do they bring to the deceived world." "And by
the living God," swears Dorantes, greatly moved, "I have seen two or
three sons or grandsons of genuine Conquistadors starve to death in this
city; and I have helped to bury them with pity that help had been so
long denied them."

No one has ever said a better prayer for the memory of Mexican
claimants, that anonymous legion that has lived and died in governmental antechambers for four centuries. Dorantes will not only tell of
their misfortunes; he helped to fold those thin hands, vainly
outstretched for so many years. Those martyrs to bureaucracy, who
would rather starve to death than dishonor their escutcheons by undertaking plebeian employment, showed the grasping viceroys a beautiful
example! "The offspring of kings and princes," says Dorantes, drawing
the appropriate moral, "must always be given help, for they are beloved
by God himself."

The protective mantle thrown over the shoulders of importunate
nobles by our chronicler did not extend to the cabin boys and seamen
who began to call themselves Don So-and-So and Don Such-and-Such
the moment they came down the gangplank in the Indies, nor to those

women who used a thousand arts, talents, and false titles, such as Doña Angela and Doña Alberta to pass themselves off as ladies. They brought their embalmed pretensions to the New World and were accepted by the weak-minded, but they scorned the country and destroyed the old-time residents.

Dorantes carries on a strange system of double-entry bookkeeping with pedantic attention to detail. He lists the good people, those who have a right to enjoy the delights of the royal treasury in one column, and the bad, the rude, the base characters whom the viceroy should sentence to exile and destitution to the other one. But he reserves the lowest circle of the bureaucratic hell for the sons of Conquistadors who cannot boast of a satisfactory family tree. Of all the damned—the bastards, the newcomers, and the toadying settlers—they were the worst. In his final outpouring, he unleashes all the hatred and scorn which the poor insular feudal lord of the Middle Ages reserved for the bourgeois possessors of great urban wealth. The Creole who was forced to spend his life hanging on the coattails of the viceroys, holding modest offices in unhealthful regions, had to endure the ignominy of walking "between the feet of the horses" that the commoners rode. His only revenge was to boast of his nobility and fling their base origins in the faces of those impudent lice. He writes wrathfully:

I give infinite thanks that the titles of respect granted to my father were granted him by virtue of his very noble nature, and that he did not come to the Indies in a lowly estate but as captain in His Majesty's infantry; and he was never anyone's servant, nor did he come as a hanger-on or dependent of any man born.

But who were the most eminent and outstanding men in New Spain now? In the case of one man, his father had been a lackey "even after the country was conquered"; in another case, the father was a black-smith. Still others were the sons of tailors, carpenters, shoemakers, drummers, fifers, buglers, sailors, and cabin boys. Today they have left behind them "the cooking fire and the blackened pans," and they eat like princes. His pen might have described the bones they were once thrown to gnaw on, but he prefers to leave that in the inkwell—he would thank me to keep still about it—and to absolve everyone, owing to "the great services rendered by their forefathers from whom these generations have sprung, root and branch."

The Encomienda, the Beloved Encomienda

At times, Dorantes is a realist, because of his post as hanger-on to the viceroy. He is too well informed about American politics and administrative resources to be guilty of anything so foolish as asking for the impossible. The dispossessed feudal lord would not have dreamed of addressing the king in the insolent manner of the Creoles of the second half of the sixteenth century; he shows his gratitude for the tutelary policy of the monarch in the rhetorical effusions peculiar to him.

From what we can winnow out of the confused rationalizations that surround Dorantes' petition, it was customary to appoint magistrates and mayors even to tiny villages but with salaries so picayune "they would not suffice to keep a hen." If such unnecessary posts were abolished and only the important provinces were staffed, with higher pay and a term of three years, in line with the provisions of the Statutes of Castile, "the Indians would be relieved of some of the heavy labor they carry on their backs." He admits that as things stood, "we destroy them with a breath." The monarch would save money, and the viceroy would not have to waste his time dealing with reports of irregularities.

In this section of his *Relación,* he sounds like a fervent partisan of Las Casas. For the Marquis of Montesclaros, he took pains to extract in his difficult style the Dominican's twenty-four proposals, and finally confided to him that his precious book had been stolen and that to recover it he would give "not only money, but the blood from my arms."

To judge by his fervor, his encomendero's heart had been touched, a miracle wrought by reading the works of the Bishop of Chiapas. He had shed the remnants of the old slave-owner and emerged as a man in the grip of a cruel remorse. "The Indies," he writes, "were lost through greed as they were won through greed." He is firmly convinced that it was impossible to hold an encomienda and to possess the land in perpetuity because of the encomenderos' ill treatment of the natives, and he is persuaded that only one of Las Casas' lapidary arguments was "enough and more than enough" to move the monarch to refuse encomiendas to the many "greedy tyrants" who asked for them.

He quakes at the thought of the destruction of the Indies. God's glory had been annihilated, his holy faith had become hateful; the provinces were turned to deserts; thousands of Indians had perished without the sacraments and their souls had gone to hell. The Lord would punish those terrible sins and might even ordain the destruction of Spain. At the height of emotion he says:

> And because our life cannot be long now, I invoke all the hierarchies and choirs of angels as witnesses, all the saints at the celestial court and all the men in the world, especially those who were living not many years ago, to bear witness to this testimony I am making and to the unburdening of my conscience herein.

In the midst of his lamentations, his prophetic divinations, and his tears, Dorantes still insists on his petitions. Alas, the encomienda is a lost treasure, a dried-up fountain, but it must not be forgotten that the viceroy still has ample resources to provide for the Creoles. What Dorantes is actually proposing here is an administrative version of the miracle of loaves and fishes, as he proves by illustrating this portion of his *Relación* with a sonnet by an unknown poet:

> *With five loaves God fed the multitude*
> *In the wilderness, and there was enough.*

Though there may not be much bread, "the dear, gentle father, who has pity on my blessed country" can feed the hungry and still have some left over, if he will distribute it prudently. Or, to put it in bureaucratic jargon, the viceroy could dispense honors, franks, exemptions, and privileges to the descendants of the Conquistadors; he could give them preferment over the upstarts; he could increase the terms and salaries of officeholders; he could include the ownership of Indians with the mayoralties and magistracies; and he could abolish the ruinous custom of announcing vacancies, for with so few favors available it was not worthwhile to spend a lifetime in the antechambers to obtain them. "And if this is done, as Your Excellency is going to do it, the kingdom will be content and no one will urge *repartimientos*."

The Creole's blood sings at the thought of viceregal grants. He envisages mayoralties, ownership of Indians, and magistracies descending on his neglected race like manna. He goes into a true administrative trance, a bureaucrat's kind of madness, and he thinks with rapture how easy it would be—and how legitimate!—to have his basket filled to overflowing with the gifts he has pictured, with the most precious jewel that any self-respecting Creole would aspire to—the encomienda. A good lawyer proves himself with difficult cases, and Dorantes goes on to extol the merits of his own; he performs the barefaced trick of making Las Casas a vehement advocate of the Mexican encomienda, although a few pages later he rebuts his decisive arguments, and even makes a sort of public expiation.

"It is true," he says in his rebuttal, "that many people solicit encomiendas for just cause and for services rendered." The Indians assigned to the Crown might very well be transferred to the claimant if such a change of control were not forbidden by law. Having stated the question thus, Dorantes goes on to destroy the legal obstacle with an irrefutable argument. The condemnatory laws had been decreed to avoid further butchery on Santo Domingo; they were meant only as a warning. The case of New Spain was different, because there

conditions are dissimilar in all respects, and particularly as these days there are no Indians who are better kept, better treated, protected, and rewarded than those of the encomenderos, who protect them in their labor and defend them before the law, who are true fathers to them in their need and doctors and nurses in their illnesses, for they heal them with medicines and gifts at their own expense.

If the holy bishop, instead of being so unfortunate as to live in those dreadful times, had had the good luck to be alive in the blessed golden age of the encomendado Indians, he would surely have advised repartimiento in New Spain. Dorantes' defense of the institution soars to the heights of eloquence; he then caps the climax by citing some exceptions made in favor of Mexico by Las Casas. The chronicler's effrontery goes even further, and he ends by volunteering disingenuously to go to court as procurator for the encomenderos—even a naked man can speak—while there is still time to right the wrong, and before we all become as unaware of what harms us as Saint Lazarus was of evil, and before we are ejected from this republic and this world as germ-carriers and pests; I pray to God that we shall not come to stink worse with time, for we give so much offense now, whenever we appear, that the governors and princes grow weary of this constant importunity and are angry with us . . . and will be unable to oblige so many paupers.

The Historian of the Indies

The fact that Baltasar Dorantes de Carranza wrote his *Sumaria relación* from 1601 to 1604 does not mean that it runs beyond the frame of the sixteenth century. His own life belonged to that century, to the first generation of Mexicans, and his work reflects the ideas of his day and the spirit that distinguished the Conquistadors' sons and the first settlers. He has much in common with Suárez de Peralta, beginning with the fate that befell their respective manuscripts. As we have seen, Suárez's was exhumed in 1878 by Señor Zaragoza, while Dorantes' remained unpublished until 1904, the year when our Museo Nacional decided to issue it. In addition, the gulf that separates their fathers' common names—plain Juan Suárez and Andrés Dorantes—from their own informs us of the social climb that one generation could make. If Suárez's roots in Spain did something to weaken his sense of being an American, Dorantes' roots in New Spain conditioned him to view the Indians with greater sympathy but without changing his ideas as an encomendero. To him, "they were the great workers and tillers of the soil." Turning to Aristotle for inspiration, he adds, "By their very nature they are peaceful and they do not covet what is their neighbor's nor do him wrong, and the work of their hands gives them pleasure and peace, "because naturally a man loves what he makes himself."

The two writers saw things in much the same way. Dorantes adorns his account with many digressions. "I stumble through all this," he writes, "not to construct history, but merely to insert here this little thumbnail sketch to relieve Your Excellency's boredom with so many names." He had planned to confine himself to New Spain, but now and again he is carried away by some other topic, and in spite of himself the manuscript grew so bulky that the author himself, usually unconcerned, realized that he had erred by excess.

"In this little notebook"—a little notebook of more than three hundred pages—"Most Christian Sir, I have been like a guest at a great banquet who, though he has firmly resolved not to eat any more than he needs, tries every course out of sheer gluttony."

Like Suárez, he felt called upon to mention several subjects which still remain unsolved puzzles, such as the origin of the Indians. His quotations and his appropriate or inappropriate allusions to Pliny, Diodorus, Plato, and Aristotle—he calls Huitzilopochtli the Jupiter or Mars of the Aztecs—betray the Humanistic preoccupation of his day, somewhat obscured and uncertain in him. At the same time, he believes firmly in the devil and his world is ruled by the belief in an omnipotent God whose judgments are inscrutable. He does not hesitate to attribute the destruction of Guatemala, a holocaust whose effects were still visible in the sixteenth century, to the "work of the demon whom God granted permission to punish men for their sins"—a modern vision of Sodom—and he was convinced that the extinction of the Indians was divinely ordained, since every means taken to increase their number had failed, "as we have seen from experience."

His weakness for anecdote and his tendency to take delightful fables about the Indies as articles of faith made his "thumbnail sketches," written to while away the viceroy's idle hours, resemble Suárez's digressions. For example, he tells this story about the curative powers of the "most temperate and healthful" Lucayas Islands. A citizen of Santo Domingo, named Francisco Monasterio, whom dropsy had given a belly like a pregnant woman and a face like a pumpkin, lived in the Lucayas for four or five months and came back "as hale and hearty" as if he had never been "ill a day."

Suárez devotes a chapter of his *Tratado* to the grace of a falcon that belonged to his brother; Dorantes finds that birds are the most beguiling creatures in American nature, and he tells anecdotes about them that had come down from the people. He mentions the *zenzontle,* that marvelous bird that spoke 400 tongues; the tiny, luxuriant *cuitlacochi;* and other amazing breeds that Clavijero had heard singing in his exile from Italy. He tells how Doña Juana Patiño de Vargas, the wife of Don Cristóbal Sotelo Valderrama, fell into a swoon one unlucky day, and the bird she had trained—a cuitlacochi—also lost consciousness. On the following day the lady had another fainting spell and the sensitive bird not only fainted again, too, but later died, because it felt its mistress's illness so keenly.

He copied from Gómara the story of the manatee, that siren of the cetaceans whose wiles are described by José Durando. It introduces into the *Relación* a touch of the medieval legend and the modern yarn of *Mr. Peabody and the Mermaid,* with the difference that nowadays such matters are handled by the psychiatrist while in the sixteenth century they were every man's imaginative heritage.

Speaking of Indian women, Dorantes says they are "very fertile and prolific," which he attributes to a complex Platonic precept. Now and then his wordy prose is embellished with a beautiful image. In his days as an encomendero, he watched the women "go to the river for water," he writes in the *Relación;* "they could serve as models for a painting called Charity, for they take with them two or three children who go before them, one or two in their arms, and still another in the womb, so that the mother hardly has room to carry the jar or pitcher in her hand, and she carries it on top of her head."

His descriptions of the flowers, the wild game, and the strange vegetation, his careful observations—the "Aztecs needed to live in the water like the waterfowl"—indicates a sensitivity to nature in America that always compensates for his pedantry and his swollen rhetoric.

Dorantes, never out of the stream of his time, was well acquainted with contemporary writers. To his habit of interpolating verses by well-known poets, we owe all the fragments of Francisco de Terrazas' poem, entitled *Nuevo mundo y conquista,* plus some fragments of Salvador de Cuenca, José de Arrázola, and some unknowns. These quotations have proved most useful to historians of the national literature. The influence of Rosas de Oquendo, whom he cites frequently, is apparent in his *Relación.* Indeed his tirades against the arrivistes and newly rich commoners, the dark picture he paints of colonial society, seem to have been taken intact from the Spanish satirist. For example, he reflects that the man who lives in the Indies "is more a creature of habit than in Salamanca and Alcalá, and all the more so if he is trapped into a lawsuit, for there are always plenty of ways in which he may be caught."

Such are the ideas that motivated Dorantes de Carranza, the Creole who sprang, pen in hand, to the defense of his people. He created a dismal portrait of his world and his class. As a sort of knight in the armor of a militant bureaucracy, he believed the salvation of his people lay in showering them with royal favors. His horizon was limited to the palace, in which he saw all answers to the public needs. His *raison d'être* was his family tree, and he based his seignorial rights on it. His fondness for plunder was a heritage from the Conquistador. Aside from that, he had no idea of the prospects to which he might aspire in his country. He knew only one truth: that his class was a class of worn-out men; and he foresaw that their decadence would become intolerable in time. That prophecy was to be carried out to the letter.

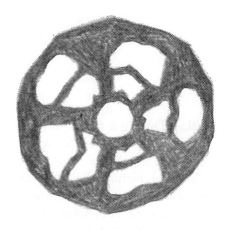

13

Poetry and the Colonial Man

They go forth in an evil hour,
Searching near and far,
Endeavoring in the Indies,
Like their fathers in Castile. Rosas de Oquendo

For the last time we see the cool foliage of the Indian paradise, bright with the yellow sun of the closing years of the century. Now comes the hour of expiation. The avenging angel, incarnate in the viceroy, has exchanged his flaming sword for a bulky file of royal ordinances with which he threatens to evict the tenant from the mansion he has been occupying with the gods' permission. The Creole now confronting the viceroy is not a rebellious tenant like the Ávilas, a genealogist like Dorantes de Carranza, or a knightly rogue like Suárez de Peralta. This Creole is a poet. He is defending his patrimony by the might of his pen, but instead of writing memoirs or ambitious but fragmentary histories, he parries the law with his epics and hurls sonnets at the royal advocates.

No duel of greater duration or less bloodshed has ever been witnessed. It was fought from the middle of the sixteenth century to the end of the eighteenth, and ranged over a field of honor which extended from New Mexico to the southern regions of Chile. Oceans of ink were spilled. During a two-month voyage "while the ship rolled," a single Creole, Saavedra Guzmán, who called himself the Wandering *Indiano*, composed a poem of 2,036 octets, which adds up to 16,288 verses.

What a picture the sixteenth-century Creole presents! He wraps himself in a metaphorical toga and from his mouth spill sonorities of the *octava real*. A metronome, set to an eight-line beat, rings in his ears; he walks with the rolling gait of the sailor in bursts of eight steps, as the words needed to fill out his lines tumble through his head. He founders on a bar of rhetoric where high seas wash in rhythmic series of eights as far as the eye can see.

Never has expiation taken quite that form. Thousands of sheets of paper aglitter with the fool's gold of song and poem, composed by these endless legions of literary ants, peep from the sleeves of Creole doublets and darken the horizon of New Spain. Their fluted ruffs were made of paper scribbled with octavas, and if ever Dante's sentence was applied in the New World—"If you will read me, I will read you"—it was throughout that century when men and horses galloped to the sleepy rhythm of octava rima.

The Creole seemed to feel obligated to cling to the theme of the New World and the Conquest, for it persisted with undiminished strength during the sixteenth century. The European Humanists were the first to be captivated by its novelty. "Bembo (a Venetian cardinal) managed to insert a chapter on the New World in his book on Venice." Mártir de Anglería's universe was unexpectedly broadened by "reminiscences of the Hesiodic Age of Gold, the island of the Amazon Women who were a gallery of heroines as in Titus Livius, Columbus in the pose of a Roman statue." The theme was to everyone's taste. Gómara, an author in search of a subject, found his hero in Hernán Cortés. To the theologians, the Conquest posed a delicate problem; to the jurists, an opportunity to revivify the law. Historiography—the labor of dedicated monks and more or less official chroniclers—"awoke and stretched herself before the spectacle of extravagant societies. She approaches the crowd curiously and plucks the flower springing from that subsoil called ethnography." Thomas More was building the shining city of Utopia upon an account by Amerigo Vespucci, out of his dream of human equality.

This leitmotiv began to disturb the people at home fairly soon.

Gómara's prejudiced approach to it gave rise to *La Conquista de la Nueva España,* by Bernal Díaz, which a professional historian has termed "an exaggerated account of merits and services." Bernal had set off in hot pursuit of lost time, burning with anger. Gómara wrote from hearsay, and he was misled. An office makes a poor observation post from which to judge battles in which death has worn the sacred mask of Huitzilopochtli, devourer of enemy hearts. Bernal, however, gathers up the loose ends and dots the i's. In his view, Cortés is not the *deus ex machina* of the Conquest; it was made possible only by his soldiers, their hunger and illness, their efforts and their deaths. He won a marquisate and immense wealth—"he was the one who knew best how to guide his destiny," as Dorantes later wrote—but what did the anonymous follower of the Conquistador gain? Contempt and poverty. He was the survivor of shipwrecks and glorious battles; the champion of the faith that conquered thousands of Indians, thereby broadening the frontiers of Christianity; the faithful servant of an ungrateful king. He was left to poverty, illness, and oblivion, while a host of upstarts raked in the prizes won by his blood.

When death plucked the magical pen from his hand—Bernal, the first Conquistador historian and the last to set down his own exploits—the sons of his old comrades in arms picked it up from the floor and went on with the epic. An odd thing happened then: The veteran's prose was transmuted into the octava real, and the full-blooded evocation of life became a literary game. Yet the man who left the legacy and his unexpected heir were united by a common preoccupation: the thirst for compensation, the accounting of merits and services; but with a difference. The man of action claimed the prize owed to his efforts while the Creole asked forgiveness for blood he never shed. The son of the Conquistador was accustomed from birth to living on his ancestors' past, on the deeds of others, and to expecting everything to come from outside himself. Our Alfonso Reyes writes:

The tales and the epics of the Conquest conceal a practical objective, which was payment for services rendered. Oquendo had already poked fun at the wish to exaggerate the debt when he told of his mendacious exploits in a village of Tucumán. They say no one or almost no one is exempt from this vice.

There was hardly a Creole alive who did not keep in his desk a sheaf of verses in praise of the Conquistadors' exploits. The writing of this poem lasted his whole life long, and as often as not he never finished it, as the busy Dorantes tells us: "Those who write poems on the Conquest move so slowly," he declares, "that time consumes and makes an end to them, so that out of all their industry they leave us nothing but a strong determination and good intentions and everything goes to sleep at last and is covered over."

The First Mexican Poet

The facts that have come down to us concerning Francisco de Terrazas, the first poet born in Mexico, fall short of completing his portrait, even though he was embroiled in an Inquisitorial lawsuit that became one of the most notorious cases in the colony. His father, the Conquistador by the same name, followed the classical career of the soldier of fortune in the Indies; he was major-domo to Cortés, then a prosperous encomendero, and then mayor of the city. Terrazas' mother Doña Ana Osorio was the daughter of Mari López de Obregón, a prototype of the Spanish American matron. When she died at ninety her seventy children, grandchildren, and great-grandchildren, dressed in "black gown, cape, and hood," filled the church at her funeral; five grandsons officiated at the altar, and one was chosen to deliver the eulogy. On the maternal side of his notable family, the poet was "first cousin to Baltasar de Obregón, author of the *Historia de los descubrimientos antiguos y modernos de la Nueva España.*" The dates of the birth and death of Francisco de Terrazas, the eldest of three brothers, are unknown. But according to Baltasar Dorantes de Carranza's *Relación,* he died before 1604.

In 1563, the playwright Fernán González de Eslava addressed a *Pregunta (Question)* to him—"a typical medieval gambit"—about the validity of the Mosaic law, and Terrazas answered with four ten-line stanzas. Eslava replied, and the theological correspondence continued with six new stanzas in which our Creole restated his opinion, as follows:

> It was the hand of Scripture
> that wrote the law, which then

was falsified by men
and put to right by Nature.
Before much time had passed
the figure was recast
and the dreamed-of form took shape
when the Son of God did pay
as he took our sins away,
by dying for our sake.

Juan Bautista Cervera, the poet of Toledo, entered the fray and passed off Terrazas' decimos as his own, among "feeble-minded readers," but the mere fact that he had taken part in the discussion gave the Inquisition cause to step in and accuse him of Judaism.

Eleven years later, Terrazas again became involved by chance in a famous dispute between the Viceroy Don Martín Enríquez de Almanza and the Inquisitor Archbishop Don Pedro Moya de Contreras. The old struggle between civil and ecclesiastical authority that had gone on since the stormy period of Fray Juan de Zumárraga, and which was to be one of the distinguishing marks of the colony, was joined this time between two equally strong adversaries, each jealous of his prerogatives. Enríquez, in obedience to instructions from Philip II, forbade members of the religious orders to acquire new properties and simultaneously decreed a rise in excise taxes, both dangerous measures that affected the people and the Church alike. As usual, Moya complained bitterly and the viceroy was censured by the Council of the Indies for no reason, which exacerbated the traditional rivalry.

In 1574, Moya's efforts to establish the Holy Office won him an appointment as archbishop. Splendid ceremonies were held to celebrate his consecration. On December 8 *El desposorio espiritual entre el pastor Pedro y la iglesia mexicana* (*Spiritual Betrothal of Pastor Pedro to the Mexican Church*)—a "pastoral comedy symbolical in character"—was staged in the cathedral, along with a farcical interlude which referred to a lay brother of the Carthusian order. The *Desposorio* was the work of the Creole Juan Pérez Ramírez, who holds the title of the first Mexican playwright, though unfortunately we know as little about him as about Terrazas. The facts we have may be summed up in the brief report sent by Moya to Philip II in 1575: "Juan Ramírez, a native of Mexico, thirty years old, son of a Conquistador, speaks

Mexican, has read canon law, understands Latin well, is a skilful man and a good poet in the field of the romance, lives well and decently." The characters of the *Desposorio* included the Church, the archbishop, "Divine Love" in the shape of a priest who blesses the engagement, a choir, and the "fool" of the classical Spanish theater, "who plays a very small role in this and in succeeding Mexican works." For all this good will toward Ramírez's "graceful versification," Alfonso Reyes was forced to conclude that "the drama had not yet come out of its infant's walker, and remains half swaddled in paper."

On December 11, while the festivities were still going on, *Un coloquio en la consagración del Dr. D. Pedro Moya de Contreras* (*A Conversation on the Consecration of Dr. D. Pedro Moya de Contreras*), the work of Fernán González de Eslava, was staged, this time in the company of *El Akabalero* (*The Revenue Officer*), "a well-known work in the Lope de Rueda cycle." A charming mulatto who played the leading role interpreted it in such a way that he aroused laughter and applause from the Inquisitors. That was enough to exhaust the viceroy's patience. The allusion to the lay brother in the first interlude and a satire on excise taxes in the second made him decide to forbid the productions and to write angrily to the Council of the Indies: "All the other farces might be forgiven, but this did not sit well on my stomach; indeed no one could approve of it, for a consecration and the assumption of the pallium are not subjects for farce."

Not long afterward, the old liberties taken during the time of Hernán Cortés came to life again. A lampoon, making fun of the viceroy and the excise taxes, was found nailed to the door of the cathedral. Enríquez jailed Eslava and Terrazas; Moya de Contreras lost his nerve and excused himself on the grounds that the Inquisition's censor, Fray Domingo de Salazar, had given his approval to the presentations. Terrazas was set free, but Eslava spent eleven days in jail, and the quarrel finally ended with the Council of the Indies reprimanding the susceptible viceroy and the arrogant archbishop.

Terrazas lived in a period dominated by the influence of Italian poetry. He sailed happily through this secondary orbit of the Petrarchan system, between vigorous realism and human understanding—"too human," Menéndez y Pelayo called it—of the tragicomedy *Calixto and Melibea* and the soft lyricism of his friend, the luckless Gutierre de

Cetina. Sempronius reminds us that "Women and wine make apostates of men." In Mexico this aphorism would have seemed an unpardonable lack of courtesy, a crude blasphemy to be vigorously rejected. The poet "wounded by love" suffers from the deceit of women, their lack of love, and their slights, their scorn, ingratitude, and inconstancy. Yet he feels obliged to make some mention of their lewdness and filth, their loose tongues, their shamelessness and bawdiness, which the daring Fernando de Rojas casts in their faces at every step. The poets of New Spain did not blaspheme; they merely agreed to deplore. They were unable to buy the services of the madam—at least when they were writing—and they were forced to content themselves with expressing their pain and bewailing the ungrateful lady's disdain.

Terrazas' poetry moves freely through the tonic scale of the Renaissance lyric. Three centuries after he had written his fourth sonnet neither Icazbalceta nor Menéndez y Pelayo cared to reproduce it—the former because he found it "excessively free," and the latter because it seemed to him "a little indecent." The two greatest authorities of the nineteenth century agreed to ignore the poem, in which Terrazas glorifies the legs of an anonymous lady. But in a later day the verses of Manuel M. Flores and Efrén Rebolledo did not incur censure, even though they present the sad spectacle of men consumed by erotic obsessions more appropriate to the intimacy of the bedroom than to public expressions of dubious merit.

In the censured sonnet Terrazas says:

Ah, bases of marble, a living design
of columns translucently white,
reflecting most clearly the heavenly sight
to the earthbound, of goodness divine.

I'm jealous at sight of the beautiful arch
and the capitals, envy of kings,
for Cupid would willingly march
to his death on the altar of such lovely things.

Ah, gateway to glory for the god with bow bended,
and guard of the flower that's sought low and high
by all living lovers, the poor and the splendid,
let us know when your lock will respond to the key

when the crystalline heav'n's undefended,
and the forbidden fruit can be tasted by me.

The poem could hardly have been written by a man disposed to invade another's walled garden by violence; such discretion was seldom shown by his European models. This difference betrays the yearning and timidity which are among the most deep-rooted, constant, and outstanding traits of Mexican poetry.

Mexican literature begins with the nine Renaissance sonnets of Francisco de Terrazas. Oddly enough, only three of them have survived, and they, together with sonnets that Sor Juana Inés de la Cruz was to write in the seventeenth century on the theme of disappointed love, are the only works of the viceregal period that escaped the almost total destruction of octavas reales, the slender literary effusions, the letters, and the obscure baroque verses.

An Epic without an Epic Poet

The delicate sensibility Francisco de Terrazas shows in his sonnets vanishes the moment he seizes the war trumpet; then he changes into a grave and hyperbolical orator. His unfinished poem *Nuevo mundo y conquista* (*New World and Conquest*) starts like this:

> *Not of Cortés and his wondrous deeds,*
> *nor victories unheard-of do I sing,*
> *accomplished by the courage of those breeds*
> *whose daring made the whole world ring.*
> *Nor of those men who never felt the greeds*
> *of minor poets who'd be loath to ring*
> *the bells of fame that chime from pole to pole*
> *for glory never gained by lesser soul.*

This author of an epic, who conferred upon himself the honor of directing the vast Cortesian cycle, is not an epic poet, however contradictory this may seem. The section concerning the Conquest, which must have been the nucleus of the poem, is not among the fragments preserved by Dorantes. The only part we have in which Terrazas even timidly approaches the epic is the digressive passage where Francisco de Morla hurls himself into the sea to recover the lost rudder. Terrazas' temperament inclined him more to lyrical subjects: the abduction of the Indian girl Quetzal and the despair of her lover Huitzel; the ransom of the sorrowing Jerónimo de Aguilar; and Cortés' flowery and persuasive discourses on the subject of religion to the Indians of Yucatán.

Essentially, Terrazas views history in the same way as Suárez or Dorantes. He too faces up to the massive and worrisome contradiction between the divine intent of the Conquest and its cruel and unjust methods. Like Dorantes, he condemns slavery and even puts into the mouth of an Indian the following judgment on the Conquistadors' behavior in the wars:

> *I'll say nothing of his queries,*
> *his scorn for victims of his theft*
> *his hauteur and his furies*
> *his cruelty to those whom he bereft.*

Like Dorantes, however, Terrazas still believed that Cortés was an instrument of God, this criticism notwithstanding.

> *Cortés was he whom God selected*
> *to bring salvation 'neath his flag unfurled*
> *to alien races and a brave New World,*
> *thus serving those the Lord elected.*

Francisco de Terrazas', lyric gifts are given more freedom in these verses, where reason tries to throw light upon the inscrutable designs of providence:

> *How far away from human highways*
> *the secret paths You walk will lead . . .*
>
> *You have clearly marked the byways*
> *where all may follow You in word and deed . . .*
>
> *Thy secrets, Lord, we cannot find*
> *Thy wisdom we may not understand.*
> *We cannot follow, for we are blind,*
> *We cannot fathom the world you planned.*

It is significant that the theme of the war should elude Terrazas and that, on the other hand, he should dedicate the longest passage of his fragmentary poem to a defense of the patrimony of the Conquistadors' luckless sons. His vision of the colonial world and his thirst for reward are so like those of the author of the *Relación* that it is difficult to say which of them first had the idea and which first expressed its essence.

According to Terrazas, pagan warriors of the ancient world had been granted wealthy cities, villas, and villages in return for their victories, and "only unhappy Mexico lost out."

> *What was denied no other land on earth*
> *has sunk New Spain in grief and mourning*
> *dissolved in tears, and all undone . . .*

> *Though men esteem you, take this warning,*
> *proud Philip's never mindful of your worth.*
> *He leaves you falling like a setting sun*
> *to sink in ever greater desolation*
> *poor, hungry, and deprived of consolation.*

Such is the picture the Creole has painted of the land in which he lives. A star of misfortune rules his sky; pain, adversity, and want are his portion; and amid all this desolation, this world peopled by tragic ruins, he feels that he himself is a corpse, a damned soul bearing the guilt for all the evils that afflict the fatherland.

The octavas in which Terrazas describes the despair of colonial man are strongly elegiac:

> *Fate is now swinging her angry scythe,*
> *dealing death to end man's woe.*
> *She sheds her children by that knife*
> *and stranger nations, too, must go.*
> *If your darkness turns to light*
> *and burns with steady, even glow,*
> *you'll pay for it by dying, and I pray*
> *that death will end my plight one day.*
> *A merciful mother to strangers you've been*
> *but a hard stepmother to us.*
> *You grant riches to strangers we've never seen.*
> *You share your troubles with us.*
> *Farewell, stern Mother, reign on as queen.*

Rule ever, O Mother unjust.
Don't slacken your fierce and ruinous hand
or stop starving the stepsons who die in this land.

In prose or in verse, all the Creoles were smarting from the same wound. Of the thirteen hundred Spaniards who brought light to the dark shadows of New Spain,

. . . when from Satan's power they freed you
in the splendor of bright suns
of your grandsons, sons, and kinsmen
not three hundred now remain.

And those three hundred wander through out-of-the-way villages, broken and poor, like

some few and stunted fowl
hunted down by birds of prey
without shelter, help, or mother.

At the end of the known portion of his poem, Terrazas addresses the shade of Cortés, though he is speaking directly to the viceroy. His elegiac tone is heightened so as to veil, with skilful rhetorical manipulation, the naked revelation of his intense covetousness. Since the Conquistadors were not granted the promised titles and estates, he concludes, the perpetuity of the encomienda must be assured,

and not when most of them have perished
or their children through hunger have banished.

This lament does not conclude the poem. In the end, the Creole seems resigned. If he has been denied earthly justice, God will grant it to him for eternity, although it is not clear whether eternity refers back to the encomienda or forward to the heavenly paradise that doubtless awaits the sons of the heroes in recompense for their many misfortunes.

Like so many sixteenth-century figures, Terrazas, the youthful father of our poetry, is a melancholy shade, a lovesick handful of dust. He died very young, with a small measure of fame. His verses, which never merited the honor of publication, remain hidden in manuscript collections or in the papers of the Inquisition, whence the critic exhumed them three centuries after they were written. The quality of his work varies widely. He wrote Italian as well as Spanish verse and also wrote in Latin, the cultivated tongue of his day. His expert knowledge of languages, his literary discipline, the ease with which he manipulates poetic forms, and his discretion and good taste are his basic characteristics, and they were common to the stream of literature that ran through the colony into the nineteenth century and flows on into our time.

In the final analysis, what we have left of his work shows little originality. His *Nuevo mundo y conquista,* written with obvious discouragement, was inspired by Ercilla's *La Araucana* and lacks authentic feeling. He was not living during the Conquest; war was alien to his cast of mind and he feels it only insofar as his genealogy establishes the rights of his class. The blast of the martial trumpet was sour to the inner ear of a man who detested extremism and was appalled by the traditional trappings of glory. The poem, a slavish imitation of Ercilla, was never finished, a fact that increased the frustration of the mournful, finely bred Creole who undertook to become the singer of other men's deeds.

He was a delicate minor poet, with elegance and deliberation as his limits. His best sonnet, *"Dejad las hebras de oro en sortijas"* ("Leave thy golden hair in ringlets"), is an imitation—some people call it a paraphrase—of Camoens' famous *"Tornai essa brancura á alva assucena."* (Give back that whiteness to the pure lily"). In this, as in his other Petrarchan sonnets, he was criticized for that "minor key," that "twilight sentiment," which later critics were to consider the keynote of Mexican literature.

Criticism of our lack of imagination and of strength, in other words, our decadence, generally is expressed in those wretched commonplaces which we accept with complacency. Terrazas, the first poet of a new land, is now branded with the stigma of insipid lyricism, frankly decadent, because he writes vicariously, trying to express as his own sentiments alien to him, and because he writes for a small group of initiates in the hermetic philosophy of Petrarchan poetry. He writes of love "in the Italian style," although he lives in a small city surrounded by Indians; his descendants would later concoct Arcadias and place

Grecian shepherds in our volcanic landscape. They were to be carried away by Romanticism, quicker to grasp the pistol than Werther, to fancy themselves as *poétes maudits,* and to die bloated with absinthe. They wrote intellectual poetry and free verse, and sent their tidy little *plaquettes* to groups of initiates who practiced the art of the paraphrase "in a minor key." It must be clearly understood that this is not a question of condemning artistic servility in the name of nationalism. Nowadays the air of the world circulates freely through our country, but the bell-jar vacuum of colonial intolerance and isolation would have smothered the most gifted of writers.

But Mexicans are not all either men alive to the happenings of the world or witty, worthy poets. For some time now, a native current has been flowing vigorously through many outstanding artists. The current bears much of the picturesque, as well as much that is impure and even ignoble, because the discipline of art does not clarify or direct it. If the two streams could meet, the urgent need for expression might be met, the painful struggle of the Spanish-American consciousness; but most prescriptions turn out to be ineffective. The answer would be a change in the cultural medium that produces such conflicts. The writer is caught between two antagonistic worlds; he is a victim of the social disorganization and the cross currents in his own breast, but he has been unable to make them his own, which would be the way to reconcile them.

The Creole character seems to have been formed in the sixteenth century, the brand-new product of a new society, *sui generis.* Living in a peaceful world, he is filled with chivalric notions; and his bias toward breeding and nobility conflicts with the constitution of his society. He writes epic poems celebrating wars which he knows only by hearsay; or he composes Petrarchan sonnets about things that have never belonged to his own world. His creative work emerges as a monstrous fiction, because it does not correspond to his life and his surroundings. Naturally, if he assumes in advance that everything has achieved its ultimate form, if on the one hand he lacks freedom of thought and if on the other hand the door to transcendental action is closed to him, he is bound to sink into verbal expressions emptied of feeling—he has nothing left but the word. The word seduces his spirit, and with the word alone he builds those hollow structures, those veritable tombs, where the power of speech decays in horrible baroque writhings. In Mexico, poetry came in floods, in surface streams, and now it is petrified into a huge block of stone. We do not need any more specialists in literary archeology to decipher the layers of strata. What we need is to smash the whole thing, to grind it into the earth and let it receive the blessings of sun and water, then to rebuild it within the rules of art. That is no easy task, but it must be undertaken someday.

Social Poetry

The social struggle of the sixteenth century is reflected not only in epic poems of the Cortesian cycle but also in a flood of satire. The similarities of theme in the works of Oquendo, of Suárez de Peralta, and of Dorantes de Carranza give us grounds for believing that the sympathies of the Creole and the Spaniard were the same, once the Spaniard was deprived of profit from the colony. Both hated the newcomers; both despised the Indians and mestizos; and both mourned their inability to make a fortune through bootlicking or trickery. Oquendo, Suárez, and Dorantes, however, belonged to different worlds, even though they shared the same resentment. Oquendo could not conceal his pride in being a Spaniard, a privileged member of the empire, in a position to laugh at his own institutions and to criticize them sharply. The Creoles, on the other hand, always expressed the sense of being victimized by a burdensome system, and while they burned to epic poetry in the hope of assuring their rights to the encomienda, they did not hesitate to attack and ridicule the colony as their chief enemy. A famous anonymous sonnet of the sixteenth century portrays the Creole's proud scorn for the newcomer:

> *Across the salty sea from Spain*
> *to our Mexican domicile*
> *comes a rude man full of guile*
> *poor in health and wealth and brain.*
> *His friends delight to hang on his thoughts*
> *and treat him like Caesar or Vergil.*
> *They'd tender him laurels with demeanor most servile,*
> *though it's only his money that talks.*

There's another who once used to sell
pins and laces he brought in his pack
who's now rich as a banker and titled a count.
He's forgotten his loathsome old sack
and the fish-net he dragged, so they tell,
for he's titled, has taste, and a mount.

Obviously, not all the poetry of the period is either Petrarchan or satirical. Even the "poor and mutilated remains" that have come down to us from the old abundance—a contemporary declared that there were more poets than manure—reveal the vitality of the sixteenth century. Certainly a great refining influence had arrived, but amid all that "verbalism that looks like poetry" which was then in vogue soared some truly beautiful voices. Córdoba and Bocanegra, who embodied the "Renaissance man" in New Spain; Guevara, author of the sonnet that begins, *"No me mueve mi Dios par quiererte"* ("I am not moved, my God, to love Thee"); the still fascinating theater of Eslava; and the lyricism of Terrazas—all can convey some idea of the depth and variety of Mexican culture in the sixteenth century.

A Stranger in His Own Land

The common note of the sons of first-generation Creoles seems to have been the frustration of a rich human potential. Their failure, whether they were starting a chronicle or an epic poem, or whether they were organizing a rebellion or trying to defend their threatened patrimony, was traceable to an apparent inability to carry out any kind of transcendent action.

Seldom can history show us two human types as opposite as the Conquistador and the Creole, separated by a single generation. The man of action, the muscular warrior with the ability to hurl himself into the most unlikely adventures, the man with the truly demonic energy which made him invincible, was absent in the son. The father's very *amour propre,* the adventurer's exalted confidence in himself, became debased, in the heir, into self-esteem founded not on personal accomplishments but on another man's exploits, petrifying the wood of the family tree.

The Creole, a new-minted aristocrat in a virgin land ripe for any creative effort, attempted to monopolize the greatest of social and economic privileges, at the same time clinging fiercely to his sacred right not to work, a right won for him by his father's conquest. García Icazbalceta writes:

In short, they were a pack of idlers with the presumption of great señores, who looked askance at the Spaniards who came after the Conquest because they turned to business or tilling the land with greater resolution. The Spaniards acquired by their own industry comforts which those of Conquistador lineage looked upon with envy, and the Creoles expressed their feeling by reviling mercilessly those whom they called parvenus, and they took advantage of the ridiculous weakness of some arrogant impostors who arrived with wonderful tales of their wealth and bloodlines, meanwhile revealing the rough substance of their low and narrow cradle, visible a mile away.

The dramatic struggle between the Creole and the Spaniard cannot be reduced to a comic rivalry between spiteful idlers eaten up with spite and hard-working men somewhat given to bragging. The weakness of the Mexican and his serious limitations as compared with the Spaniard are attributable to the fact that he was born in a colony, an essential circumstance which we must always bear in mind in any serious consideration of the Mexican character.

Whether a sixteenth-century man was born in Spain or in one of the colonies was the source of radical and complex differences, even though both might call themselves Spaniards, have the same blood, speak the same language, and practice the same religion. To put it briefly, one man was the other's master; one had the privilege of commanding, and the other the obligation to obey; one could choose and impose, the other could either accept the imposition or rebel and lose his head on the block.

The grim conception that the Creoles, almost without exception, had formed of their own world corresponds narrowly to the steaming, florid, tropical nature of the colony. They felt they were putrefying bodies, living cadavers, inmates of a carnival charnel house where everything rotted noisily and inescapably.

The colony is an alien world; the will of a nation to forge its own destiny in the face of adversity did not exist in the viceregency. The Mexican, a Mexican without a Mexico, a Mexican of New Spain, breathed the air of a land which was owned by a landlord, owing to certain divine and political imperatives. The failure of the Conquistadors to obtain a reward worthy of the great services they had rendered the Crown, a phenomenon for which they could find no explanation, embittered their days and darkened their lives with dissatisfaction and resentment. The encomienda, the Creole's reason for being, the foundation of his wealth and his aspirations to pre-eminence, was never his in the eyes of the law. The encomienda—the land and labor of the Indian—the only spoils of the Indian wars, was forcibly imposed by Hernán Cortés, and the Crown opposed it from the beginning. Independent of the fact that kings might not look kindly upon the consolidation of a new and dangerous feudalism in the Indies, they could sustain their stubborn opposition to the establishment of the encomienda in perpetuity by pointing to their catastrophic experiences with it in the Antilles, where the abuse of the encomienda had annihilated the Indian population, and especially to the impassioned defense of the natives by the first missionaries.

From the very moment of the Conquest, Charles V had "ordered Cortés not to establish them in New Spain . . . because God had created the Indian free and not subject"; yet in 1526 the encomienda was legalized amid grumbling and reluctance, then distrained in 1530. "Soon afterward, in 1536, the encomenderos succeeded in obtaining grants to their encomiendas through the Law of Inheritance for Two Generations, which still seemed to some of them a short time, and they petitioned for perpetuity." In 1542, the encomiendas were restricted again, thanks to the tenacity of Fray Bartolomé de Las Casas, and the abolition of slavery was decreed; but in 1546 the emperor restored them both. The ideals of justice and human freedom struggled in vain against practical considerations. The encomienda was the only encouragement to colonial prosperity and it could not be destroyed. No one would want to live in the Indies deprived of the Indian's labor. The encomenderos' opposition to the New Laws of 1542, which had cost Viceroy Blasco Núñez Vela his head in Peru and which brought on the abortive revolution of 1562 in Mexico; the work of procurement agents sent to the king; the dispersion of the Conquistadors and settlers, which often threatened the colonies with extinction; the circumstance that outstanding men and the powerful Franciscan, Dominican, and Augustinian orders took the side of the encomenderos—all tipped the scales in favor of retaining the encomiendas, not as a permanent property, but as the usufruct of a gracious loan, which might be snatched back at any moment.

The results of this "precarious constitution of the public wealth" have been visible throughout our study. The conviction that nothing belonged to him was creating in the Mexican a feeling that he was living on borrowed time. Even the Creoles who were overlords of villages, like the Ávilas and Francisco de Terrazas, understood with disappointing clarity that New Spain was a stepmother. They had an accurate conception of their complete subordination to the higher powers of the colony.

The slow bureaucratization at work throughout the sixteenth century ended by destroying the hidalgo's system of values. His absolute dependence on the viceroy, the Inquisition, public officials, and usurers made a rogue of the Creole, like the Spanish pícaro of the period of decadence. The feudal lordling had to turn to the money lenders whenever he took part in a tournament or a cavalcade, or merely tried to keep up appearances. Gaming, parties, and great banquets led to his ruin—not that he struggled to avert it by going to work. The conviction in America that wealth dissolves "like smoke or like salt in water" shows a blind and paralyzing fatalism. The lowest rungs on the bureaucratic ladder were reserved for the impoverished Creole. He had to practice deceit and to fight hand to hand against the cleverer aspirants merely to obtain the poorest paid mayoralties and regional offices, in the smallest village or the most unhealthful sections of the country. If he entered the clergy or the monastic orders, his prospects were not much brighter. Open fights broke out between Creole friars and Spanish friars over the choice of prelates in the sixteenth century. The authorities intervened repeatedly and forcefully to spare the city the unedifying sight of its spiritual mentors killing one another. Even the laws of alternatives decreed by Philip II to regulate clerical elections could not keep the Spanish friars, in most cases, from making the Creoles feel their absolute predominance.

The struggle to survive, that fierce, hidden struggle that went on in governmental antechambers and involved every ignoble means, made a cynic of the Creole. The abuses of servility and flattery, the tricks and the bribes, the hatred and the venomous intrigues that tainted the atmosphere of colonial administration gave him the psychology of an arrogant pensioner.

For all that, he was living off miracles, through favoritism, through the good humor of the current officials, and the insecurity of such a life, the constant fear of a misstep, the endless haggling over property with others who believed they had the right to it, in the end made him indifferent and resentful.

The Creole cherished no illusions about his colonial position. As far back as the first generation, he labeled it accurately "a bank where everyone fails, a depository of lies and deceit, a picture of hell, the sweet kiss of peace to the newcomer, and the lash and the knife to its own sons." Poetry and the study of history offered a highly prestigious escape to the man of letters, and we see him taking refuge in Petrarch's universal rationalizations or burying himself in the past of the Indies. But in his attempt to flee the inferno, this newly created being was turned into a pillar of salt, and stood with his eyes fixed on the outer world and the past. His limitations, his hatred of the bastards and the plebeians, his stubborn opposition to the new colonist—one of the active elements of nationality—and his disdain for the mestizo, that mestizo who was to give Mexico in the course of time her incorruptible outline, all contributed to the weakening of the Creole's position by depriving him of his natural allies.

Survival of the Colonial Man

The son of the Conquistador or of the first settler born in New Spain—that is, the first Mexican—is not entirely dead. We note with surprise that his attitudes toward life, his ideas and sentiments, his approach to his world survive today in our contemporaries. We observe this phenomenon of the colonial man's survival after the disappearance of colony as both witnesses and participants. Of course, the man himself is not the surviver of a remote age. To us the old Creole is a man shipwrecked in the sixteenth century who, like Robinson Crusoe, saved what he could from the wreck.

The colony is closer to us than we think. The "deep sense of worthlessness," the Mexican's famous inferiority complex which is the basis of "all his virtues and all his defects," is an offshoot of the colony. He was convinced that whatever was foreign was best merely because it was foreign, largely because he was politically subject to a foreigner who governed as God's vicar. He was completely dependent economically; he had little opportunity to take part in public life or in the administration of commercial or industrial enterprises, and he was inferior to the Conquistador's skills and cultivation.

How many consequences can arise from a brutal and oppressive slave system? We shall list only a few. With the clairvoyance of the poet, Octavio Paz writes in *El laberinto de la soledad,* "Perhaps dissimulation was born in the colony. Indians and mestizos had to sing softly, as in the poem of the kings, for the mutterings of rebellion have a sinister ring. The colonial world has vanished, but not its fear, distrust, suspicion." The fear of compromising oneself by one word suggestive of rebellion, the distrust inspired by the professional advocate of slavery, the suspicion that one is being deceived, mocked, and scoffed at by a superior, the constant scrambling for advantage—all of which were common to the Creole—transformed the Indian and the mestizo into men who seemed the embodiment of reticence and grim, mysterious suspicion. "Confirmed in his sullen loneliness, at once thorny and courteous, everything serves him as a defense—silence and speech; courtesy and disdain; irony and resignation." Everything is an act of defense but also a scornful surrender to annihilation. His terrible violence and his spirit loaded with repressed hostilities lose meaning through indifference, that sort of immobility with which the Mexican chooses to destroy himself. Indifference is not only the result of mistrust in his hostile world; it is also the desolate certainty that he is defenseless, that it is futile to become involved, and that everything is bound to go wrong and nothing is worth worrying about.

Undoubtedly, indifference is the fruit of an age-old conviction that the goods and pleasures of the world are not for him. A man who was born in a colony where everything is owned by a foreigner becomes an indifferent man, in the grip of dark and destructive intentions. We have before us an instance of nihilism that embraces the tree and the earth, the government, enterprise and sloth. The Mexican may watch a forest burn without lifting a finger. He may witness an act of destruction or waste without opening his mouth. He knows that the burned forest, ruin and destruction, plunder and injustice are all obedient to a system of despotism, to superior and untouchable interests. The system of concessions, or bosses, monopoly, and favoritism, which are the colony's vices, create a reality against which he considers himself powerless to fight.

Essentially, his attitude toward politics can be considered similar to that held by the Creoles of the sixteenth century. In the colonial period administrative appointments were viewed as legitimate spoils to which certain privileged men might aspire; today they are still regarded as the patrimony of an equally privileged group, although for other reasons. Even though any Mexican may hope to hold a high position in administration, his low opinion of government remains unchanged. To him all authority is spurious, immoral, and tyrannical, and all laws are inimical to his interests.

This clear sense of government as an immoral imposition, both the personnel and the acts of governing bodies, seems an out-and-out contradiction of the Mexican's "apathy as a citizen" and his indifference to political action. He looks for some way to mock whatever has to do with the law, to render it inoperative, and he revenges himself with refined malice on public officialdom and all its works. The anonymous lampoon painted on Hernán Cortés's house—"white wall, the fool's writing paper"—the venomous allusions to Viceroy Enríquez, and the popular discontent shown in the theatrical productions of 1578 have been revived today in anonymous jokes that pass from mouth to mouth, appear in newspapers, and are acted in sketches in popular revues.

The Mexican never looks political matters in the eye. He moves cautiously, full of suspicion, carrying forbidden weapons and speaking in whispers, as though still threatened by the repressive apparatus of the colony. His antagonism, and the dim view that he, like the Creole, has always taken of any and all government, militate against a resolute participation in politics. Yet what a servile spectacle he makes of himself! The scenes in the government antechambers at the end of the sixteenth century and the sticky adulation of Baltasar Dorantes de Carranza are phenomena common to the bureaucracies of that day and this. The colonial man believed not only that the government was alien to him, but that his country's wealth and her affairs were equally beyond his reach. Doomed to live in sufferance in a world lacking opportunity or stability, he scorns money, and when he can scrape some together, instead of being concerned to increase his slender patrimony, he squanders it, hurling himself into sad and bestial orgies like a depraved peasant in a Russian novel, crushed by the certainty of his own impotence and guilt. The upper classes throw their money away on much the same sort of things as in the time of the second Marqués del Valle de Oaxaca. Today money is wasted on luxurious automobiles, on outdoing other rich exhibitionists, on gaudy pretensiousness, on prodigality that opens the way for such violent and shameful contrasts as those shown by the census of 1940. "Thirteen million Mexicans sleep on the ground; seven million wear white cotton trousers; six million go barefoot; four million wear huaraches; and nine million wear shoes." The revelation of so much poverty among the people, "the poverty that has been established and sanctioned since the first days of the colony," more than justifies the fatalism of the Mexican, his contempt for life, his resentment, his longing for any kind of miracle, burning a candle to the Virgin and placing under her pedestal the lottery ticket on which he has spent his last centavos in a baseless hope.

If the colonial man has survived because his colonial condition has survived, he will only disappear when the circumstances that have formed him shall disappear through the passing of time. In point of fact, his old traits are disappearing, being broken by the march of history like a familiar and repulsive mask. The Mexican has tentatively begun on the conquest of what is his. Much of what was once foreign belongs to him today, and he is beginning to see much of what he considered alien through the eyes of a lawful owner. The metamorphosis of the oppressed and enslaved man—who used to live on sufferance—into the master of his life and his property will be completed on the day when he feels that the blossom and the earth, freedom and knowledge, government and the pursuit of happiness are all his. That will be the day that Mexico ceases to be a stepmother to her children and becomes their mother; in another word, their motherland.

Glossary

Audiencia Primarily a judicial body, although it had other functions; the highest court of appeal in the colonies.

chirimía An Aztec clay flute or flageolet.

comisario An administrator of the Holy Office.

comisario general Inspector general of the Franciscan order.

Council of the Indies An advisory board that, with the courts and the king, handled colonial problems and performed administrative functions under the Code of the Indies, codified in 1680.

encomendero Holder of an encomienda by royal grant without the right of inheritance except by statute or feudal entail or a Crown extension of the grant.

encomienda A Crown grant to Spanish individuals, chiefly the Conquistadors. The encomienda did not convey property in the soil. The grant included the Indians living on the land, who were required to pay tribute to the encomendero and who were to all effects and purposes slaves. Many had been enslaved by their chieftains, who paid the encomendero in Indians in lieu of goods or gold. The encomienda was granted specifically as a reward by the Crown and as the Conquistadors' share of the booty of the Conquest. The grants were not in perpetuity, but were meant eventually to revert to the Crown.

Hibueras The sixteenth-century name of Honduras.

indiano A Spaniard who lived in America or one who had returned wealthy to Spain from America.

Indies The Spanish colonies in America.

Law of Inheritance for Two Generations A law passed in 1536 decreeing that the encomiendas granted provisionally by the Crown could pass to widows or legitimate descendants for one lifetime. This law was rescinded in 1542 and the New Laws promulgated, according to which the Crown would declare an encomienda vacant on the death of the encomendero. The New Laws were revoked in 1546, at which time the Crown promised grants in perpetuity. No settlement was made, however, until the encomiendas had reverted to the Crown except in special instances in which inheritance extended into the fourth or fifth generation with severe limitations on the encomendero. The sixteenth century passed without any grants in perpetuity.

licentiate A general title for lawyers and university students given to holders of degrees between the baccalaureate and the doctorate.

oidor A judge of the Audiencia.

repartimiento A labor battalion of Indians.

teponaxtle A large Indian drum.

tigrillo Wildcat.

visitador A commissioner or inspector of the king or the viceroy, often affiliated with the Holy Office.

Selected Bibliography

Cervantes de Salazar, Francisco, *México en 1554* (México, 1875). Three dialogues, originally written in Latin and published in Mexico in 1554, translated into Spanish by Joaquín García Icazbalceta.

Díaz del Castillo, Bernal, *Historia verdadera de la conquista de la Nueva España* (México, 1944). Introduction and notes by Joaquín Ramírez Cabañas.

Dorantes de Carranza, Baltasar, *Sumaria relación de las cosas de la Nueva España, con noticia individual de los descendientes legítimos de los conquistadores y primeros pobladores* (México, 1902)

Gallegos Rocafull, José M., *El pensamiento mexicano en los siglos XVI y XVII* (México, 1951)

González Obregón, Luis, *Los precursores de la independencia mexicana en el siglo XVI* (Paris, 1906)

Icazbalceta, Joaquín García, *Bibliografía mexicana del siglo XVI* (México, 1886)

———, *Don Fray Juan de Zumárraga, primer obispo y arzobispo de México* (México, 1947)

———, *Opúsculos varios* (México, 1896–98)

Kubler, George, *Mexican Architecture of the Sixteenth Century* (New Haven: Yale University Press, 1948)

Méndez Plancarte, Gabriel, *Humanismo mexicano del siglo XVI* (México, 1946)

———*Poetas novohispanos: Primer siglo, 1521–1621* (México, 1942)

O'Gorman, Edmundo, *Reflexiones sobre la distribución urbana colonial de la ciudad de México* (México, 1938)

Orozco y Berra, Manuel, *Noticia histórica de la conjuración del Marqués del Valle* (México, 1853)

Pereyra, Carlos, *Hernán Cortés* (Buenos Aires, 1947)

Reyes, Alfonso, *Capítulos de literatura española* (México, 1939)

———, *Letras de la Nueva España* (México, 1948)

Suárez de Peralta, Juan, *Tratado del descubrimiento de las Indias* (México, 1949)

Toro, Alfonso, *La familia Carvajal* (México, 1944)

Walsh, William Thomas, *Felipe II* (Madrid and Buenos Aires, 1943)

Index

294